T0265807

A PART OF THE HEART
CAN'T BE EATEN

TRISTAN TAORMINO

A PART OF THE HEART CAN'T BE EATEN

A MEMOIR

Duke University Press Durham and London 2023

© 2023 Tristan Taormino

All rights reserved

The events and dialogue are portrayed to the best of the author's memory.
Some names and identifying details have been changed to protect the
privacy of the people involved.

Printed in the United States of America on acid-free paper ∞

Project Editor: Bird Williams

Designed by Aimee Harrison

Typeset in Minion Pro and Helvetica Neue by
Westchester Publishing Services

Library of Congress Cataloging-in-Publication Data
Names: Taormino, Tristan, [date] author.
Title: A part of the heart can't be eaten : a memoir / Tristan Taormino.
Description: Durham : Duke University Press, 2023.
Identifiers: LCCN 2022061109 (print)
LCCN 2022061110 (ebook)
ISBN 9781478020226 (hardcover)
ISBN 9781478027218 (ebook)
Subjects: LCSH: Taormino, Tristan, [date]- | Lesbians—United States—
Biography. | Lesbian authors—United States—Biography. |
Sex educators—United States—Biography. | BISAC: BIBLIOGRAPHY &
AUTOBIOGRAPHY / LGBTQ | LCGFT: Autobiographies.
Classification: LCC HQ75.4.T36A3 2023 (print)
LCC HQ75.4.T36 (ebook)
DDC 306.76/63092 [B]—dc23/eng/20230417
LC record available at https://lccn.loc.gov/2022061109
LC ebook record available at https://lccn.loc.gov/2022061110

Cover photo by Rachel Crowl

FOR **QUEER PEOPLE** EVERYWHERE

CONTENTS

ACKNOWLEDGMENTS

In 1997 a book agent reached out to me and asked me to lunch, so I met him at Zen Palate in Union Square. He had read something on Nerve.com that piqued his interest, a mention about me writing a memoir about growing up with a gay dad. Talk about playing the long game. Andrew Blauner, you have championed, supported, and challenged me and are one of the kindest and most ethical people I know. You never gave up on me, so I never gave up.

To Dean Smith, Ken Wissoker, Ryan Kendall, Bird Williams, Aimee Harrison, and everyone at Duke University Press. It was truly an honor to work with such an amazing team. Ken, I've never felt so respected, valued, and nurtured as a writer as I have with you. To my readers, three people whose identities aren't known to me: it was an absolute gift that you took the time to read and critique the manuscript. You went above and beyond, offering ideas that significantly reshaped parts of the book. Reader 1, you should be credited as another editor with the care you took. Reader 3, your take on the book brought me to tears and propelled me forward just when I needed it. To Tina Horn, the unofficial *other* editor, who read an early draft: you are an insightful teacher and provided invaluable notes. To Michael, who applied his keen eye for detail and ear for dialogue in the polishing stage. To Ignacio Rivera, one of the first readers of a very early draft, who shaped my thinking about this project plus numerous others. To Keiko Lane, who served as a Queer Nation historian to help me with the 1990s timeline. To those who edited my earlier work and published pieces that eventually became parts of this book: Anne-christine d'Adesky, Joan Larkin, Felice Newman and Frédérique Delacoste, Doug Simmons, Carly Milne, Catherine Reid and Holly Iglesias, Noelle Howey and Ellen Samuels. To teachers, formal and informal, who have had a profound impact on my writing: Dr. Claire Potter, Dr. Gary Comstock, Dr. Ann duCille, Heather Lewis, Amy Scholder, Patrick Califia, Joan Nestle, Susie Bright, Cherríe Moraga,

Dr. Constance Penley, Dr. Mireille Miller-Young, Dr. Celine Parreñas Shimizu. To the photographers whose work appears in these pages: Richard Kern, Dick Mitchell, Janet Ryan, Rachel Crowl, and Michele Serchuk. To everyone mentioned in these stories; whether you are mentioned by your real name or not, you know who you are, and I appreciate the ways you influenced my life.

To my Patreon patrons, who financially and emotionally supported me through the writing and editing process and kept me accountable. To the memory of Gabrielle and Dee Dee, who died while I was finishing this book. To all the dogs who have cared for me: Reggie Love, Jordan, Harley, Ceiba, Moxie, and Bodhi. To friends and chosen family for bringing so much love and joy into my life: Amber, Audrey, Dara, D.J., Elissa, Holly, Jennie, J.D., Jordan, Joshua, KD, Kelli, Nicoletta, Roberto, Winston, and Wyndi. Eli, you were by my side through the entire process to cheer me on. To Aunt Joanne and all the Barbas I finally met, who welcomed me with open arms into their family. To my mom, Judith Pynchon: you deserve all the credit for raising me on your own. You and I have our own story, which is yet to be written. I love you deeply. Thanks for putting up with random fact-checking text messages and for sharing memories from your past with great care, even the painful ones.

To my dad, Bill Taormino: this story is ours, and I hope I have honored you with it. I miss you every day.

Tristan Taormino

CONCEIVED

I was conceived in a moment of queer love and confusion. At least that's how I imagine it—obviously, I wasn't there.

My mother was born in 1940 and raised in Oyster Bay, on Long Island, New York, where she was the only girl in her class until sixth grade. She did everything the boys did, including playing on the basketball team. By high school, she was known only as the younger sister of her brother, whom some teachers believed was a genius. Her classmates voted her the wittiest. It wasn't until she got to college that anyone told her she was really smart.

When my father graduated high school in 1961, he joined the army. No one knew when the Vietnam War might end, and the possibility of combat terrified him, but anything was better than sticking close to home with his big Italian family. He liked playing Superman with his cousins at the beach in Coney Island, and he loved TV and movie stars, but his childhood was more profoundly marked by his mother's bouts of mania and depression. Her episodes were punctuated by violence and threats: *You better lie to this ER doctor about how your arm got broken. I'll send you to the home for bad boys and leave you there forever.* He needed a way to pay for college, and his family said the army would make him a man, which was both appealing and repulsive to him for different reasons. Being straight, in every sense of the word, was drilled into him by slaps of the ruler at the hands of the Catholic school nuns and the never-ending onslaught of homophobic jokes from his relatives. So off he went to basic training at Fort Dix.

Figure 1.1 Dad (left) and another soldier in the army, Okinawa, Japan, circa 1962

When he got back to the States in 1964, he enrolled at Suffolk County Community College on Long Island. The first time he saw my mom, she was wearing stylish Italian shoes and a chartreuse wool tweed coat as she got out of her MG convertible, where the ashtray overflowed with fuchsia-ringed cigarette butts. At twenty-four, she had spent the summer in Europe and was returning to campus for her second year as an English professor. She saw him onstage in a school play and was intrigued. They went to a concert together and bonded over their love of a then mostly unknown Dionne Warwick. Shortly after, they started dating and fell in love. An older, stuffy male colleague of hers said about their relationship, "Well, you two certainly have moxie."

After the community college, she got a job at Long Island University's C.W. Post campus, and my dad enrolled there. He graduated, and she taught there for one more year. My mother, whose mind is sharp at eighty-two, told me, "I can't prove it, but I think my contract wasn't renewed because he was such

Tristan Taormino

Figure 1.2 Dad's acting head shot, Brooklyn, New York, 1968

Figure 1.3 Mom, Long Island, New York, circa 1969

a troublemaker in the drama department." He aspired to be an actor. He was born a troublemaker.

I have a single photo from their wedding day, twenty months after they met, taken at her parents' house in the backyard among my grandfather's prized rosebushes. She looks fashionable in a white column dress with her nearly black hair cut in a short pixie style framing her thin face. Standing next to her in a dark suit and tie, my father is handsome, with thick dark brown hair and intense eyes. They both look stunned. Not caught off guard that someone had taken their picture at that exact moment; no, more like serious and slightly confused. There are no smiles. But someone preserved the photo along with a photo of my grandparents from that day; they sit opposite each other in a gold-edged double frame with a hinge between them. Decades later, my aunt gave me a copy of their wedding album which featured a similar photo from the Catholic church where they were married.

While my mom was pregnant, ultrasound to determine the sex of the baby wasn't yet widely available, but it didn't matter because my parents wanted to decide on my name before I was born, regardless of whether M or F would be checked on my birth certificate. Instead of poring over baby name books, they created a contest for their friends and family, which they called "Name the Little Creature," complete with a mimeographed flyer. Typed on the page, among scattered baby clip art, are the guidelines:

> You can pick only one *multi-purpose-unisex* name. Prizes will be awarded for originality, bizarreness, and in some cases a refreshing tackiness. Winners could receive two weeks with the creature, a Tony Perkins album, a collared peccary, or 3/8 of a bushel of garlic salt.

No names from the contest spoke to them, and they instead decided on Tristan, the tragic hero in *Tristan and Isolde*. Best known as a Richard Wagner opera, *Tristan and Isolde* is a story that dates back to the twelfth century that has been retold in many different versions and languages and references King Arthur mythology. The gist is that Tristan, a knight, is tasked with going to fetch Isolde and bring her back to marry King Mark of Cornwall. Tristan and Isolde drink a potion that causes them to fall madly in love (Was it intentional? Was it an accident?). Isolde ultimately marries Mark, who loves Tristan like a son, but she and Tristan carry on an affair. There are several versions of what happens once King Mark finds out: they escape but are caught; or he sentences them to death for adultery (hanging for him, burning at the stake for her); or Tristan leaves the kingdom so Isolde and the king can be together.

Figure 1.4 Mom and Dad's wedding, Oyster Bay, New York, 1966

Figure 1.5
Huntington
Station,
New York,
1971

My mother tells the story of my birth on Mother's Day in 1971. She had taken Lamaze classes, learned the breathing, and decided beforehand she didn't want any drugs. She labored for a long time, all night, until she finally gave up and said, "Give. Me. The. Fucking. Epidural." Then she pushed and pushed and had a clear vision: I was coming out of her, head first, with my arms folded against my chest and my eyes wide open. I was holding a sword. She said it must have been the drugs.

In 1972 they decided to flee Long Island so they would have more distance from their parents and so Dad could get his master's in film. We moved to a rural town thirty miles north of Hanover, New Hampshire, and lived in a church they bought with a mortgage from the Veterans Affairs (va) home loan program. It was a tall brick building with big windows and a wooden steeple painted white. A hand-painted sign still hangs under the window at the top of the entrance to the building. There is an ornate filigree in the middle, and black lettering that reads:

1837 Meeting House. 1859 Abandoned.
1875 Village Hall. 1968 Dwelling.

When my parents moved in, it had already been converted to a living space. They were hippies and thought it was cool. *Look at us, we live in an old, broken-down church!* Heavy doors in the vestibule opened into one big space with a stage at the back of the room—the original pulpit. Stage left were the kitchen, a bedroom, and a very DIY bathroom. A wooden staircase led to a small loft. There was a narrow balcony opposite the stage that ran the entire width of the building, where I'm told I spent hours running back and forth. The whole living situation was deeply ironic since both my parents were raised Catholic but had consciously rejected and abandoned the religion. They found it entirely too dogmatic. To them, Catholicism crushed souls, it didn't save them. They didn't baptize me or raise me with any religion. So when people ask me about the first time I went to church, I tell them I lived in a church. In North Haverhill, off the main road, with a big field behind it.

Figure 1.6 Roslyn, New York, 1974

Tristan Taormino

In 2015, en route to a queer wedding between two dear friends, I made an uncharacteristically spontaneous detour. I saw Haverhill on a sign on the highway and urged my partner to exit. I called my mom, and she guided us to the place from memory. I found the imposing brick building standing majestically among tall grass that hadn't been mowed for months. It looked the same as the photos I'd seen. I got out of the car and walked up to the front door; when I turned the knob, it opened to the vestibule. I ventured inside to see that it had once again been abandoned. It had been used as a dance school, and much of its recent past—posters of ballerinas, tiny pointe shoes, dusty tutus—had been left behind. It was a little spooky, like I could be walking into a Stephen King novel. I looked around, climbed the stairs to the balcony, took some photos. I wanted to feel some connection to the place, a body memory, but I didn't. So I went on Zillow, which listed its value at a little over $100,000. It recently sold for $27,000. Probably at auction.

Before my second birthday, my dad announced to my mom that he was moving out. He didn't tell her he was gay, but she overheard him telling his mom on the phone. He moved in with his lover, a local priest. A church was apparently also the best place to find single gay men in New Hampshire. When he took off, she became a single mom in the middle of nowhere with a toddler and no job (they'd been living off his student loans). He told her she could have the church, but that meant monthly mortgage payments she couldn't afford. She decided to go back to Long Island, the place and the people they had initially fled. 1973, abandoned. Before we moved, she baked pies and sold them from the front yard to support us. She still makes her apple pie at holidays; it's got a cinnamon crumb topping that could bring you to your knees.

My dad never put on a tutu like some budding gay boys, but when he was growing up, there were other signs that he might be queer. He had his first male lover when he was stationed in Okinawa: a marine whom he was deeply ambivalent about, in his own words. He knew his desire, but he fed it reluctantly. I had always assumed he kept this secret from my mom. Many years later, when I was home on winter break from college, we were at the new apartment she moved into when I graduated high school. I sat longways on the couch that had followed us from place to place, which she had reupholstered for the fifth time. The new fabric was a flamboyant jewel-toned flower print. She was in the kitchen baking Christmas cookies.

"Did you ever suspect that Dad was gay before you got married?"

"Well, he told me he was bisexual."

"Really?" I hadn't expected that.

"It wasn't at all surprising to me," she said, being very casual, and followed that up with: "It was the late sixties, wasn't *everyone* a little bit bisexual?"

It was amazing my dad could say that much out loud since the homophobia in his family was not subtle or unspoken; every day was a new opportunity to shame a man with feminine traits or use the word *fag* to eviscerate someone. *Do you know why queers all have mustaches and goatees? To make their mouths look like pussies!* I believe he married my mother in a complex web of emotions: certainly there was love, a want for a partner, but marrying her was also a way for him to hide from his desire for men. Marriage *was* a good cover story.

As I write this memoir, I am living through the second pandemic in my lifetime, the one after AIDS, a word that stings like a fresh wound. Most of my work as a sex educator is on hold, so I have something that ordinarily eludes me: time. I call my psychiatrist, and he ups my meds. I bake lemon bars, binge *RuPaul's Drag Race*, and read the books of authors I will interview in the next weeks for my podcast: *The Not Wives*, *The Ultimate Guide to Seduction and Foreplay*, *Female Husbands*, *Crossfire* by the poet Staceyann Chin. I update the PowerPoint graphics for my polyamory workshops, catalog photos and letters from old lovers, organize my copies of *On Our Backs* magazines, rearrange the cabinet that holds my Feminist Porn Awards. And I decide, finally, to read my dad's memoir, which is dedicated to me. As I am writing my own story, I am delving into his. Printed on a dot matrix printer, the title, "Lies and Circumstance," is still remarkably dark on the page after all these years. I stare at the typewriter font as I type the manuscript into Word on my MacBook Air, and I hear his voice, low but animated, whispering to me. It brings me comfort and renewed grief.

I have had this manuscript, which was never published, since he gave it to me in 1991, but I never read it all the way through until now. There are so many reasons why, and probably more I have yet to uncover. I miss him too much. I might find answers in these pages to questions I never had or solve mysteries I didn't know existed. It's scary to read about his troubled childhood, his complicated desire, his transgressions, in black and white. Fearing the nuns at school would catch him with another boy. Watching his hypermasculine cousin Bubby shave his face in the nude. Ducking when his mother hurled a frying pan at him for talking back to her. Losing his virginity to an Okinawan sex worker. Leaving his family and never looking back. What's written into

Tristan Taormino

his DNA, my DNA, emerges in stark details. It's disconcerting to see a line that connects his trauma and mine. The story ends in 1973, so it doesn't contain any of the closeness and joy we shared. It's painful to be with him through only words and memories. I should be thankful that he left behind this archive. It is my inheritance, the story of my life before me.

MRS. C.'S

From 1973 to 1976, I went to Mrs. C.'s house every day with five or six other kids whose moms worked. Mrs. C. was a kind, round woman with a bowl haircut who wore colorful hand-knit shawls. She had a daughter named Valentine who was born on Valentine's Day, but everyone called her Val. Val had the kind of short haircut where you could see through her hair on the sides, and she often wore jeans with a chain attached to the wallet in her back pocket, a T-shirt, and a leather jacket. Like a uniform. She worked at a mechanic's fixing cars, but her real passion was boxing. I had never before seen such a handsome, strong woman. She looked like she could handle herself in any situation, including beating someone up if necessary (to defend her honor or maybe mine).

I had my own tiny room in the front of the house for nap time, with a twin bed and yellow-flowered bedspread. I was a naturally high-strung five-year-old, so it was hard for me to fall asleep on command; I usually just lay there, restless. One day, I began moving my right hand between my legs, and it felt really good, so I kept doing it. I'd explored touching myself before, but this time I was more deliberate; I rubbed my vulva through my underwear and could feel myself getting excited. I flipped over on my stomach and kept rubbing, now putting my left hand over my right hand to apply more pressure. My body started to tense up, almost like a cramp, and there was an explosion inside me, like an electrical current coursing through my entire body, like my skin could start a fire. The feeling washed over me. Afterward, I was breathing quickly, like I had run around a park for hours, and I was exhausted. I drifted off to sleep easily. When I woke up, I heard rustling in the hallway because the other kids were awake and doing stuff. My young brain thought I had found a secret weapon: I could put myself to sleep whenever I wanted. Or maybe I was the secret weapon, like the Bionic Woman. Certainly that would come in handy in the future?

There were two boys my age I liked at Mrs. C.'s: Brian and Nicky. Brian was a poised and confident boy; my mom called him "alarmingly sure of himself." He had wavy blond hair and was clean and neat. It seemed like he didn't have a ton of time for anyone, so when you got his attention, you were lucky and basked in the glow of his strong five-year-old ego. Kissing him felt exciting and made me tingle all over. I knew in my tiny heart that Brian was out of my league; thus, it was really cool that he picked *me* to kiss.

Nicky had a mop of dirty, sometimes greasy, blond hair cut in the style of The Monkeys. He had the kind of body you might call *string bean*. His go-to outfit was a maroon turtleneck sweater over goldenrod bell-bottom corduroys. He had beady brown eyes that made him look like a mouse. Nicky was a free-spirit hippie kid who never had a care in the world. Once I saw tears stream from his eyes when he hurt his hand, and it was clear he wasn't embarrassed to be crying in front of grown-ups and other kids. (I was sure Brian could have an arm broken in six places, and he'd never shed a tear.)

When I learned to read, my mom got me a copy of *The Little Mermaid* by Hans Christian Andersen, which came with a cassette of someone reading the story, which I listened to again and again on a tape recorder. When the witch took away the mermaid's voice in exchange for giving her legs so she could be among humans, she warned her that each step would feel like she'd been cut in two. I imagined the pain like shards of glass deeply embedding themselves in her feet. I could picture it, I could feel it. The mermaid pined for a prince, who fell in love with another, but the witch had told her that if that happened, it would seal her fate. She died. Everything had its price. It was a model of love, and it was pretty bleak.

One night, Nicky and I were sleeping over at Mrs. C.'s, and we plotted to find each other after everyone went to bed. I took the risk of cracking my door open, trying not to wake up the dog. I tiptoed across the hall to the den. I crawled inside his sleeping bag on the floor, and we giggled softly. I put my index finger on his lips to say, *Don't make noise*. His body was warm against

Figure 2.1 Brooklyn Aquarium, Brooklyn, New York, 1976

mine as we kissed. He tasted like Tater Tots and ketchup, sweet tomatoey breath. I thought it was weird to taste the inside of someone else's mouth. We'd had hot dogs for dinner, but that was hours ago, so I wasn't sure why ketchup lingered on his tongue. I liked Nicky, we fit together nicely, but I was sure he wasn't my one and only because I would never put ketchup on a hot dog.

Tristan Taormino

ARTICHOKE HEARTS

My mother comes from a long line of white Anglo-Saxon Protestants and Catholics, the Bennetts and the Pynchons, and they go *way* back. My grandfather's side of the family are some of the original colonizers who arrived in America from England in the early 1600s; I call them the *Mayflower fuckers*. I am a direct descendant of William Pynchon, considered the founder of Springfield, Massachusetts, after he "bought" the land in 1636 from the Pocomtuc tribe to create a trading post on the Agawam and Connecticut Rivers. Pynchon's son founded several other towns in western Massachusetts and Trinity College. I imagined they owned slaves and burned witches at the stake, but there are no records of that. I *am* a Daughter of the Revolution, just not that one.

William Pynchon's claim to fame was authoring *The Meritorious Price of Our Redemption*, the first book ever banned in the New World and burned in Boston Common. Considered a theological layman, Pynchon dared to interpret the Bible differently than the New England clergy, arguing one could earn God's grace rather than have the fate of your soul be predestined. He wanted people to work for it. Charged with heresy, he fled back to the Old World before his trial and never returned.

His descendant, my grandfather Thomas Ruggles Pynchon, was orphaned at the age of three and raised by a series of relatives. He settled in Oyster Bay on Long Island, where my mom and her brothers were raised, and he was a local Republican politician for a while, appointed the superintendent of highways, then town supervisor. He was well liked and sincere; he loved golf and his rosebushes, and all of us called him Poppie. My grandmother, Katherine, was raised upstate in Frankfurt, New York, also by relatives, because her mother died in childbirth when she was three. What a thing to have in common. Katherine became a nurse in 1926 when it was a big deal for women to get a higher education and work outside the home. She referred to her own grandmother, one of the women who raised her, as a *battle-ax.* Both my grandparents stayed on-brand: they were very stoic, stiff-upper-lip kind of people. Sometimes my grandmother was sharp-tongued, caustic, mean even, especially when she drank too much. On holidays, which is mostly when I saw her, she'd often blurt out whatever was on her mind. My mom's favorite story to tell is that her mother often repeated with a certain resignation, "I always wanted three sons." (My mother is her only daughter.)

My mom is a strong woman despite having delicate hands and exceptionally tiny wrists. She could lift heavy things and paint an entire room by herself. I watched her as she dressed up for meetings in a stylish poppy-colored suit with shoulder pads and a silk shell underneath. Her dark hair followed what was fashionable at the time—a pixie cut, a perm like Cher's, a mom bob once her hair went fully gray in her forties. She styled it and wore makeup every day, but she never adopted the 1980s glamour of Linda Evans or Joan Collins. She didn't successfully blend in with the other moms in a way I wanted her to. She never dated like other divorcées. *Does she no longer believe in love?*

I asked her, "Why doesn't Dad give us any money, like kids in other divorced families?"

She replied, "I don't need a man to support me. I am a *feminist.*" She didn't mention that he didn't have any money to give.

Unlike every other adult woman I knew, my mother never wore a bra, and I found that embarrassing. Especially if she wore a thin turtleneck, and you could see her nipples obviously visible through it. Fem-uh-niz-um. To me, it had something to do with being single, broke, and braless.

In the summer before I began first grade, we moved to a house on Cherry Avenue in West Sayville. Sayville was a sleepy little town in Suffolk County on the South Shore of Long Island, considered "far out east" since it was much less densely populated than other parts of the island. The fact was, the further east you went, the cheaper things got; keep going on the Long Island Expressway, and you would hit farmland waiting to be transformed into housing developments, condo complexes, and strip malls. Sayville had a quaint, movie-set Main Street with a pizza parlor, a ladies' lingerie shop,

Figure 3.1 Mom at my grandparents' house, East Norwich, New York, 1977

Greaves Stationary, Fritzsche's Bakery, plus a movie theater, a public library, and a Friendly's restaurant. Past Friendly's, under the overpass, the town sprawled into housing developments.

West Sayville was the part of town with a mini strip mall, a funeral home, and one short block of weathered shops—less fancy than Sayville. It was best known for its high-end restaurant, the Lake House; its golf course; and LaSalle Military Academy, a school for boys from rich families in need of discipline. The West Sayville Fire Department was housed in a picture-book brick building at the end of our block, where Cherry Avenue dead-ended into Main Street. It was staffed by volunteers, so when there was a fire, we heard the loud wailing of the sirens in every room of the house.

Our two cats moved with us: one was a neurotic calico named Splash with big circles of rust and black on her white fur, whom my mother had found crouched under a car in the rain one day, malnourished and frightened. Splash could be moody and scratched me badly several times, but I loved her like she was my baby. Friday, named for the day he came to live with us, was Splash's foil: an affectionate, laid-back boy we got from a friend's litter; he was snowy white except for a circle of gray on the middle of his head, another one on his back, and a gray tail.

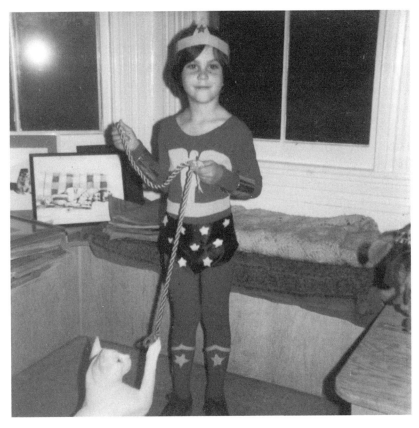

Figure 3.2 In Wonder Woman costume made by Mom, West Sayville, New York, 1977

As soon as we moved into the two-story Cherry Avenue house, my mom started to fix it up; she wallpapered my bedroom with a lavender flower print and set up a home office with her own desk and typewriter. After being in what seemed like other people's spaces, I thought this house might be *ours*. We lived on the first floor in one apartment and rented out the upstairs and the back unit. On one side of our chain-link fence was a huge corner property with an actual mansion with black shutters and two chimneys. People said George Washington stopped by to rest there in 1790 on his way to somewhere else. Maybe we'd stay a while in our place?

Sayville was 99 percent white and Christian. It was hard starting a new school, especially when it was clear that everyone knew each other from kindergarten. On the first day, I didn't have much of a plan to make new friends, but I noticed that I was wearing the same shoes as another girl: a

Tristan Taormino

pair of brown Stride Rite Mary Janes with a cartoon character painted on the rubber soles. Her name was Dana, and soon we were inseparable. The first time I went to her house, her Doberman pinscher jumped up on me, scaring me so much I peed. The urine ran down the legs of my thick red tights, and I was embarrassed, but Dana laughed off the whole incident. Dana moved away at the end of the school year, and I was devastated.

I loved my first-grade teacher, who treated me like I was one of the smartest kids in the class. During recess I'd create elaborate productions of plays, pick the cast, and direct them. No one expected me, the new girl, to land the female lead in our production of *Do You Know the Muffin Man?* right off the bat, but I knew I nailed my audition. I had way more stage presence than the Man himself. On my first-grade report card, my teacher wrote, "Tristan is well-motivated toward doing her best. She completes her work quickly and generally with great care. Tristan is a fine leader and well liked by her classmates. She is a sensitive child and always willing to help anyone in need. She enjoys writing her own stories." I have to give it up to Mrs. Tresham for calling me, a girl, a *leader* in 1978 rather than bossy and demanding, which were the terms other adults used to describe me. Both are true. I've been bossing people around my whole life.

When my mom said I could have a party for my eighth birthday, she asked me what we should serve my classmates. I knew right away that I wanted my favorite food.

When I was a toddler, we lived in an apartment above a movie theater in Roslyn with floors that sloped and a raccoon that lived in the dormers. As a single mom, she didn't go out much. But once in a while she treated herself to a nice dinner at a local Italian restaurant. She didn't have money for a dinner out *and* a babysitter, so she took me to the restaurant with her, where there were rarely any other babies or children. She placed her order as the waiters sat me in a high chair and fussed over me, draping me with several stiff white napkins. The first thing that arrived was a single steamed artichoke. She would take off the leaves one at a time and place them in front of me. After she showed me, I caught on quickly about how to eat it. I'd pick each one up, dip it in a sauce, and begin scraping the flesh off with my tiny teeth. It took me several tries to do one leaf. Apparently this occupied me for more than an hour while she enjoyed an appetizer, salad, entrée, and dessert. She finished with a tiny glass of clear liquid that had two coffee beans floating in it. She lit a cigarette from her pack of Parliaments and sighed, full and content.

In third grade, I still loved artichokes so I wanted them for my birthday party. Mom raised an eyebrow but accepted the notion that she was going to feed artichokes to a bunch of third graders. She decided to make a lot of different sauces for dipping, like barbecue sauce, mayonnaise with relish, and her special Dijon vinaigrette, to entice them to try this strange food that none of them had ever eaten. The condiments worked, and once everyone got the hang of scraping the flesh off the leaves, we had a blast sitting around the big round table in the living room.

Artichokes are a wonderful paradox, made of light and shadow, hard and soft, inviting and repelling at the same time. The thing about an artichoke is that on the surface, its leathery leaves don't exactly scream "Eat me, I'm delicious!" Some even have sharp tips, so you have to proceed with caution and a little faith. As you work your way from the outside leaves to the inside ones, they soften and submit to your teeth more easily. There's a payoff for getting through the rough parts because once you're at the center, you're left with the heart—the best part, with the most meat to dig into. But there's a catch. It's covered with prickly, almost hairy, inedible stuff (the *choke* in its name). How could something so nearly perfect have such nasty parts to it? Once you think you've hit the soft leaves and reached truly pliable territory, a new form of armor appears. You have to scrape off that bitter, fibrous part, and then underneath you find the magical tenderness of the heart. It's kind of a commitment. When all of us were done with the leaves, she took the hearts, scraped the bad stuff out, cut them up, and returned them to us on a platter, where we grabbed at them with our messy fingers. Kids talked for months in school about the weird artichoke party I had.

Even though she was raised by two motherless parents, my mom had some mom skills. We had a place to live, and I never went hungry. When I needed a ride, she drove me. She showed up for parent-teacher conferences. But when it came to my health, things were confusing. I felt very in touch with my body from a young age and therefore knew when something was wrong with it. I had constant upper respiratory issues and sinus infections, which were usually assumed to be colds. I learned much later I was actually allergic to cigarette smoke and cats. When I told her I felt sick, that Protestant keep-going-and-work-til-you-die sentiment she was raised with kicked in. I was confused about why my mom would dismiss or diminish my symptoms, why I had to bug her to take me to the doctor. All I was asking her to do was

Tristan Taormino

mom me. An overthinker from a young age who blamed myself for a lot, I started to question my sense of reality and my own intuition. *Can I not trust my gut to know things about my own body? Do mothers really know best?* I didn't know that because she never had a traditional job, we never had health insurance. She did a lot of different work—technical-manual writing, board-game development, academic research. When she got paid was unpredictable. What I saw as a simple trip to the clinic was financially dicey a lot of the time. She hedged her bets that I would get over whatever I had so she could pay for things like the artichoke party. I can't imagine the pressure she faced as a single mom trying to make ends meet and give me what she had: a nice middle-class life like everyone around us. There was an equal disconnect when it came to my moods. I recall only a handful of times my mother cried or raised her voice. But early on, I felt my emotions intensely, and often they enveloped me. Sometimes I got so worked up, I couldn't calm myself down. She couldn't calm me down either.

FIRST TIME

A last name is supposed to tie us to our ancestors and a rich history passed down through generations. Mine is derived from the people of Taormina, a town on the east coast of Sicily that sits on a dramatic cliff and is known for old churches, an ancient Greek theater, and its active volcano, Mount Etna. Family lore tells the story of a relative emigrating to the United States, where he decided Taormina sounded too feminine, so he simply began telling people his name was Taormino and signing official documents that way.

But my dad and I are not really Taorminos. My dad's mother was Catherine Barba. Her father, an Italian immigrant, died at fifty-one, and several stories circulate in the family that he was murdered on the roof of the building where he owned a restaurant because of a bad gambling debt, an affair with a bartender, or a street fight gone bad. Catherine's Irish mother died three years later, leaving Catherine, age ten, and her eight siblings to raise themselves. In 1943 Catherine married James Clancy, who went to fight in World War II. Ten months later, on Halloween, as children dressed as ghosts and goblins walked around their neighborhood in Brooklyn, my dad, William James Clancy, was born. Supposedly, James was messed up from the war, and the marriage lasted only four years; his adultery is the reason listed on the divorce document filed with the Kings County clerk's office. In 1948 Catherine married Anthony "Nino" Taormino (everyone on that side of the family had a nickname), and my father's name was legally changed; there is even a revised baptism and birth certificate for him with Anthony listed as his father. Catherine was a devout Catholic, and I am not sure how she managed to make it all happen without anyone batting an eye, but she did. She essentially erased James Clancy from the picture with some paperwork.

Decades later, my father tracked down his biological father, who was shocked to see him. James hadn't told a soul about his marriage to Catherine; in fact, he had a whole new family, including another son named William James Clancy. James told him to go away, that he didn't want anyone to know my dad existed; the reinvention of his life, where the characters' names remained unchanged, rendered my father impossible. My dad was heartbroken. Nino raised my dad from the time he was young, but my dad told me very little about him.

"My mother ruled the house, and Nino never stood up to her," he said. I never met my grandparents.

From an early age, I devoured any book I could get my hands on and one of my favorites was *The Juniper Tree and Other Tales from Grimm*. There was a story about an "obstinate and willful" girl who disobeyed her parents and went to visit a lady named Mrs. Gertrude ("People say her house is very strange and they say there are such queer goings on there"). The girl could see the true nature of people and spirits, including Mrs. Gertrude, who was both witch and devil. Mrs. Gertrude turned the girl into a log and set her on fire, but that's not what I focused on. I wanted that power: the power to see someone's true self. My father did not shy away from the truth in his memoir. Page 138:

We had been friends for about two years. Tomorrow he was getting married. He asked, "Bill, will you stay with me here tonight? I know it's too late to call Judy, but she'll figure it out. You can call her first thing in the morning."

"Ed, I already told her that I was probably going to stay over."

"Oh, good. Thank you."

He got up and stripped down to his boxer shorts and went off to take a shower. I got undressed and got into bed.

When Ed came back into the bedroom, he had a beach towel wrapped around his waist. His black hair and mustache were dripping. He said, "Jilly said not to use the new towels yet." He turned away from me to put on a clean pair of boxers.

He had a football player's body. He went off to the kitchen and came back with two oranges.

I realized that we had both been waiting for this. I noticed that his hands were shaking slightly; my stomach and voice were gone. I reminded myself that his marriage ceremony was just hours away. The timing seemed insane. My wife was pregnant and due any day. The timing was insane.

"I would like to kiss you," I said.

"Well, why don't you?"

"I'm not drunk, Ed. I'm not stoned."

"I know," he said.

Above Ed and Jilly's brass bed, there was a huge American flag. It made me think of the crucifix above my parents' bed. I always thought it was out of place and ominous, like a coffin at a party. Surely it must be unpatriotic and possibly illegal for two men to be going at it under the red, white, and blue Stars and Stripes of Old Glory.

When I woke up, Ed was gone. Off to get his tuxedo. Off to his parents' house. Off to say his vows. His boxer shorts were on the floor. There were orange peels in the bed.

As the music signaled the bride's entrance, everyone stood and turned toward the back of the church. I stood up, but I did not turn around immediately; instead, I watched as Ed entered the altar from a side door. We stared at each other. I have no idea what he was thinking. Finally, I turned and watched Jilly. She was appropriately radiant. I was elated. I had no guilt. None.

Outside the church, the newlyweds descended the granite steps, the well-wishers threw rice. I had some orange peels in my pocket, and I tossed them at the bride and groom.

A few days later, our daughter, Tristan, was born. More elation. And then, very quickly, I felt it all slip away, and I crashed. What am I going to do? But instead of coming up with some answers, I did what I had programmed myself to do. I kept running.

My dad sporadically sent letters to my mom and me. A postcard from 1974:

Am planning on spending Christmas by myself . . . I love you both very much. Growing up at last.

I saw these brief communications for the first time when I went through a dense archive of his papers.

Tristan Taormino

Our Cherry Avenue house was strangely shaped. On the right side, it jutted in and formed this little space between the driveway and the house where a car fit perfectly, so that's where my mom parked her shit-brown Pinto. It freed up the rest of the driveway so our tenants could use it. The Pinto was eventually recalled because if another car hit you from behind, your car caught fire and exploded. One day when I was about eight, we were sitting in our Pinto, which hadn't yet exploded (ours eventually did, on the shoulder of the Long Island Expressway). My mother touched the gearshift to put it in reverse. *Y.M.C.A.* by the Village People was playing on the radio.

I turned to her and asked, "Hey, where is Dad? Can I see my dad?" I have no idea what prompted the question or why I asked it then.

She just replied matter-of-factly, "Yes." She didn't say another word.

My mother drove me about three and a half hours from our house to Jamaica Plain, a neighborhood in Boston. It was less suburban than I was used to, and my mom had a hard time finding a parking spot. You had to walk up wide steps to get to my dad's apartment in an old building. He greeted us at the door, hugged my mom, and looked down at me.

"I am so happy to see you!" He smiled, and his cheeks formed two plump little circles of pink on either side of his nose.

He was thin, his face was round, and he had pale skin like mine and a prominent forehead. His hairline was receding, but where the thinning stopped, dark, bushy brown hair grew wild in the back. He was wearing jeans, a plaid shirt, and a gray sweater vest. *His eyebrows look like mine.* Already very sensitive, I felt for any tension between the two of them, but there was none. That was unusual based on what I knew from the few kids who had divorced parents.

"I made us lunch," he said, and I realized I didn't recognize his voice, as if I had never heard it before. A friend once said to him, "You have this strange foggy, raspy, husky voice. It's very AC/DC. I can't decide if you sound like Aldo Ray or Lauren Bacall." He replied, "If those are the choices, I prefer Lauren Bacall."

We walked into the kitchen, and the walls were painted a pale but cheery green, like gum and ice cream. The color was a little darker than mint chocolate chip, which was my favorite flavor. *Maybe that is also his favorite flavor. Maybe this is a sign?* There were archways throughout the place, including the kitchen, and it was very stylish, not like our cramped kitchen back home, which was just a long hallway of appliances. There were three place settings at the kitchen table. He served us homemade pea soup. I thought: *We are eating green soup in a green kitchen, and that seems very coordinated. I like it.* There were pictures on the wall of people I didn't know. A black-and-white portrait of a topless woman with her hair in a ponytail staring straight at the camera. A picture of two men standing next to a broken-down white Volkswagen Transporter van; one of them looked like a young Albert Einstein. Then I saw it: a black-and-white photo of me when I was a toddler. I recognized the tall grass my small body was nestled in—it was behind the church in New Hampshire. I wore a cardigan with the top button buttoned over a printed turtleneck with a white collar. My hair was parted unevenly in the middle, held back by two plastic barrettes, and there were wisps on my forehead they hadn't managed to catch. I was there. In his apartment.

Soon Dad moved to a different neighborhood in Boston. I asked to see him again, and we had to drive over a bridge to get to his condominium in Charlestown, which my mother remarked was not a very safe place.

"It's changing," he said when we got there.

"There are boarded-up buildings," she replied.

Figure 4.1 Photo by Dad, North Haverhill, New Hampshire, 1973

Tristan Taormino

He was living with his roommate, a man named David, who was very tall. David looked a little like my Uncle Tom, with the same thick black hair. He and David had the casual banter of two people who were very close. Their place needed some work, and they were doing it themselves, so there was peeling paint and a shower full of mold. David's mother, who lived in Connecticut, worked at the Lender's Bagel Factory, so their freezer was stocked with an endless supply of frozen bagels, which I thought was the coolest thing in the world. It was summer, and I wore my purple tube top because it was my favorite. David and my dad noticed right away and complimented me on it. My mom and I stayed the night, and we all had meals together around a square table. I was beginning to note the differences between my parents; he greeted me with a big, warm, squeezing hug—not the kind of hugs anyone else in my family gave each other—and loved to tell me that he loved me.

After that visit I began to see him a few times a year, mostly around holidays and school breaks. His absence from my life until that point was never discussed or explained by either of my parents.

THE BUNK HOUSE

I grew up in a pretty unremarkable town with one very unique element.

The media images I saw of Long Island in the 1980s were entirely foreign to me. Snooty country-club types having cocktails at lush, rolling Gatsby-like estates in Great Neck and Manhasset. That was *Nassau* County, practically an entirely different world. Sayville was full of preppy, solidly middle- and upper-middle-class folks with what people from Great Neck would call *new money*. We were ordinary: a homecoming king and queen rode on the back of a pickup in a parade; we painted the windows of local businesses during the holidays; we joined Key Club and Students Against Drunk Driving. But there was one thing that set us apart from other towns: the ferry.

Across from Long Island's South Shore between the Great South Bay and the Atlantic Ocean sits a tiny sliver of an island called Fire Island. It is made up of small communities dotted along its thirty miles, and each one has its own culture and vibe. Since Fire Island's origin as a summer vacation spot, the Pines and Cherry Grove have been known best for being all or mostly populated by LGBTQIA+ folks and businesses. To get to any part of Fire Island, you have to take a ferry. To get to the Pines and Cherry Grove, you catch that ferry in Sayville.

Beginning on Memorial Day weekend, like clockwork, every Friday, Long Island Railroad trains would arrive at the station packed with queer people headed to their rental shares or homes for a weekend, a week, or the whole summer.

When I was growing up, my mom had several close friends who were gay, including Chickie and Alan and a French couple, Jean and George, who cooked scrumptious meals. My dad also had gay friends, and there was usually one gay guy whom he spent a lot of time with. When I heard my mom or dad say we were going to a couple's house for dinner, I never assumed the genders of the people.

There were also rumored-to-be-gay people at my school. Ms. B., the tough elementary school gym teacher who barely cracked a smile, wore her salt-and-pepper hair closely cropped and dressed only in tracksuits. She was not a Mrs., that much we knew, and she never wore makeup. Once a year, we took a special square-dancing unit in gym that culminated in a dress-up night of dancing with a professional caller. Even then, she wore a light blue polyester pantsuit with a blue-and-white-checked button-down shirt underneath. In high school there was the chorus teacher, Ms. Peal; when Ms. Peal wore a dress or skirt (which happened only when there was a concert), she looked like a female basketball coach dressed up for a game on TV. *All wrong.* If any of the male teachers were gay, they were deep in the closet, or maybe I wasn't paying as close attention as I was to the women.

Sayville relied on gay people for tourism dollars, to spend money on groceries, booze, and beach stuff before they got on the ferry. My classmates worked various jobs for the ferry service or on Fire Island. You needed a car to get to Long Island beaches, so the ones in the Pines and Cherry Grove were the easiest to get to: we just loaded onto the ferry, surrounded by queer people. It was part of our world: the gays arrived for the summer and confronted us with their difference. Some folks snickered and made homophobic, hateful jokes, and others were pleasant in that WASPy way. But no one didn't see them, that was for sure. It was a given that queer people (the majority of whom were white gay men) passed through *our* town in order to get to *their* town. When I went to the deli across from the train station, I saw them ordering heroes and cold salads and eavesdropped on their conversations, filled with names and places I didn't know anything about: Keith Haring, Laurie Anderson, Jesse Helms, New St. Mark's Baths, the Limelight, the Piers. The men had sharp haircuts and were well dressed in bold 1980s fashion: tight short-shorts and crop tops or something straight out of the International Male catalog. They dragged suitcases behind them or carried bags overflowing with brightly colored flowers and beach towels. I lived off a main road that ended at the water, so I could see as many as forty or fifty in a day. It was, dare I say, like a parade. To me, these people lived exciting, happy, flamboyant lives, and they knew something the rest of us didn't. I wondered what it was.

Every night after I punched out from my shift at Friendly's in my sweaty polyester navy-blue-and-white houndstooth dress, I made a Happy Ending sundae to go (chocolate chip ice cream and Reese's peanut butter topping, whipped cream, nuts, no cherry). I sat on the curb in front of the to-go window eating it and staring at the building next door. The Bunk House. It was a solid square brick building with a door but no windows, so it had a certain mysteriousness to it. It had been open since the 1970s, so it was a fixture, a part of the landscape, by the time I moved to Sayville. It was not rumored, but *confirmed*, that the Bunk House was a gay bar. It was packed during the summer because of the Fire Island crowd, although it was open year-round, and the parking lot was never empty. In high school, kids would dare each other to try to get into the Bunk House. The jokes and comments I heard about gay people ran the gamut—some people thought the gays were entertaining weirdos; others knew they were social deviants who were going to hell. *Don't bend over in the Bunk House! Guys are fucking each other up the ass at the Bunk House!* As I pictured the inside of the bar, there were actual bunkbeds where men had sex with each other. And it was impeccably decorated.

Tristan Taormino

BUTTERCAKE

"**U**se your fingers. You're telling him you want him to open his mouth," said the instructor, a beautiful brunette teenager named Mary with soft, midlength feathered hair who wore a polo shirt tucked into her jeans. She looked like Tatum O'Neal in *Little Darlings*. First, we practiced bridling Mo, a brown horse with a black mane and tail. When it was my turn, I put my fingers under Mo's lips, wet and slobbery, until I felt his teeth move apart. It was such a simple gesture, but he knew right away what I wanted. I slowly slid the shiny metal bit into his mouth as I slipped the stiff, dark leather bridle behind his soft ears.

In the summer of 1979, I had convinced my mom to let me attend Suffolk Day Camp, on Nicholls Road, ten minutes from our house, for one reason: the horses. I wasn't athletic, into sports, or even very coordinated. Gym class was hell on Earth for me. I preferred reading, and devoured any book about horses I could get my hands on. I loved Marguerite Henry's *Misty of Chincoteague*, about a band of wild horses who live on Assateague Island; each year, the locals do a roundup on Pony Penning Day and swim the horses over to Chincoteague Island, where people bid on them. Two kids, Paul and Maureen, save their money and buy a mare named Phantom, who had eluded being caught for several years, and her foal, Misty. The next year on the same day, Paul wins a race riding Phantom. But Phantom longs for the herd she left, so they let her swim back to be with them on Assateague, and Misty stays behind. Sometimes the wild must stay wild. At eight, I was ready to bring the books I'd been reading to life and turn my obsession with all things horsey into a reality.

"Now buckle that part, the chin strap, on the last hole and tuck it into the loop," Mary said in a high-pitched sing-songy voice, sounding like she could repeat that same phrase all day and never get frustrated. Standing next to me, she turned to the small group and continued, "We want to make sure all these different parts fit correctly . . ."

When I saw the bridle up close for the first time (instead of in an illustration), I thought, *This delicate series of straps is what I'm going to use to control this massive animal?*

"Find one that fits your head," said Mary, pointing to a pile of worn black velveteen-covered helmets. I picked mine, then got in line to take my turn. Standing on a tall wooden box, I put my foot in the stirrup of the flat English saddle, and Mary hoisted me up and onto the back of the horse. She held on to the reins down by the horse's head.

"Take a rein in each hand with your thumbs up, lying on top."

I wrapped each of my tiny hands around the strips of braided leather, slightly oily against my skin, and slid each side of the reins between my pinky finger and ring finger into my palm, then looped it back through between my index finger and thumb, mimicking what she showed us.

The first time I got on a horse, I felt small. I became conscious of my body in a way I had never experienced before. I was very aware of my butt tucked in the slope of the saddle and my thighs spread apart like they might snap. As I attempted the right posture, I put my shoulders back and felt my chest open up and my spine curve. I didn't usually sit up this straight; my neck was longer, and I felt regal. My fingers tingled as I held the reins.

"When you are ready, squeeze your legs a bit to start him walking." Her sugary voice was reassuring. "Press on the reins very gently to guide him where you want him to go." I did as she said, and Mo and I headed to a well-worn path next to the fence in the dirt ring. This 1,100-pound horse and I were having a conversation with our bodies, and he was responding to just a squeeze of my hands and legs. I had no choice but to surrender to his massive strength, but he listened to me. There was a kind of magic between us. I was still small, but I was *powerful*. For a week, we practiced sitting correctly, steering, and asking the horse to stop. One day, there was an older girl in the ring on a palomino horse the color of Farrah Fawcett's hair, and Mary gestured toward her.

"Dana is going to demonstrate how to *trot*," she said, punctuating the word with excitement, and Dana and her blond horse started moving at a pace slower than a gallop that still looked pretty fast. I eventually got the hang of it myself, pressing my legs deep into the stirrups to move my body up and down in the saddle in a rhythm to match the horse's stride. I moved my wrists ever so slightly, squeezed my legs as if to wrap around him tighter, shifted my body weight subtly, dug my heels into his flanks. We talked without words, only the occasional clicking sound I made when I moved my tongue against the roof of my mouth. Sometimes I said, "Good boy." We were speaking our own language, we were dancing, and he was responding exactly as I wanted him to. We were in sync, moving as one. I was alive and connected to another living being. It was exhilarating.

I asked my mom if I could continue horseback riding lessons after camp was over, and I was so excited when she said yes. (I had no concept that this would further stretch the already tight budget). The day camp was located on the grounds of Suffolk Farms, an equestrian center on a sprawling property with several barns, paddocks, riding rings, and a large indoor arena. She drove me there every week for a one-hour group lesson. When I got out of the car and breathed in the barn's smells, I experienced two conflicting sensations: a swarm of bumblebees erupting in my stomach and a wave of calm washing over me. Mona, my riding teacher, lived in a small house on the property. She had curly brown hair that framed her round, open face and big smile. She was earthy and grounded, full of the wisdom and passion of someone who deeply understood the equine–human relationship. She encouraged me to cultivate that connection, taught me it was just as important as perfecting my riding skills. It wasn't just the lessons I loved, but all the rituals that happened before and after. The scent of Murphy Oil Soap filled my nostrils as I cleaned the leather gear. I brushed the lesson horse with a black rubber currycomb and mucked stalls, using a pitchfork to pick up piles of shit and pissed-on patches of dusty chunks of wood shavings. I would get back into my mom's car smelling of sweat and manure.

I was jealous of the kids who could ride whenever they wanted, but I knew owning a horse was *very* expensive. I'd been taking lessons for about a year when Mona told me that another student named Matthew had outgrown his pinto pony, so his parents had recently bought a new horse for him to continue competing in horse shows.

"He doesn't want to sell the pony, so maybe they would consider leasing him to you? Leasing is when you pay a monthly fee, you take care of the

Figure 6.1 First year at Suffolk Day Camp, Bayport, New York, 1979

pony—you could ride him as much as you want. I think it would be a good match," she said. My mother and his mother, Sheila, a woman perfectly put together, elegantly dressed, and busy, agreed on a price. Once we dropped off a check at their house, and it looked like a mansion.

The pony's name was Buttercake, and it was love at first sight. To be fair, his unique pattern of white-and-chestnut-colored patches made him stand out. He was bright and energetic and had deep brown eyes. The first day I rode him, we joined together like puzzle pieces. He anticipated what I wanted, and I honored his experience as a seasoned show pony. He was a show pony!

Beyond the barns and riding rings was a huge grassy field with hills and valleys à la *The Sound of Music*, where all you could see was green for miles. One day, I decided to ride bareback, and we took off cantering across the vast expanse. I felt strong enough to conquer anything when I rode him and free. It was becoming a familiar sensation with him, like the first time we jumped a higher fence than we usually did. We were braver together than we were on our own. Nothing scared me when I was with him.

Buttercake stumbled slightly on some uneven ground. It is much more difficult to ride a horse without a saddle, so all it takes is one good jostle. I slipped off his back and landed on my ass with a thump. He could have taken

Figure 6.2 On Buttercake at a horse show, Sagaponack, New York, 1982; photo by Leslie Wilson

off running, but he stopped abruptly and stood waiting for me to dust myself off. A fall reminds you how magnificent a horse is, how you've made a deal with an animal that could easily crush you. We respected each other despite the difference in our size. I fell more times than I could count over the years, but I never hesitated to get back on.

Nearly every other kid at the barn was older than me. They arrived in fancy cars, wearing sweatshirts emblazoned with the names of private schools and custom-made boots as they perched on their shiny, well-bred horses. I felt scrappy and poor compared to them. I yearned to feel like I belonged there.

Eventually, I found my people. Stacy was a plump girl with white-blond hair and slightly crooked teeth. She leased a black quarter horse named Bullet, and they were a good match: stocky, practical, and tough. When I confessed my crush on Matthew to her, she said, "Don't waste your time on boys like Matthew. You deserve someone hotter, smarter, and super into you." Stacy had a kind of wisdom beyond her years. Stacy's friend Jillian had permed, frosted, feathered blond hair; a lot of pimples on her face; and strong, thick thighs. She bought her horse, Warlock, at an auction, dirt cheap because he was entirely untrained. One of the tallest horses I'd ever seen, he was an Appaloosa, which is a spotted breed with a distinctive patterned coat like a cheetah. Warlock's coloring wasn't the traditional black or brown and white; his spots weren't neat and uniform like those on my plastic Breyer horse. His coat consisted of a lot of different colors in random, changing patterns, and he had a long, unruly mane. He was high-strung and sometimes hard to control. If he were a dog at a shelter, they would probably consider him unadoptable, but Jillian loved him with such devotion. We became an inseparable pack of misfits who rode for the sheer joy, pleasure, and freedom of it. None of us had perfect skin, hair, or horses. As an only child, I had older sisters for the first time. They loved me unconditionally, held me when I cried, and taught me how to use a curling iron so my hair could look like Blair's from *The Facts of Life*.

My mom and I arrived at the stable like usual one day, and Mona's pickup truck wasn't parked in front of her house. I went into the barn, and Matthew told me that Mona was gone. I was crushed. Mona knew me; she knew Buttercake. No one told me what was happening. Rhonda arrived the next day, a nationally known trainer, and she brought her star pupil with her, a girl named Patricia who consistently won top honors at shows and had even had a magazine article written about her. Rhonda's plan was to transform Suffolk Farms into a top-notch facility.

Rhonda was an athletic woman with a blond bowl haircut and slightly sinister eyes who reminded me of Martina Navratilova. She was no-nonsense, strict, unyielding. She would have made a great dominatrix. It was clear in her lessons that the students she'd inherited weren't up to her standards, but she was ready to whip us into shape. I had to adjust. I didn't know what else to do. One of the first shows we attended together was on the beautiful, pastoral grounds of Sagaponack Farms near Bridgehampton. Bright white-painted fences surrounded paddocks, and each show ring was an endless swath of neatly trimmed grass. I stood on the sidelines as a girl entered the ring on a small white pony with a precisely braided mane. I focused on visualizing the Pony Hunter course: start with the combination at the far side, then go around the corner to the oxer, the blue and yellow, the green fence on the diagonal. I'd ridden in horse shows before and typically, I'd get nervous, but I was extra anxious this time. Our warm-up wasn't spot-on; Buttercake and I were having an off day. When I was up, we made our way around the course, jumping each fence in the proper order but not very well. I slowed him to a walk and leaned over to pat him on the neck gently as I exited the ring. Rhonda had an angry look on her face.

"That was awful," she said. I agreed it wasn't my best.

"I am embarrassed to be standing next to you right now as your trainer," she said, then turned and walked away. I burst into tears. Rhonda continued this training style, one of reprimand, degradation, or what people might call *tough love*. Some riders thrived under her tutelage. As a sensitive eleven-year-old, I took her words to heart. She made me feel awful about myself, and I lost some of my confidence. Tough love still doesn't work on me. But I loved to ride, and I discovered I loved to compete, so I was determined to work harder. I dug my heels in determined to get better, and Buttercake and I had some success showing in the Pony Hunter division. Then the inevitable happened: my body grew, and I was too big for Buttercake.

SEX ED

I went on my first real date in sixth grade, with a boy in my class named Mike Jupiter. He was smart and funny and came to pick me up at my house. I wore my favorite jeans and a blue Members Only knockoff jacket I got at a thrift store. We walked to the pizza place, where I ordered one cheese slice and a small Coke. We stood against the counter and ate our pizza as "Billie Jean" played on the radio. About a half hour later, he walked me back to my house and told me he had a good time. I felt giddy at the idea he might become my boyfriend. When I got to school on Monday, my friends asked for the full details of my date, but really they only wanted the answer to one important question:

"Was Mike a good kisser?"

The moment they asked was the moment I realized: we didn't kiss. It never occurred to me, and he never made an advance. But something told me that was not the tale I should tell, so I simply said, "Yes," and left it at that.

While my dad was in the army during the Vietnam War, he had his first relationship with a man. Page 62:

I was in the PX looking through record albums. Some folk singers were whining over a defective PA system. They sounded like they were underwater.

This guy next to me, a Marine, said, "Do you like Judy Garland?"

I said, "Excuse me?"

He repeated, "Do you like Judy Garland?"

I started laughing.

"What's so funny?"

"I didn't think Marines were allowed to like Judy Garland."

"What?"

"I mean, I didn't think Marines liked Judy Garland."

"Well, this Marine does!"

I started laughing again.

"What's your name?"

I pointed to my name tag.

"No, your first name."

"Bill."

"Will?"

"No, Bill."

"I prefer Will. In fact, much better than Will, I like Willy. Willy!"

"Whatever. You're the Marine. It's done. Willy it is." We both laughed, and I began to relax.

He then looked into my eyes, so directly, so receptively, and for so long that I flinched. He seemed to be juggling a question and giving an answer, reassuring me and taunting me. He was the first man to look at me so candidly. I felt exposed. I turned away.

The Marine walked me back to my barracks, and the next day, after work, my houseboy handed me a package that had been delivered earlier. It was a Judy Garland album. No note. No card. I played it over and over again on the company's miserable hi-fi. I found it emotionally intense and addictive.

The following week I did two things: I started dating a WAC named Paula, and I began to hang out with the Marine. I was lonely and horny. Paula and I had nonverbally agreed that there would be no sex, no romance. We went out once a week. I saw the Marine the other six nights. There wasn't much to do on the island. Mostly we got drunk on sake and 7-Up.

I was teased by other students throughout elementary school. Patrice Harris, the ultimate dirtbag-bad-girl-who-looks-older-than-she-is, called me out, announced to the class that she was going to beat me up after school. She ended up pushing me down hard on the concrete, and my new purple sweatshirt skirt from the Gap got dirty. Kids taunted me for being smart; they taunted me because I was one of the shortest, smallest kids in my class;

Figure 7.1 With my friend Kathy (left) and my cat Splash, Sayville, New York, 1985

they taunted me for what I wore; they taunted me for my acne and my often frizzy, can't-quite-get-the-hang-of-the-curling-iron hair. But things really heated up in sixth grade. They began to make fun of me because of my flat chest (since this was a time when many girls were hitting puberty, and I, quite obviously, was not).

Their favorite thing to tease me about was that I was excused from all gym activities except for swimming. By the time I was ten, my knees began to

Tristan Taormino

randomly pop out. I didn't twist it or trip or hit something—it seemed like it happened for no reason. I called it *popping out* because that was the sensation: my leg gave way underneath me suddenly, and I felt a searing, excruciating pain. The medical term for this is *patellar subluxation*, which refers to a partial dislocations of the kneecap. Unlike when I had yellow snot running out of my nose, my mom took this medical problem seriously. After a few incidents, we went to a doctor, but she declined the recommended orthopedic surgery on the grounds that I wasn't even fully grown yet (also, there was no way we could afford it). She opted for physical therapy, and I got out of gym class, which for uncoordinated me was a good thing. But kids loved to call me a weak cripple. At some point, I got fed up.

One day, we were all lined up outside our classroom after recess, boys on one side of the door, girls on the other, waiting for Mrs. Kuehn to let us in. José and Mike (the boy I went on a date with who became my boyfriend briefly) began saying mean things to me, and I just snapped.

I gave them the middle finger and said, "José gets hard when he sees a hole in the wall."

I have no idea where I heard it, but I knew it was something damning about his sexuality. He came over and deliberately kicked me hard in the knee, which predictably dislocated instantly, and I fell to the floor. We all got called to the principal's office, me with an ice pack from the nurse, but I got in more trouble than José and Mike. This prompted my mother to type a letter to the principal:

> Tristan made that obscene gesture out of provocation and frustration.... José and Michael, and possibly others, have repeatedly taunted Tristan about her "handicap" this year. As you [and several teachers] know, Tristan and I have worked very hard to deal with her disability, and you have all been very cooperative and helpful. If all that effort is to be blown away by a malicious boy with an overactive sociability, I am beginning to wonder: Are you, even unintentionally, giving tacit approval to José's contempt for disability and "differentness"?

When she was provoked, you couldn't mistake her outrage and the middle finger in the subtext. It was a moment of her protecting me, which I cherished.

I was invited to be the guest speaker at our twenty-year high school reunion; because I use my legal name in all my work, everyone I went to school with has found me on Facebook, and they are all pretty titillated by what I do. Two decades later, most of them were drunk and seemed exactly the same.

José pulled me aside with clear eyes and apologized for being mean to me when we were kids. It's so weird, the things you hold on to.

Although I knew what I said to José was about sex, I didn't know much else about sex. My mother never said a word, my peers never buzzed about anything beyond making out, and, like for millions of other young people, there was no real sex education at my school. One day, all the girls and boys were rounded up and taken to separate classrooms for what the teacher called *health class*. The girls' group was shown an old film about female anatomy, menstruation, and reproduction. I hadn't gotten my period yet, so none of what was discussed seemed at all connected to *my* body or what I knew about it.

I had been rubbing myself several times a week ever since I first discovered self-pleasure, to feel the rush in my body, to fall asleep, or both. No one mentioned masturbation in the presentation in sixth grade. By then, I had been fooling around with girls in their basements when their parents weren't around, feeling sparks and shocks in my body similar to when I touched myself. We were curious to explore each other's bodies, and I would've loved some more information. But there was no *sex* in the *ed* we got. All I remembered from health class was where my fallopian tubes were, hoping that might come in handy later. It didn't.

My mother did take one interesting approach to my sex education. She had a ton of books all lined up on built-in bookshelves in our living room. Among her Ngaio Marsh mysteries, the autobiography of Lillian Hellman, and Betty Friedan's *The Feminine Mystique* were several sex manuals, including a book with a soft beige cover: Alex Comfort's *The Joy of Sex*, a bestseller in 1972. I could take any books off the shelf and disappear them for months at a time, and she wouldn't say anything about it. On one shelf, propped against a book, was a polished wood drink coaster with a photograph of a gorgeous auburn-haired naked woman posing against a scarlet-red curtain. Her back was arched, her head thrown back with one arm up covering half her face, her knees bent, and her breasts fully jutted out. It was the iconic Tom Kelley photo of Marilyn Monroe that became *Playboy*'s first centerfold in 1953. My mother displayed it as an art piece. My dad wrote in his memoir that his stepfather, Nino, had that same photograph hung in a makeshift pinup gallery behind the bar in their basement, and he thought it was demeaning.

There was no big sit-down on the birds and the bees, just a tiny naked woman and an all-access library. I consider *The Joy of Sex* to be both the first sex education I read and the first porn I saw. I am not sure anyone else would call it porn, but it fits a definition: explicit images of people having sex—where you could see naked bodies, genitals, and penetration—that turned me on. Most kids I knew engaged in the age-old ritual of finding their dad's stash of *Hustler* magazines, breathlessly flipping through pages of glossy naked women, hoping not to get caught. *The Joy of Sex* accomplished two goals at once: material for me to recall when I touched myself and words that brought sex to life and piqued my curiosity: *friction rub, mouth music, chastity belt, perversion.* The men in the drawings had long hair, the women had full bushes, and they all looked relaxed and connected, like they were having a good time. Sex appeared to be really fun. Today more than a hundred sexuality books line the walls of my living room, organized by subgenre: instruction manuals, sexual politics, porn scholarship, kink classics, nonmonogamy, art and photography, and erotic fiction. Along with *The Good Vibrations Guide to Sex, Whores and Other Feminists*, and *Speaking Sex to Power* sits *The New Joy of Sex.*

When someone asked me what I wanted to be when I grew up, I always gave them the same answer:

"A *Solid Gold* dancer or a teacher."

I really liked school, and teaching was a very practical job I could do. But I was obsessed with *Solid Gold*, the 1980s TV show hosted by Andy Gibb and Marilyn McCoo. It featured pop music hits and guest performers, but its unique hook was a multiracial troupe of dancers who performed original numbers to the top 10 songs of the week. It was the closest thing to sex I could watch in prime time.

The costumes were everything: skimpy gold lamé ensembles, skintight hot pants, beaded bodysuits, bikini bottoms with suspenders, shiny headbands, fingerless gloves, and sequined tube tops and leg warmers. Darcel, the lead dancer, was a vision in long braids that swept the back of her knees; she often wore some embellishment to set her apart, like a bejeweled belt or headpiece. The men wore see-through tanks, open shirts, and spandex pants that drew attention to their dicks. The guests themselves were trendy and daring, like Boy George in his signature black derby hat and full makeup with killer eyebrows.

I was mesmerized by the way the dancers moved their bodies together while wearing clothing that looked painted on to songs whose meanings required no translation. *Tonight She Comes.* The dance styles moved seamlessly from jazz to lyrical to modern. The choreography was athletic and risqué, expressing desire and sexuality: performing frequent splits, showing their butts to the camera, gyrating in pairs or groups, writhing on the dance floor. One night Sheena Easton lip-synched to her hit "Strut":

Strut pout, put it out, that's what you want from women
Come on baby, what'cha taking me for
Strut pout, cut it out, all taking and no giving
Watch me baby while I walk out the door
I won't be your baby doll, be your baby doll

I liked the message of a woman being in charge and not letting a man walk all over her sexual autonomy. I also wondered what it might be like to be someone's baby doll. In my adolescence and tweens, I had crushes on boys and boyfriends and loved making out with girls my age as each of us took the role of boy or girl (I played both). Eventually, we got to an age where none of the other girls were initiating that kind of play and focused all their attention on boys. I was still interested in kissing girls, but it seemed like no one else was. Well, not no one.

In junior high I used to mess around with a girl named Angela. Angela was one of those girls who developed early; in sixth grade she already had big breasts. She lived in a one-bedroom apartment on Main Street above the fancy lingerie store where her mom worked. When we got home from school, we had the place to ourselves. We mostly kissed and touched over our clothes, and we played out various scenarios. With her, she was always the boy, and I was the girl—my early femme roots.

"Please come into my office," she said sternly.

"Yes sir," I replied. I walked past the Japanese screen to where her bed was.

"You know that your work hasn't been up to snuff lately. You need to prove to me that I shouldn't fire you. For starters, suck my dick."

I knelt in compliance, and she pushed my face unmercifully into her crotch. I could smell her scent through her thin poplin pants—it was musky, it was salty, it was overwhelming. My body reacted on its own. I didn't want it to end. I liked being bossed around, too. The drama of it all—the force, the degradation, the games—really got me off. After that, there was no going back to simple kissing and groping. I was hooked on the power.

THE BEACH HOUSE

My mother and her best friend, Dee Dee, were pregnant together at the same time in 1970. Dee Dee's son, Dalton, was born a month before me. Dee Dee and my mom both got divorced when Dalton and I were young, and that further cemented their bond. Dee Dee got remarried to a man named Gene, who had two children from his first marriage, and the whole bunch was like an extended family for me and my mom. Dee Dee was a stunningly gorgeous woman who reminded me of Elizabeth Taylor. Her shiny black hair and makeup were always done, especially a perfect red lip, which I never saw her without. Dee Dee was short and voluptuous and weighed about 250 pounds, and no one ever said a word about her body or her weight. She never talked about dieting, never abstained from eating or drinking whatever she wanted, and seemed immune to society's fucked-up standards about what a perfect body was. She was beautiful, and she knew it. Gene was a stocky guy with a wild laugh. Gregarious, affectionate, teasing, he's the kind of guy who picks you up to hug you and could break a rib out of sheer enthusiasm. He was like Jack Tripper from *Three's Company*, a little less madcap but still the life of the party. I couldn't put words to it at the time, but Dee Dee and Gene had palpable chemistry; they touched each other with equal amounts love and lust. They were early role models of parents and partners who were undeniably sexual.

Dee Dee's son, Dalton, was like a brother to me since we'd grown up together for so many years. He had dark wavy hair; a sweet, slightly mischievous smile; and an athletic body (as soon as he could run, he became an avid soccer player). We spent lots of time at their summer beach house, a pale yellow Cape Cod in East Marion, a town just outside Greenport on the east end of Long Island. Within walking distance of their house was a "private" beach, meaning only the residents of that area could use it. It wasn't a gated community or what we think of now as exclusive, just a bunch of people with modest houses on or near the water. The beach was a small sandbar, set on the Peconic River, which leads to Gardiners Bay. Down the street, Dee Dee and Gene docked their speedboat, which they named Jasmine after a stray dog that lived around the docks. They spent the whole summer in East Marion hosting their friends and friends-of-friends and their families. It could be a small group, but more often it was something like fifteen adults and ten kids.

That Dee Dee managed to host, feed, and house twenty-five people in a small two-bedroom cottage seemed impossible. She and Gene slept in their room. The blue room, named for its pale beach-glass-blue walls and ocean-colored bedspreads, had two single beds and room on the floor for two more people to sleep. There was a pullout couch with a TV in a small room off the living room, which had a wicker sofa with olive fabric cushions. The adults had priority for something that approximated a bed, and the kids mostly slept in sleeping bags in tents in the backyard or in the breezeway (a closed-in porch that had a long table where we ate dinner). Inevitably, someone slept (or more like passed out after too many drinks) in the rope hammock in the front yard, and one or two people crashed for the night in their cars. There was one bathroom. Really. And an extra shower stall in the garage.

Dee Dee's entertaining was legendary. As we gathered beach chairs, towels, the bocce ball set, and whatever else we needed for the day, she would meticulously pack five or six coolers of food. Grown-ups would pile into a couple of cars, and most of us would walk or ride bikes three or four blocks to the beach. Somehow our group got the prime spot, dead center in the strip of sand. The parents would get out their books and magazines; children were told to put sunblock on. The kids would run full speed for the water and begin splashing and playing in the cool, greenish bay. They would swim out quickly far beyond where they could reach the bottom to an anchored wooden float the size of a double bed that some guys in the neighborhood had built out of plywood.

Although I was young when I first started going to the beach and I could swim, I was not one of the first in the water. I wasn't as confident as the other

Tristan Taormino

kids. I usually waded in up to my thighs or waist, but that floating structure looked very far off; sometimes I dunked my head, then waded back to shore.

My favorite thing about the beach days was the spread of food. When you opened up Dee Dee's coolers, it was like a fully stocked deli: sweet rolls and bread, cold cuts and cheeses of all varieties, even lettuce and a tomato you could slice on a small cutting board. There was Dee Dee's famous tuna salad, made with tiny diced carrots; potato and macaroni salads; bags of chips; and fruit. Oftentimes, there would also be leftovers from last night's dinner, like London broil sliced thinly that morning for sandwiches or cold barbecued chicken and grilled vegetables on skewers. Another cooler would be packed with beer and soda.

Besides Dalton, there were usually a bunch of kids at Dee Dee's who were around my age or a little older: Dalton's stepbrother, James; his stepsister, Elaine; and Jessica, Bev, and Brandon, the kids from another family whose parents Dee Dee and Gene were very close to. All six of them played soccer together, they were allowed to drive the speedboat by the time they were twelve, and they all water-skied. They were athletes, strong, physical, and confident. I felt like an outsider. I was bookish, obsessed with horses, usually outgoing but shy around them.

The party never stopped with Gene, Dee Dee, and crew, and it was the only time I ever saw my mom get drunk. They would start early at the beach with beer and wine coolers, then head back to the house for cocktails, and get what my dad called *really shit-faced*. No one had to drive anywhere, so there appeared to be no reason to hit the stop button. By the time the kids were eighteen, the adults let them drink freely. I would be offered a beer or a mixed drink, but alcohol tasted bad to me, so I stuck with Cokes.

From an early age, whenever I visited Dalton at his house in Huntington and we were the only two kids there, we'd eventually wander off by ourselves and mess around. I was very curious about sex and pleasure, and even though we were the same age, I saw him as more experienced than me. He initiated most times, and I was flattered because he was really handsome. It occurred to me that if we went to the same school, he wouldn't give me a second look. But we didn't, so we spent a lot of time making out and exploring each other's bodies. At his house we'd go up to the attic, which had been converted to a rec room, like Greg's bedroom on *The Brady Bunch*. We'd play air hockey or Monopoly and eventually ended up on the daybed or sunk into the giant green faux leather beanbag. We kissed, and he'd grab my nonexistent boobs, put his hand between my legs, and rub me over my pants. Everything felt safe and mutual. Although the house was pretty small and our parents were right downstairs, no one ever came to check on us; the only time they acknowledged us was when they shouted from the bottom of the stairs that dinner was ready. We'd pull ourselves together and descend the carpeted stairs nonchalantly. I did wonder if all the kids I knew had their own Dalton (or their own Tristan), someone to be sexual with on a semiregular basis without hand holding or note passing or labels. I liked to imagine that our relationship was special and that I was the only one he did these things with, although, looking back, I probably wasn't.

One day at the beach house, he and I ran home to beat everyone else to the shower in the garage. It was this kind of DIY shower stall, with a cement floor, a flimsy pink shower curtain, a tiny metal tray that held a bar of soap. My skin tingled with heat when the water hit it; I probably should have reapplied sunscreen. I came out of the shower, and Dalton was standing there. Although we'd been intimate for years, we didn't spend a lot of time seeing one another naked. But being naked to me felt pretty normal. He was standing in his board shorts, and he leaned in to kiss me. This was unusual because our hookups happened in private, in secret, really. Even though we were the first ones home, someone could come around the corner at any point. His mouth and skin were salty from the beach. He pulled me into him, and then our flesh touched, and I got turned on. His dick grew against my thigh as we kissed, and he rubbed my nipples with his fingers. That move was unexpected, but I went with it, and I started to feel less self-conscious.

He moved back from me and said, "I'm going to jump in. Put some clothes on, then I want to take you somewhere."

I got dressed in a T-shirt with a Pegasus running in front of a rainbow on it and green terry cloth shorts; my skin still felt sensitive, so I looked in the bathroom closet for some aloe vera gel. He came out of the blue room and said, "Let's go!" I still hadn't asked where we were going. We walked a few blocks, past several houses, and then he took my hand and led me into an empty meadow that veered into the woods. The sun would set soon, but there was still enough light for us to make our way through the thick bushes and tall trees. There wasn't a path, so we were pulling back branches and scraping our way through. We came to a small clearing, and he stopped. He resumed making out with me. I thought, *Oh, he knows everyone's coming back to the house, and he wants some privacy. Cool.* He got hard again against my leg, and I let his dick just be there, not really paying attention to it.

Tristan Taormino

"I want to put my mouth on you," he said. I looked up. This was new. No one had done that to me before. But I was game. So we sat on the dirt, and I shimmied off my shorts. He knelt between my legs, and his tongue zipped right inside my vaginal opening. For the first time, it was like I could feel the inside of my pussy through his tongue. It was a shock, and my body jolted at the surprise. He moved his tongue around, in and out, and I thought, *Hmmm, this is okay.* (My attitude toward anyone going down on me remains the same. Feels nice, doesn't get me off.) It lasted for maybe a minute. He came up and kissed me. His mouth was salty. Then he put my hand on his crotch.

"I want you to suck it," he said, matter-of-factly. It worked for me because we really didn't have a romantic dynamic. There was a directness to our interactions, no seduction, teasing, or postplay cuddling.

He wants me to suck it. Right. I also hadn't done that before. I knew what it was. Several of the drawings in *The Joy of Sex* showed fellatio and sixty-nining. I should have reread those passages and memorized them. He pushed his shorts down, and there it was: my first in-the-flesh hard cock. Looked about right. It wanted something, *he* wanted something, from me. I moved my head down and first just kind of licked it. Licked the tip with my tongue in a haphazard sort of way. The sky began to get darker, and I started to notice how the dirt felt against my knees. Slightly damp and grainy. For a split second, the voice inside my head asked, *How will we explain why we are dirty?*, but I dismissed the thought.

"Really suck it," he whispered. It was pretty big, and there was not a lot of room to maneuver once I had it in my small mouth. I tried an actual sucking motion, but that was difficult. It wasn't like a jawbreaker. He offered no direction whatsoever. Then I felt it. A little snap of fire started to rise up on the back of my waist, which was exposed since my shorts still sagged on my thighs. Then another itch erupted on my ankle. The mosquitoes were out. It was dusk at that point, and we hadn't thought to spray ourselves down with Off before we left the house, which we did every other night. There was a bite on my butt, then another on my leg. *Well, this is not ideal. I am in the woods, trying to give my first blow job, and I'm being eaten alive by mosquitoes.* This was not helping my concentration or my technique, which, let's be real, was pretty nonexistent anyway. Dalton didn't say or do anything except for some moans once in a while. He sat back. I couldn't tell if he was enjoying my efforts. I tried the sucking thing again, but it didn't really get a reaction. Finally, the itching took over, and I couldn't think about anything else.

I sat up. "It's dark, and the mosquitoes are getting me. We should probably go." He agreed and pulled up his pants. We brushed the dirt off each other, then headed back to the house. When we arrived, happy hour was in full swing. People were out on the deck drinking and laughing, and Dee Dee was passing around a tray of hors d'oeuvres. We walked through the garage, and I made a beeline for the bathroom. I wanted to see if any dirt lingered on my knees and shorts, and I had to pee. I pulled my underwear down and sat on the toilet. I looked down, and there was a streak of wetness on the double-reinforced crotch. *Oh, that's why the fabric is thicker there.* I reached with my fingers and found a slick wetness. Like when I masturbated. I peed and checked myself out in the mirror. Then I looked in the cabinet for some calamine lotion.

Our sexual exploration continued until we were about fifteen or sixteen. We never had a conversation about it, just one day when my mom and I went to their house, a beautiful brunette who looked like Alyssa Milano was introduced as his girlfriend; she had shiny hair and wore a fashionable outfit straight out of *Seventeen* magazine. And that was that—no more fooling around.

Dalton and I eventually went away to college. We still saw each other for family gatherings, but it became clear we were headed in different directions. He played soccer and lacrosse and belonged to a fraternity at Bates. I was taking women's studies classes and hanging out with the theater crowd at Wesleyan. Several years after graduation, we were both living in New York City, and I wondered: Now that we weren't obligated to see each other because of our parents, would we have any interest? It turned out we did. We both worked uptown, and we'd get together for lunch. I was fascinated by the young Republican's stories about investment banking, expensive suits, and playing golf with clients. His was such a foreign world to me, and mine to him, of course. He was entranced by my adventures cruising girls at Meow Mix, the dyke bar on the Lower East Side; the sex zine I was putting together; the open mics where I read smutty poetry. We'd talk about our dating and sex lives openly, with both curiosity and sometimes disbelief.

Dalton revealed to me that when he really liked a woman, to further seduce her and convey a desire for something deeper, he'd buy her a pair of shoes. And he had impeccable taste in women's shoes. So we'd window-shop on Fifth Avenue, and he'd point out his picks. They were very expensive and

Tristan Taormino

luxurious, sexy without being too obvious about it. He preferred sling-back pumps and peep toes in black, deep wine, or red. He loved the curve of a shoe, imagined how it would look on a foot, and drooled over Bruno Magli, Marc Jacobs, Gucci. He always zeroed in on a shoe for a strong woman that said, "I HAVE TASTE AND FUCK ME."

I was single at the time, and Dalton had a live-in girlfriend. His family adored her, but he confessed to me over lunch one day that he didn't think she was *the one*. After we ate, we got in a cab and went to his apartment in Murray Hill and had sex. We were back to a familiar place, but this time we were grown-ups. The chemistry was still there, even though I'd lost most of my interest in sex with men once I began fucking women. We started an affair that lasted a few months. We'd mostly meet during the day when we could get away from work. For me, there was the novelty of it all and the story it would make eventually, like *Can you believe we did that?* He loved blow jobs still, and he wasn't shy about asking for one after he went down on me. By then, thankfully, I knew how to give good head. You'd think I'd want to prove to him that I had certainly upped my game in a decade, but I mostly wanted to fuck. I would reluctantly suck his dick, and I wouldn't even cover over that it was boring and slightly tedious. I am not sure why he tolerated this, but he did. I would just look at him, roll my eyes, sigh, and put his cock in my mouth. Eventually we'd get to fucking, and that's what I craved. He had a nice-sized cock (so I wasn't wrong all those years ago, it was big!), and he had some skills. It was back to being a secret that only the two of us shared, just like old times, and that was part of the thrill. It ended when he decided to ask his girlfriend to marry him. It seemed like the right thing to do. They never ended up getting married.

FOXGLOVE

By 1983, I had outgrown Buttercake. He was such a singular source of joy and freedom for me that I felt a little lost. Jane, another trainer at Suffolk Farms, was opening her own stable further east, a twenty-minute drive on the Long Island Expressway from our home.

"Everything is brand new, and the next project is building a house on the property," she said, as we passed the last stall before walking into the office. She had just taken my mom and me on a tour of Foxglove Farms with great pride, and I could tell it was her lifelong dream realized. Jane had calming, grounded Earth Mother energy with a strength just below the surface that meant she would take no shit. She was a tall, wide woman whose body could have been trained to deadlift at the Olympics, but was softer, better suited to envelop you in a warm hug. It was unusual to see a fat rider and trainer, especially in the horse show world, where beauty standards rivaled those of modeling, and I was often surrounded by young Christy Turlingtons in tailored jackets and jodhpurs. Jane was neither glamorous nor snooty. Her long, stringy brown hair was often unwashed and hidden under an army-green knit hat. She wore the same pair of dirt-covered jeans and a ratty orange puffy coat. I imagined it was difficult to find nice clothes in her size.

Jane was a smart and caring teacher, the opposite of sadistic Rhonda; she knew how to hold you and push you forward at the same time. Plus, she had the ability to calm me down when I panicked about making a mistake and re-focus me. She understood that I was sensitive and encouraged me to use that to my advantage to be super in tune with the horse. At Foxglove, I quickly found my favorite lesson horse, a bright-eyed chestnut with a white star and blaze down his face and white markings on his back legs named Chipper. Most people thought of him as average and even-tempered, and they didn't see the special spark in him that I did. I didn't know if I could ever find such a strong connection as the one I had with Buttercake, but I was beginning to build one with Chipper. We fit together in a way that can't be forced. When I looked deeply into his eyes, I could tell he was up for a challenge. We created a pact that we would each try our best and care for one another. He would not let me down. I wanted to lease Chipper, have him all to myself, but he couldn't leave his post as a working horse, so Jane agreed I could ride him on his time off.

I spent every ounce of time I wasn't in school at the barn, and I became best friends with three girls my age who all owned horses: Renny, Donna, and Hailey. We'd go on long trail rides together in the woods cantering over logs we set up as makeshift jumps. We had sleepovers and made friendship brace-lets. We got into as many shenanigans as budding teen girls could, including going to all-ages clubs on the weekends. We decked out in lace headbands, tight skirts, and black rubber bracelets to look like Madonna in *Desperately Seeking Susan*. We danced and mouthed all the words to "I Wonder If I Take You Home" by Lisa Lisa and Cult Jam.

Jane's star student at the barn was Patty, a very mature sixteen-year-old. She had a magnificent, graceful gelding named Forever Amber, which elicited raised eyebrows from anyone she told because it was apparently the title of a steamy romance novel. She was wealthy but never a snob. I looked up to her like a big sister. She was a beautiful, gifted rider but faced an obstacle in her show career. There was talk that judges discriminated against her because she was short and a little chubby, which I thought was preposterous and unfair. Once again, I felt most at home in a crew of misfits and outsiders.

I got back into the horse show circuit, where Chipper and I began to exceed Jane's (and everyone's?) expectations. A dusty lesson horse—who lived outside when the barn was full with paying boarders—and I held our own alongside rich kids with brand-new Saabs and expensive mounts, some worth six figures (in the 1980s). My proximity to this level of wealth was a crash course on the class system. Other people had much more money than we did, so there was a part of their world I would never have access to. Mine was not a Hollywood story where my talent could transcend these constraints.

Figure 9.1 With Chipper at Foxglove Farms, Medford, New York, 1984

I had an unstoppable work ethic, I threw myself in completely, but that would never be enough.

Chipper and I had a great run for several years, but we got to the point where he had taken me as far as he could. I'd outgrown him in a different way—I needed a bigger, more athletic horse who could jump higher fences and partner with me to get ready for Medal Maclay, the next level in equitation. My best bet was to find a deal on a green horse that needed lots of blood, sweat, and tears. I knew I could put in the work; I just needed the cash.

Jane had a creepy boyfriend named Len, whose face and clothes were covered in dirt and grime. He always wore a crumpled, dusty hat and had a cigarette dangling from his mouth. His breath smelled of liquor. They lived together in a cramped trailer on the property where every surface was covered in empty beer bottles and ashtrays overflowing with cigarette butts. My mother said, "They are in a codependent relationship." I didn't know what that meant exactly, but it was obviously no fairy tale.

Len and I were the only ones at the barn on a Sunday when the others were away at a show. He invited me into the trailer to warm up. For some reason,

Tristan Taormino

he started asking me about sex and said, "I bet you've never seen an adult one before." I was fifteen. I tried to change the subject, but he persisted, and I was weirded out by his emphasis on the word *adult*, which implied I had seen lots of nonadult penises. I quickly changed the subject. Later, as he walked down the aisle feeding the horses, I didn't want to make eye contact as he passed me, so my eyes dropped, and I saw the zipper of his pants was down. He was wearing a pair of greasy, thin hunter green work pants, no underwear, and I could make out his penis in the shadow of his open fly. I wondered if he had planned this or if it was simply a mistake, but the talk about penises earlier made me uneasy. When my mom picked me up, I told her what had happened, and she said, "He can't get away with this." She sounded very upset. She immediately took me to the police station to file a complaint.

"I would like to speak with an officer, please," said my mom to the woman in uniform behind the counter.

"What is this about, ma'am?" she asked, almost casually.

My mother seemed annoyed. Picture Christine Baranski, a woman with a caustic wit who can conjure an I-am-not-fucking-around attitude in a flash. My mom lowered her voice and spoke slowly. "It's about child molestation," she replied.

The woman's eyes grew wide, and she said, "I'll have someone come out to get you."

I recounted my story to an officer sitting at a desk with files piled high everywhere. He wrote it all down.

"So what happens now?" asked my mom.

"Well, truthfully, ma'am, the only thing we could really get this guy on is indecent exposure. Because he never actually touched your daughter . . . He didn't touch you, right, hon?"

"No," I said.

"I want him arrested," said my mom.

"We'll go out there and have a talk with him. Is he at the address you gave us now?"

"He should be."

"Okay, we'll pay him a visit, and you can call me tomorrow for an update. Here's my card."

We drove home in silence. *Why did my mom say* molestation? *I don't think that's what happened. Maybe he just peed and forgot to zip up. Or maybe Len was just being his usual creepy self which everyone else seemed to tolerate. Is he going to get in trouble? What will Jane and everyone else think when they find out we went to the police?* No matter how dumb, dirty, or drunk he was, Jane loved Len, and there was no tearing them apart. I knew that for sure.

I heard from Renny that the cops arrested Len at the barn and brought him down to the station. Maybe he even spent a night in jail? He pled to something and paid a fine. *What will I tell Jane? Should I blame it on my mom?* I decided to say nothing, a tactic my mom and dad seemed fond of using when what you had to talk about was hard or uncomfortable. And Jane pretended like everything was normal. But nothing was the same. How could it be?

I was about to turn sixteen, and several realities sunk in. It was clear there wasn't a horse at the barn for me to ride. Mom's financial situation was more precarious than it had ever been. Buying a horse and sustaining my place on the horse show circuit seemed impossible. I'd broken Jane's trust. I couldn't see a way forward. One day, I told my mom I didn't need her to drive me to the barn. A day turned into a week and then a month. My mother and I never talked about it. Jane never called me, but I suspected she was furious about the thing with Len. At the time, I blamed this disappearing dream on the money. There was a price to pay, and we couldn't afford it.

In the tack room at the barn sat my old brown trunk with worn brass trim that my mother had found at a secondhand shop. It was filled with dandy brushes, a shedding blade, a mane-and-tail comb, a black currycomb, a rubber glove with textured nubs, a bottle of shampoo, a red bucket, a metal hoof pick, a blue halter, and a few rags. My saddle sat on one of the wooden posts that jutted out of the wall. Although I got my boots and show clothes from a consignment store, my mother bought the saddle for me brand new. I painstakingly cleaned and oiled the leather of my prized possession and polished the small brass engraved nameplate on the back where the seat curves up. No one asked me if I wanted to keep any of those things or give them to someone else. I suppose if I kept my saddle, it meant I was leaving the barn but I would one day ride again. I longed for some kind of resolution, even just an explicit goodbye to my friends. I cried without knowing or naming my emotion as grief. Mom and I never talked about how painful it was for me to let go of my love, my one true passion. That barn was my home for more than four years, and the people my family. We stayed in touch for a little while, but eventually, I never saw any of them again.

Tristan Taormino

P-TOWN

"**S**ummer is peak tourist season here. I'll talk to some people I know, but I think it will be easy to find you a job," said my dad. He'd sold his place in Charlestown, Massachusetts, and moved to Hyannis for a few years, waiting tables and working retail, then found his way to Provincetown—P-town—on the tip of Cape Cod. At fifteen, I wanted to spend more time with him, plus I was still riding then and needed to make money for my dream-horse fund. So we decided I'd go live with him on summer break.

I packed my diary, my Sony Discman, my favorite pair of Jordache jeans, and too many black rubber bracelets. He told me he was so excited to show me his new condo, which he had just painted and decorated before I arrived. During the tour I took note of his paint choices. Light gray. Medium gray. Concrete gray. Darker gray. He had found an antique wooden church pew, which served as the living room couch, gorgeous but really shallow and uncomfortable (typical for the Catholics). No matter how vehemently he rejected the religion, he thought the artifacts were beautifully made and said, "It brings a sense of irony to the living room, don't you think?" Hanging in my room was a five-by-seven-foot abstract print of a blue horse galloping across a yellow background. He picked it just for me. The photograph of the topless woman with long, wispy hair pulled back in a ponytail, the one I'd seen the first time I visited him in Boston, hung in the hallway.

Commercial Street is the hub of Provincetown, jam-packed with shops, restaurants, galleries, and bars and crowded with tourists day and night, who

Figure 10.1 With Dad, Provincetown, Massachusetts, 1987

came to shop, eat, lie on the beach, and, above all, party. He worked at a leather shop called Northern Lights on the east end of the street. The owners of the store, a married couple named T. and Celine, welcomed me like family and gave me a job. They were both high-strung, gregarious, and focused on their business. They carried top-of-the-line leather clothing that sold for hundreds of dollars and handbags made of leather so soft it felt like silk. I spent my days upstairs above the shop, unpacking and inventorying luxurious things and packaging mail orders; occasionally I'd cover a shift at their Yucatan hammock store down the block. I'd never been away from riding that long before, but when I opened a box of stunning purple leather jackets or smart messenger bags, the smell filled the air around me and reminded me what I was working for. It was also soothing in a way I couldn't articulate. That calm was often interrupted when a staffer came up to take a break from the sales floor.

One guy, Don, ate his lunch upstairs before his shift and would announce, "It's almost time. Let's get worked *up*. I am going to sell like crazy today!" Then he'd do a shot of ginseng and a shot of vodka. All the staff who worked there were similarly energetic and stressed out much of the time. They sold a lot of leather. A lesbian bike messenger named Nina visited regularly to drop

Tristan Taormino

off and pick up packages. She was a cross between a grown-up tomboy and a biker chick with long, kinky jet-black hair and muscled, tattooed arms. I grinned too wide when I saw her. I had a crush.

Although he hadn't lived there for very long, my dad knew a lot of people, but then again, everyone in P-town seemed to know everyone else, especially those who lived there year-round. As we walked down the street, spontaneous family reunions happened all around us, with folks embracing, kissing, catching up, and making plans. I mostly hung out with adults because the only other kids my age were townies, who considered me a mere working tourist. They were dirtbags anyway, hanging around with their skateboards and causing trouble outside Spiritus Pizza late at night. One of the first people I met was my dad's friend Paul. He worked at Mad as a Hatter, a hat shop across the street from Northern Lights. Like many stores at that end of town, it was in an old house with two huge picture windows, which were full of felt fedoras, wide-brimmed floppy hats with giant bows, and outrageous top hats straight out of *Alice in Wonderland*. When Paul was redoing the window and I was outside on a break, we'd catch each other's eye and wave, and sometimes I'd cross the street and check out what he was doing. He was a short guy in his thirties, well dressed, with a deep tan and electrifying aqua-blue eyes. There were a lot of beautiful people in Provincetown.

My dad invited Paul over to our house for dinner and cooked squiggly pasta with peas, chicken, Parmesan cheese, and ground pepper. After we sat down to eat, Paul began to tell us a story.

"It was our first date, and the guy and I really hit it off. After the movie we went back to his place. We started kissing, then he told me the couch was a sofa bed, so we pulled it out together. We fucked on top of it, and just as we were done, his roommate came home. It was one of those totally weird moments," Paul said, and he blushed a little like he was reliving it.

"I wanted to get up and take a shower, and I suddenly felt shy because I didn't know either of these guys. But we were right there in the living room, and his roommate didn't scurry away or anything. *Do I stay under the thin sheet and wait or get up?*"

"So what did you do?" my father asked.

"I got up and walked to the shower, buck naked with the guy's cum on my stomach. Kinda awkward, right?" Paul laughed gently.

I thought, *Yeah, that does sound kind of awkward. I wonder if these men had ever been to the Bunk House.* It happened sometimes that adults would talk to me like I was one of them, but no one had ever spoken so freely and matter-of-factly about sex in front of me like that. No one. I had questions. *How did they decide to have sex after they met? What did he mean by "we had sex"? There weren't enough details to get a full picture. Why was the roommate so nonchalant? Why was there cum on Paul's stomach?* I was riveted and curious but also felt very grown-up that I was even a part of this conversation. And I had a little crush on Paul, so hearing these intimate details was titillating. I imagined his naked body, toned and tan, intertwined with another man's.

One night after we got off work, Dad took me to a show called *Sadji and Company* at the Pilgrim House. Most days, dolled-up drag queens would stand on the sidewalk in the middle of town like barkers promoting their shows. The Pilgrim House was a bar, and I was way under twenty-one, but my dad knew the owner of the club, so he walked me right in. We found a table in the middle of the room; a small placard read Two Drink Minimum per Person. I knew that money was tight, so paying $40 for two tickets and two drinks each was expensive for my dad. We each ordered Cokes. I never saw my father drink alcohol.

The lights went down, and soon it was a whirlwind of beautiful queens in long, shiny wigs and sparkling gowns. Each one "impersonated" a well-known singer in a choreographed, lip-synched dance number. One Black queen was more than six feet tall and looked exactly like Diana Ross with her huge Afro and long, skinny body as she sang "I'm Coming Out."

This was my first drag show, so I was taking in the spectacle of it all: the bodies squeezed into dresses, the curves and cleavage, the eyelashes and sweaty temples, the overdrawn lips. I was enthralled. Sadji's dark brown skin glistened against her silky blue slip dress, and you couldn't tell her curly hair was a wig. She was the headliner, so they saved her for the last showstopping number, "It's Raining Men," by the Weather Girls. At the time I didn't know that I would hear that particular song at nearly every drag show I attended thereafter.

We went to many shows that summer, and I got to know the queens because my dad was friends with many of them. Some of them were hard to recognize out of their costumes, but others appeared to be very feminine offstage; some were transsexual women, my dad explained, which I promptly looked up in the dictionary when we got home. There was a Latina queen named Lola. When we ran into her at the grocery store, Lola didn't wear heavy makeup or a fancy dress like onstage, but she was a woman. She had gentle eyes and smelled like spiced apples and vanilla. I finally got the nerve to ask her what her perfume was. I was never into perfume that much, but this scent captured her femininity in a way I'd never experienced before.

"Do you like it?" she said coyly.

"I do," I replied.

She started fishing for something in her oversized pocketbook. "I get samples whenever I visit the counter . . ."

"Here, you can have this one," she said, and she handed me a small glass vial of Estée Lauder's Beautiful. Although the majority of the tourists were white, like nearly everyone in my hometown (and the horse show world), many of the queens were people of color. I didn't have the language to articulate my feelings then, but it is one of my earliest memories of acknowledging I was white, although not understanding what that meant exactly. Except that being surrounded by whiteness had affected my ideas about gender, especially femininity.

One night on our way to the Pilgrim House, my dad announced, "The show we are going to see tonight is *different*. It's not a showcase. Only one performer will be onstage. He's a friend of mine named Jimmy James, and he's known for doing impersonations of iconic female singers. He's known for doing Marilyn Monroe."

From the moment she stepped onstage, I was awestruck. Unlike some of the drag queens with cheap jewelry who didn't know all the words to their songs, Jimmy *sang* Marilyn's songs and talked to the audience in Marilyn's voice. It was exhilarating to sit in the audience as she teased men in the front row and sang "Happy Birthday" to one lucky gentleman. In the second half of the act, Jimmy did Judy Garland, Cher, Bette Davis, even Madonna. He did their voices, facial expressions, and signature movements impeccably.

My dad took me backstage to meet Jimmy after the show, and I was completely smitten with his Southern accent and big smile. He put us on the permanent guest list, and we went to see his show a half dozen times more. The first time I ran into him during the day on Commercial Street, I saw a tiny, slightly plump, effeminate white guy wearing black Lycra bike shorts, with the front of his light brown hair bleached. He was cute, perky, and witty, and he talked to me like I was a grown-up. His nightly transformation was magical. When he got himself in that peach-pink sequined dress, blond wig, and diamond bracelets, he *embodied* Marilyn Monroe. His makeup was flawless. *How did he do his eyeliner like that?* He played her as a smart woman who used her sexuality very deliberately to get what she wanted, and often the joke was on the audience. In a pure illustration of camp, Jimmy's Marilyn

Bill
Take care
Jimmy James

Photo by:
RICHARD ARMAS
Unretouched
"Biting Scarf"

MR. JIMMY JAMES

New York
Ans. Service
212•730•1188

A Live Visual and Vocal Impressionist
Recreates Marilyn Monroe and Other Famous Legends

Figure 10.2 Performer Jimmy James, signed publicity photo, 1986

demonstrated a calculated gender performance, and because he played her so well, it made you think that the real Marilyn was probably doing drag all along. Jimmy as Marilyn was gorgeous and sexy and naughty and brash, and I wanted to be her. Not the Marilyn I'd seen in *All about Eve* with my dad, not the Marilyn on posters and cheap T-shirts at souvenir shops. I wanted to be the Marilyn Jimmy was. She was the most exciting, most glamorous person I had ever met. I was beginning to figure out my gender aspiration, and I had a name for it: drag queen.

At the end of the summer, I went back to Sayville and began tenth grade. My dad called a month later to tell me that Paul had been diagnosed with AIDS. By then, my dad had started working as an administrative assistant at the Provincetown AIDS Support Group. Until that point, I'd only read a handful of articles about the so-called homosexual disease in the *New York Times*, I didn't know any actual person with AIDS. There was no cure. People with the disease were being ostracized. They were dying. Paul was going to die.

THE PRIEST'S BROTHER

I n the winter P-town goes into hibernation: the herd thins out to about
10 percent of its summer size, drag shows end, shops close or reduce their
hours, and Commercial Street gets blanketed in snow. Then Memorial
Day rolls around, and everything picks back up where it left off. It was the
same when I returned the next summer, except that Paul was gone. Of course,
many others were gone too. I didn't understand just how many. P-town and
AIDS raged on.

By then, I knew the rhythm of the place, how to zigzag my way down
Commercial Street and make it through all the tourists holding hands. I was
ready to see what queens had returned to strut their stuff for the season. I
wanted to work as many hours as I could to save for my horse. When my dad
lived in Hyannis before P-town, we hung out with his friends Fran and Andy
a lot. Andy was over six feet tall with jet-black hair styled like the guy from
A Flock of Seagulls. He wore pants with vertical black-and-white stripes and
geometric-patterned shirts. Fran was at least a foot shorter than him, and she
dressed like an MTV VJ. Her clothes were bright and fashionable; she changed
her hairstyle a lot, but it was always something daring and asymmetrical.
We went to their house one night and stayed up late to watch *Stop Making
Sense*, a concert documentary about their favorite band, Talking Heads. The
lead singer wore this oversized suit that looked like something Andy could
totally pull off. Fran and Andy opened a store in P-town across the street from
Northern Lights that featured their own line of hand-silk-screened T-shirts.

Working in their store was pretty easy, and my coworker Danny made it an adventure. In the early 1990s, Mattel released a new doll called Earring Magic Ken. It was the original Ken doll, but he had a pierced ear and wore black denim jeans, a purple PVC mesh vest, and a silver ring around his neck that looked remarkably like a metal cock ring. He was meant to be *urban* and *cool*, according to the ads, but he was so obviously gay. Danny looked like Earring Magic Ken with black hair: gym buff, fashion forward, obviously gay. I refolded T-shirts as Danny played DJ, mixing Crowded House, XTC, R.E.M., and the Pet Shop Boys. Sometimes he'd clock out just before five so he could head straight to the Tea Dance at the Boatslip, get drunk, and hook up. Then he would drag himself in the next morning, hungover, in sunglasses, to tell me about it.

"I flirt, I cruise. I like the daddies." I was fascinated. His stories featured barrel-chested bears in thongs, messy flirts with boyfriends, DJs who only played Madonna and Whitney. There were men doing lines of cocaine off other men's asses. Sweaty dudes bumping and grinding against each other, packed together so tightly you could barely get to the bar. He used to say, "You have to dance, there's no other choice." When tea was over, more drinking, more dancing, sex.

My father had a new close friend he introduced me to soon after I arrived: a Jesuit priest named Patrick who was probably in his mid-thirties. Patrick's much younger brother, John, whom everyone called Boomer, was staying with him for the summer. Although Boomer was two years younger than me, my dad and Patrick thought maybe we could hang out. Boomer was a tall, lanky guy with brown hair like Duckie in *Pretty in Pink* and big blue round-framed glasses. He seemed very cool and mature for his age.

One day Boomer and I were at the condo alone making tuna fish sandwiches on toasted Lender's onion bagels for lunch. We sat down at the kitchen table and started to eat.

Boomer finished chewing a bite and asked nonchalantly, "So, when did you find out your dad was gay?"

My eyes widened, and my stomach jumped. The movie montage appeared in front of me, as if it was from an old projector, the kind where you can put your hand through the light and block out certain spots.

Never remarried, never even a girlfriend. He loved the theater. He wrote a play about people with AIDS. Judy Garland and Barbra Streisand. A lot of his friends were gay and lesbian. Drag queens. He loved fashion, art, and decorating. Oh my God, my dad is gay! That really makes sense and explains a bunch of things. The way Boomer asked the question made it clear he believed I already knew. *Oh. Because he obviously knows his older brother, the priest, is gay. My dad and Patrick the priest are gay. Wait, are Patrick and my dad a couple?*

I was embarrassed to admit to Boomer that I didn't know until that very moment, embarrassed that I hadn't figured it out, embarrassed that a fourteen-year-old kid knew more than I did. I felt clueless. I didn't want to look clueless. I stared at the framed photograph of Bette Davis smoking that was hanging on the wall behind Boomer's head.

"Oh, a while ago . . ." I tried to sound as chill as I could.

"Patrick came out to me last year. What is it like having a gay dad?" *He is obviously trying to bond with you, Tristan. You both have gay family members, after all.*

"It's cool. Do you want some more potato chips?" Inside, all I could think was *My dad is gay, my dad is gay, my dad is gay, my dad is gay, my dad is gay, my dad is gay, my dad is gay, my dad is gay, my dad is gay, my dad is gay, my dad is gay, my dad is gay, my dad is gay, my dad is gay, my dad is gay, my dad is gay, my dad is gay, my dad is gay, my dad is gay.* Whoa.

It was confusing that neither my mother nor my father had told me he was gay. They both had openly gay friends in their lives that I grew up with. *Why was this a secret?* I began to catalog all the gay and lesbian people my parents had introduced me to. Her close friend Chickie was the one we saw most often. *Did Chickie know?*

Chickie was a six-foot-three auburn-haired goddess who'd been in my life for as long as I could remember. He had an exceptionally well-groomed mustache and beard. His hair was unbelievably shiny, as if he came straight from Vidal Sassoon. I never saw him in the same outfit twice and couldn't wait to see his ensemble the next time we saw him. Once he wore tight jeans that showed off his ass, a half-buttoned blousy shirt that looked like it was made of expensive fabric, and a wedge heel. Rings on nearly every finger and lots of bangles. He wore Shalimar perfume. He said *doll* at the end of his sentences, like "Get me another cup of tea, will you, doll?" Imagine meeting Jonathan Van Ness in the 1970s. Chickie had a longtime boyfriend, a gray-haired older

Tristan Taormino

man who loved to decorate and redecorate their house; they lived together for decades like any married couple. Chickie worked as a guard at a psychiatric prison on Long Island, which was strange to me since that sounded like a very scary place, where you'd have to be really tough. He was tough, but his toughness was very much on the inside, and I was pretty sure that only people who knew him for a long time, like me and Mom, could see it. Plus, I thought some of the prisoners must be crazy, so they would have an even harder time seeing it. He said he went to work in something called "butch drag." Long before I'd ever heard terms like *genderqueer, nonbinary,* and *genderfluid,* there was Chickie. My mom's fabulous friend.

From a very young age, I loved Chickie's sense of freedom and confidence— he was 100 percent himself; he didn't look, sound, or act like any other men I knew. He was gorgeously effeminate, a proud peacock in a world of chickens. Later, when I met drag queens in P-town, I realized Chickie was a little like them, except his gender expression was not about performing on a stage. The only time he got into drag, he went the other way, into performative masculinity in order to exist in a *man's* job where he was surrounded by guys—the prisoners and the other guards. Away from work, Chickie felt safe to play with his gender and embody a mix of man and woman. He was the first person in my life who proved gender was more complicated than other people were letting on. He made me curious about my own gender.

My dad wasn't as blatantly girly as Chickie in the way he dressed and moved, but I still recognized some elements of traditional femininity in him. In fact, I longed for qualities he had that I didn't find in the rest of my family: he was emotional and nurturing. There was a softness about him. He could be sweet and affectionate. His love was gentle and fierce at the same time.

Once I knew my dad was gay, I acted as if I had known all along, like, *Of course I am spending the summer in P-town with my gay dad!* I went back through all his close friends I'd met over the years, trying to determine who could have been a lover. My dad could be flirty and physical, and I figured out that I had watched him subtly cruise other men in public. We'd stop, and he'd introduce me to someone as if he were winking at them. My dad was effusive and affectionate, so I didn't think anything of it. He moved his hands a lot when he talked, and sometimes he'd slide a finger across a guy's rib cage, looking him right in the eye. I can see why men fell in love with him.

Figure 11.1 With Chickie, West Sayville, New York, 1982

I didn't know if I should tell my mom that I knew. *What would that ultimately change?* She obviously knew. If my parents had never shared this crucial piece of information with me, then I probably wasn't supposed to blab it to anyone else, like my friends. There was utter silence on the subject, although one message came through clearly: secrecy (and shame?) surrounded who my dad was. What did that mean for my mother? And what did that mean for me?

Tristan Taormino

MR. MELTME

When I got home from P-town, I was hoping maybe I'd find a green horse with a good disposition or an older horse with a generous owner who'd cut me a deal. I had kept track of what I'd made that summer and the summer before, which totaled about $4,000, and I asked my mom to confirm that.

"Let's sit for a minute," she said. "I don't have it right now. I used it to pay the mortgage and some bills. But I will put it back in the bank as soon as I can." My heart sank. Things were worse than I thought.

A few days later, she said, "I'm tired of doing all this landlord shit." She sold our place on Cherry Avenue, and we moved to a blue colonial with an enclosed front porch on Hampton Street. My dream of buying my own horse was slipping away.

Because my life revolved around the barn, I was never fully immersed in my school social scene. There was a well-defined cool crowd in high school, and I wasn't in it. I hung out with the nerds because I was smart and the drama geeks because I was into theater, and these were often the same people; I was friends with the new wave kids, who dressed all in black, smoked pot and took mescaline, and listened to the Cure, Depeche Mode, and Echo and the Bunnymen. I was still close to Kathy, the best friend I made in seventh grade, a gorgeous athletic girl with a round face, icy blue eyes, and sandy brown hair with blond highlights. In junior high we wore matching best-friend shirts (a hot trend in the 1980s)—red-sleeved white raglans with comedy and tragedy masks ironed on the front and our names in black fuzzy letters on each arm. Kathy was a style icon. She couldn't shop for new clothes every week like the cool-crowd girls, yet she managed to put together outfits that could be on the cover of *Seventeen.* She could really accessorize. We bonded when she lent me nail polish in social studies class, but it quickly deepened. She was a good listener. She understood when I had big feelings; she often quieted my inner critic with love and reason, which I needed badly. But she also wasn't afraid to tell me when my hair was way too big for the ninth-grade formal, when I was being a bitch, or when I should lay down my sword in a battle. By high school Kathy had become a cool girl but wasn't exclusive like most of them.

The weekend culture in Sayville was about getting drunk, smoking pot, and hooking up at Lotus Lake, an artificial lake surrounded by woods behind one of the newest housing developments. I was a bit of an enigma because I was a nerd who drank and got high at parties and fooled around with lots of different boys. I wasn't the most popular or the hottest girl, but I was horny and, instead of simply willing, assertive about my desires. So I got plenty of kissing-groping-grinding action. I followed my sexual impulses. I was slutty and unashamed.

Figure 12.1 Mom helps me with a corsage before a prom, Sayville, New York, 1987

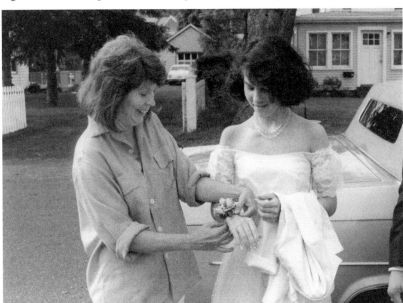

Tristan Taormino

Sometimes these trysts were recurring, like when Kathy and I hooked up with two brothers a few years apart in age. I got the younger one, Eli. His older brother was sophisticated and intellectual, but Eli had blue eyes and blond hair, an athletic body, and charm for days. Our chemistry was white-hot and stood out from all the others, except maybe boss man Angela. Once, Eli and I were having a furious make-out session in my bed, and I was on top, rubbing myself against his leg. I was so turned on, my brain quieted; I stopped thinking, which was rare, and I just *felt*. My body took over, and then I experienced that same release I got when I masturbated. It actually surprised me because I hadn't connected what I did by myself to what I did with other people. It was the first time I came with another person. I wasn't bored by Eli the way I was by other guys. I couldn't put it into words at the time, but I began to notice a pattern. I didn't experience that ache in my body about the boys who emotionally or intellectually stimulated me or made me laugh. The ones I lusted after didn't give great conversation. There was this strange divide for me between the boys I liked to hang out with and the boys I wanted to fuck. They weren't the same boys.

I was a smart, straight-A student and loved all my classes. My precalculus teacher in my junior year was Mr. S., a man who was at the center of a scandal several years before. He had an affair with the sister of Debbie, one of my classmates, and left his wife for her. He married Debbie's sister after she graduated, and his wife committed suicide shortly after the wedding. It's all anyone talked about. True love (if that's what it was) seemed to always have a dark side.

As we settled into our seats on the first day of class, Mr. S. was standing at the front of the classroom with a young guy who looked to be in his early twenties and was dressed in khakis, a blue button-up shirt, and loafers. He looked like a blond Tom Cruise. I did a double take, like in the "Papa Don't Preach" video when a short-haired Madonna first spots the bad boy in the park who will go on to become the father of her baby.

"Class, I want to introduce you to a special guest. This is Mr. Meltme. He is going to school to get his degree in teaching. He is student-teaching another class of mine and sitting in to observe this one." He turned to Mr. Meltme. "You can sit at that desk."

Then Mr. Meltme came straight for me. I occupied the second to last seat in the last row, and he took the one behind me, where he sat for four months. I made it a point to get to that class early, no dawdling in the halls, so we could chat before class started. All the girls talked about him with giggles and swoons. He was not a teenage boy; he looked me in the eye when he talked to me and didn't break my gaze. I wanted him.

As it got closer to winter break, my classmates decided we should have a going-away party for Mr. Meltme. I volunteered to be in charge: I organized the event, arranged for the cake, and—most important—created a giant card made of oaktag that the class signed. I drew Mr. Meltme standing at a blackboard, and we, the students, were all around him, represented by giant blocks of melting ice.

Mr. Meltme smiled wide when we presented it to him. He knew I was the one who made it. We ate cake and made small talk until the bell rang. I was doing a fundraiser for Key Club where you get people to order cards and wrapping paper from a catalog, and then all the stuff comes to your house, and you hand-deliver it to your customers. Mr. Meltme had ordered something from *me*, which was significant because nearly every junior was doing this fundraiser. The day classes ended, I realized that, unlike for the rest of the folks who ordered from me—my mother, her friends, my neighbors—I had no way of getting Mr. Meltme his purchases, since he wouldn't be coming back to school after break. This gig was temporary: he was finishing up his studies to become a real teacher. I saw him in the hallway outside the teachers' lounge.

"Hey, Mr. Meltme! You ordered that stuff from me, but everything comes next week, so should I send it to you or . . ."

He smiled. "Why don't I give you my home number, and you can call me? Then I can come pick it up from you. I live in Patchogue, very close by."

"Your number, right. Good idea. Give me your number, and I'll call you." Inside I was dying. He handed me a piece of paper with the name Matt on it and his phone number. Matt. *His first name was Matt, and he was indicating that now that he wasn't a student teacher at my school, I should maybe call him by his first name? Oh Mr. Meltme!* I tried to act nonplussed and said, "Great, so I will call you."

His eyes held mine for a moment, and he nodded slowly and said, "I look forward to it." I picked up on some kind of vibe. *Was I thinking wishfully, or was Mr. Meltme flirting with me? Maybe he wanted to be friends. But he was off-limits otherwise. He was a teacher . . . well, a student teacher, but he wasn't* my *student teacher . . . Tristan, that's crazy.*

As soon as the boxes arrived, I only had one thing on my mind. I went to my room and dialed his number on my banana phone from Spencer's in the mall. After two rings, he picked up.

Tristan Taormino

"Hi . . . Matt? It's Tristan. Taormino."

"Oh, hi," he replied.

"I am calling because the things you bought from me have arrived . . ."

"How are you?" he asked. "How is your break going so far?"

"Oh, um, good. I'm glad I get to sleep in every morning. How are you?" I was definitely caught off guard. *Were we just chatting like normal people?*

"I still have one more final left, so I am studying a lot."

"Oh, right."

"But we have a break too, and I am looking forward to just hanging out. Do you want to maybe hang out some time? I could come by, pick up my stuff, and we could have lunch or something?"

My heart stopped. *What? Was this crush mutual? Was an actual college guy wanting to go out with me? Not one of the hot girls from the cheerleader set but me? Holy crap.* I had no idea what to say. I was so flattered, but I also knew this would break some rules. He was twenty-one. A student teacher at my school, temporarily. It had trouble written all over it.

"Are you there?" he asked.

"Yeah, I'm here. Sure, lunch sounds good. That would be really nice. I would love that."

"How about Wednesday around noon?" I didn't need to check my calendar or anything.

I gave him my address, and I hung up the phone. I took a deep breath. *This was a date. This was definitely a date. I was going on a date with Mr. Meltme. Uh . . . Matt. I can't wait to tell . . . oh shit. Maybe I shouldn't tell anyone. I didn't want to get him into any trouble. And if I told one of my friends, it was as good as telling the whole school. It would be a secret. It would be* our *secret.* My body tingled all over.

I made sure my mom wasn't going to be home when he picked me up. I freaked out about what I was going to wear because I did not want to look like a high school girl. This was not the time to wear the miniskirt and black lace headband that I wore to the all-ages clubs I went to with friends. I chose a pair of mauve pants, a rayon shirt that matched, and white flats I got at Marshalls that had pointy toes and raised embroidery in the shape of scrolls. They looked *mature*. I washed my hair and scrunched it with my hands to make sure the curls were neat and defined.

When he pulled into the driveway, I came out, looked both ways, and got in beside him.

"Hey," I said. I had wrapping paper and a four-pack of scented candles in my hands. "Thanks again for buying this stuff."

"Are you ready to go?" he asked. *This is really happening.*

He took me to a nice seafood restaurant that was right on the water. Fancy. Definitely grown-up. Once I let myself relax, our conversation flowed easily. I hoped my makeup looked all right. I could already feel the blisters forming on my feet in the narrow shoes. When we finished lunch, he drove me home. *This could still be lunch, and we could be friends.* He pulled into the driveway and turned off the car. I wasn't sure I wanted him to come in and see our stupid little house.

"That was really fun," he said.

"I had a good time," I chimed in. Then there was a pause and silence. I looked at him. He leaned in to kiss me. His lips were soft, and his kiss was deliberate. He held my face in his hands confidently. This was no drunk, fumbling high school boy. My body came alive. We kissed a few more times.

He broke the embrace and asked, "Can we do this again?"

"I'd like that."

"So, listen . . . we should probably talk about . . ."

"I haven't told a soul—not my friends, not my mom, no one. I understand that this is important. I don't want to wreck your career before it starts. I know what people will think. I won't tell anyone."

He seemed surprised that I had thought it all through. *I'm no dummy.*

"Okay," he said, "I don't want to make you lie . . . I just, I just think that's the best thing."

"I agree." He kissed me one more time.

"I'll call you." I was floating for the rest of the day. All I wanted to do was talk to my friend Sadie or Kathy or Gabrielle. But I couldn't. I couldn't.

My mother and father also met at school. Page 86:

Judy had just gotten back from Europe and was teaching English. She was thin, with Irish skin and frosted hair. The students that liked her regarded her as extremely intelligent, ironic, and funny. The students that did not like her considered her extremely intelligent, sarcastic, and cold. Her older brother, Tommy, was a critically acclaimed writer. Her best friend was a man, an abstract painter. She lived in the woods in a converted carriage house. She smoked like an editor and cooked a perfect moussaka. Her record collection included Anita O'Day, Pablo

Casals, Nina Simone, Van Cliburn, Nichols and May, and *New Faces of 1952*. She could finish the *New York Times* Sunday crossword puzzle before lunch.

On that first day I followed her, and lost her, oh Leona Ducy, I went back to her car and hung around. There was a silk scarf on the red bucket seat.

I began to plot to get her. There's pressure on everyone to get married. I couldn't wait to get married. I needed more credentials. I went after Judy with a vengeance. I also realized that there would be a slight trace of scandal—the professor seduces the student, or, better yet, the student seduces the professor. My family and friends would be impressed. I was ready to get the blood tests.

Mr. Meltme and I continued to see each other, but it was beginning to get difficult to explain where the hell I was to my mom and my friends, so we decided together that I would tell one friend. I picked Gabrielle. Gabrielle dyed her thick hair a fiery red that complemented her pale, freckled face. She hadn't been in Sayville since elementary school like most kids, but I liked her as soon as we met. She hung out with the all-black-wearing crowd and had a wicked sense of humor. She seemed like she'd been through some stuff; she had a lot of responsibility because her mom worked nights, and she had to take care of her little brother and sister. Gabrielle would not judge me. Gabrielle would keep my secret and not have a problem lying for me. When I told her, her green eyes got big.

"Tristan. Mr. Meltme???"

"I can't believe it either. You are the only one who knows."

"Good for you!" she exclaimed. "I want to hear details, I want to hear *everything*." She agreed to be my cover story so Matt could pick me up at her house, and she'd tell my mom I was with her if she asked. She could smooth anything out with our other friends.

I had finally found the right combination of emotional connection and lust. The secrecy gave it an extra charge. He and I made out, used our hands and mouths on each other. I had done all that with plenty of boys, but he was never tentative or clumsy. His fingers slid inside me with care, made me slick, electrified, and wanting more. He knew what he was doing. I wanted to have sex-sex for the first time with Mr. Meltme. Matt. *He hasn't brought it up or even hinted at pressuring me. We already said "I love you" to each other. He treats me like a woman and respects me.* I was naive about the power dynamic because I was focused on being the one who was going to initiate it. I was making the decision myself.

Figure 12.2 With my friend Gabrielle, Sayville, New York, 1988

The following Friday night, he picked me up to go grocery shopping before our date and said he'd cook for me at his place. As we walked down the pasta aisle, he started throwing out dinner suggestions. I already had a different plan in my head.

"How about a nice steak?"

I shrugged.

"Grilled chicken with some veggies?"

"That would be fine."

Between the shopping, the cooking, and the eating, this is going to take way too long. There is no way I am going to last. I want what I want, and I want it now.

"You know what? Why don't we keep things really *simple*?" I said. I looked past him to the shelf.

"SpaghettiOs. Make me SpaghettiOs."

He grinned, ready to laugh at my joke.

"I'm serious," I said. He looked surprised but went with it. We grabbed two cans off the shelf and headed back to his place.

He shared a quad dorm at Queens College with four single bedrooms and a common living room and kitchen. Only one of his roommates was home

Tristan Taormino

when we got there, and after we were introduced, he promptly left. We ate our SpaghettiOs.

"What do you feel like doing now?" he asked.

"Going to your bedroom," I said. I was both confident and terrified. *I feel comfortable with him. I am in love with him. I want to do this. But I don't know what I am doing.*

He put a U2 tape in his stereo, and "With or Without You" began playing. We laid down on his bed and started to make out. Just kissing him turned me on. He began to pull my dress over my head, and when it came off, I took off his shirt. We hadn't talked about it. I had no idea if he knew I'd never had sex-sex before. I didn't want to set the whole thing up as this big deal. *I'll tell him later.* He went down on me. His mouth was warm; I felt the rub of his five-o'clock shadow against my labia. He sat up and took his jeans off, and then he laid on his back. I slipped his underwear down and took his cock in my mouth. He moaned, and I kept going. I knew I was wet and swollen from his tongue, and I felt an ache and urgency deep into my body. I popped my head up.

"I want you inside me," I whispered. I was holding his dick in my hand, and it jumped, that cool thing a cock does, as if it was reacting to my words. He heard me. I sat up and rolled over on my back.

He got on top of me, and we started kissing again.

"Are you sure?" he asked me.

"I'm sure." I paused. "I want you. Get a condom."

He reached over to the nightstand drawer and grabbed one. I watched him roll it down over his red cock. He wasn't nervous.

He returned to me, holding his cock. He guided himself inside my opening, and I felt a searing pain. *Deep breath.* More pain. I was expecting it, so it didn't surprise me, but it was still hard to reconcile the sensations of arousal and excitement coupled with hurting. He went slow, took his time moving in and out just about an inch. My pussy felt really tight and constricted, like he was having a hard time getting in. He was patient.

"Is this okay? Does it feel good?"

"Uh-huh." I went back to kissing him, which did feel good. The penetration hurt no matter what he did, so I resigned myself to tolerating it and grabbing whatever fleeting moments of pleasure I could.

"You feel amazing," he whispered. He got in further until his full weight was on top of me. I loved *that* feeling—of him pressed against my naked body. I felt trapped, in a good way. The hot-poker sensation subsided for a few minutes. He moved inside me more smoothly, and his moaning and breathing got faster.

"Oh fuck..." he muttered. I grabbed onto his butt and pressed him into me.

"Yes..." he groaned. He was taking quick strokes then, and his noises were turning me on. *Mmmmmmm.* His butt cheeks clenched as his hips bucked into me a few more times, then stopped. He came. He kissed my lips, my face, my neck. His back was slippery under my hands. He pulled out, sat up, threw the condom away, then crawled back into bed next to me.

"I love you," he said. I wrapped my legs around his.

"I love you too."

"Did that feel good for you?" He really did give a shit about my experience, which I thought was hopeful. It was definitely the reason I picked him over my other options for my first time. The sex didn't blow my mind or anything, but it was a start. *Just happy to get that out of the way. Hopefully, we do it more, and it feels better.* We did do it again, and soon the pain receded, making way for the pleasure. My experience can't escape all the cultural baggage and symbolism of heteronormativity that weighs down the act, renders it cliché. A penis in my vagina for the first time didn't create any cosmic shift in me, but something else did. The next time Matt fucked me, and every time after, he talked dirty to me. No one had ever done that, and it absolutely drove me wild. When he told me he loved my wet pussy, I was shocked and excited. Language brought sex to a whole other level for me. You never forget the first person who says the word *pussy* to you with adoration in their voice.

Tristan Taormino

TIME IN A BOTTLE

I eventually tired of sneaking around with Matt, knowing that we'd never be able to be public if he wanted to teach for a living, so I broke it off. My sights were on bigger things anyway. My mother read the *New York Times* from cover to cover and did the crossword with a felt-tip pen. One Sunday, I saw an ad for a summer program for high school students to take *actual* college courses at Cornell University. I didn't want to spend the summer busing tables at the Sayville Inn and drinking at Lotus Lake. I applied, was accepted, and got a full scholarship to cover all the costs.

My mother's older brother had gone to Cornell as an undergrad, and I pictured him walking through the quad to class, carrying a book bag, with his head down, being his antisocial self. *But what he learned there made him a bona fide writer, an author.* My mom told me that his books were reviewed in the *New York Times* and studied at colleges all over the country. I just knew him as Uncle Tom, the only one of my relatives I could relate to. He was tall and lanky and had a wild, overgrown, thick head of graying black hair that matched his quirky personality and made him faintly resemble Albert Einstein. He was smart, with a wicked sense of humor, and he seemed to know something about *everything*, from the Tiananmen Square protests to *The Simpsons*. He was the only grown-up I knew willing to engage in thoughtful critiques of pop culture. It wasn't fluff to him. *Footloose*, Madonna, *Bosom Buddies*—it was all layered with imagery and meaning; it was worth dissecting.

I wanted to be a writer like him when I grew up. Years later, I was delighted to find out he read *On Our Backs* when I became the editor. I felt less weird when I was around him because he didn't fit in either.

I had some trepidation going into the summer. *Am I smart enough to be here?* I took a journalism and an acting class, went to guest lectures and concerts, made friends with kids from all different backgrounds, did late-night runs to the food truck on the edge of campus. I wrote an article for the school newspaper on why sexuality and safe-sex workshops should be mandatory at colleges.

Meg was one of my close friends. She was a striking, brilliant, ethereal redhead from Hawaii, the only person my age whom I could truly call mysterious. I was in the dining hall, standing at the spinning fruit conveyor belt deciding between sliced cantaloupe and pineapple chunks, when she walked up with a boy.

"Hey, this is Ethan. Ethan, this is Tristan."

"Hey," I said, struggling to think of something to say that made me sound smart.

Ethan had a thick head of brown hair, light brown skin, and beautiful blue-green eyes. He had a prominent nose (and I have a thing for big noses). He wore round horn-rimmed glasses that looked like they cost a fortune. His willowly body was in a long linen shirt and rolled-up khakis. He was the Jewish J. Crew model of my dreams.

"What program are you in?" I asked him.

"Architecture," he said. Notoriously one of the most prestigious and rigorous at Cornell.

"I'm going to be an architect and make the world a better place than I found it." I was smitten. To my surprise, he liked me too. He invited me on a picnic where he wore a neat button-down shirt and a bowtie. That's all it took.

After classes, I used to sprint past the Victorian Gothic chapel with its tall peaks and stained-glass windows, up the old stone steps to his dorm. His room was cluttered with rolls of plans, the words penned in his perfect, graphic handwriting. The neat, precise lines and angles of an architect's writing still turn me on.

He read to me from *The Prophet* by Kahlil Gibran. He wrote his own poetry. We talked for hours about politics, literature, art. He had a depth I'd never experienced before. He also expressed his masculinity in a different way than the other boys I knew. He was smarter for sure, and a bit softer. He didn't have that insecure, puffed-up bravado I had become used to. He was interested

Tristan Taormino

in what I had to say. He wanted to know my every thought. He was sensitive and easily expressed his feelings.

"You're not like other girls who have to be wooed in specific ways that make me feel self-conscious and awkward. You know what you want. It's refreshing." I never play coy. He got me.

He slept in the bottom bunk, and when we fucked, my thick, curly hair got tangled in the wire-mesh platform of his roommate's bed above. New Order or General Public played on the stereo as I rode his cock, he looked at me intently, and everything else in the world just melted away. The sex was off the charts. It was my first taste of real passion *and* partnership and nothing to be kept secret. He told me he loved me.

The Cornell program had lots of rules, and breaking them could get you kicked out. The one drilled into us the most: never go to the Gorges, a spectacular place with bedrock formed by glaciers, dramatic waterfalls, hiking trails, and a suspension bridge high above the cold, deep waters. There was a rash of student suicides there in the 1970s. It was forbidden, so Ethan; his roommate, Manny; his friend John; Meg; and I decided we would sneak out there once it got dark. We didn't go up to the bridge; we just hung out in one of the shallow pools, splashing each other. At one point, I bent down to scoop the chilly water up toward Manny, and at the same time, he kicked some water at me. I was knocked backward. Manny and Ethan rushed over and carried me to the rocky shore. My right eye was throbbing in pain. I closed both eyes for a moment, and when I opened them, I couldn't see anything out of the eye that hurt. The group freaked out, and they quickly walked me back to John's dorm room. We weren't yet in violation of the 10 p.m. curfew. John decided that we all needed to be dry before we did anything so no one would figure out we had been at the Gorges. The way seventeen-year-old brains work. Meg blow-dried my hair, then Ethan called an ambulance. I had scratched my cornea, and I left the ER with eye drops and ointment, a patch over my eye, and the order to take it easy for the next two weeks. One week later, Ethan scratched his cornea with one of his contact lenses. In photos, he has his arm around me, and we are each wearing an eye patch. We were one. Inseparable. At least until I had to go back to Long Island and he to New Jersey. We weren't that far from each other, but he didn't want a long-distance relationship. I was heartbroken.

Ethan and I stayed in touch through our senior years. We did see each other a few times and picked up where we left off: blissed-out love, long talks, marathon sex. He was the first boy I could see myself marrying. We'd have a life together of season tickets to the opera, volunteer humanitarian work, travel to exotic places, our dream home designed by him, and fucking that brought me divine orgasms.

I met his parents, who were warm and intelligent. Hanging on the wall in their house was a framed gift his father had made especially for his mother. A beautiful illustration with lyrics from "Time in a Bottle" by Jim Croce written in calligraphy.

That was the kind of love I wanted.

When I got home, I asked him what they thought of me.

"Oh, they liked you." There was some hesitation and a definite pause.

"But?"

"Well... they sat me down after you left and said, 'We are not judging in any way, but do you think Tristan might be on drugs?'"

I was crushed, then confused, because he was the heavier pot smoker, not me, and we didn't smoke while we were there. And I'd never done any other drugs.

"I..." I didn't know what to say. "Why do you think they said that?"

"They thought you were... moody or something, like you had a kind of heightened energy. I really don't know. I assured them nothing was farther from the truth."

I had no idea how to process this information. By high school I did have more mood swings, but when my mother acknowledged them, she used her one tactic of telling me to calm down. No other adults in my life had ever commented on my mood. In hindsight, maybe Ethan's parents could pick up on my growing anxiety and depression—it actually may have been *that* obvious—and they were genuinely concerned that something wasn't right. But I also interpreted their worry as reflecting some classism, something about me not being good enough for him.

Tristan Taormino

THE SHOWER

"**M**y parents are going out of town, and we have the whole house to ourselves. You should invite Ethan to come down and have him bring a friend."

Sadie and I had been casual friends, but things deepened in high school, and soon we were spending all our time together, sharing secrets and dreaming about the future. She wanted to go to Rhode Island School of Design and become an artist, a path no one in her family took. She was a quiet rebel.

Ethan and our friend John from Cornell came to spend the weekend with Sadie and me. No matter how much we talked about being friends, I was still madly in love with him. We cooked fresh ravioli for dinner at 9 p.m., drank Tanqueray and tonics, played games, and talked for hours. We were pretending it was our house, we were adults, and we could do whatever we wanted. It was thrilling.

At Sadie's place there was a living room at the front of the house where no kids were allowed. It was her parents' rule, and we had never disobeyed it. The room looked like a museum, with expensive, pristine furniture: chairs covered in lush fabrics with ornate designs, a stunning piano you could see your reflection in. When we were drunk that weekend, we ventured in. Ethan set his camera up on a tripod, and we wriggled around and squished together on one of the forbidden couches for a dozen shots. Then we blasted the Cure on the stereo and danced our faces off until we collapsed back on the couch.

"God, I'm sweaty," said John. We were all pretty sweaty.

Figure 14.1 (left to right) With Ethan, Sadie, and John, Sayville, New York, 1988

Sadie said, "Then let's all go shower."

We ran up the stairs to the bathroom and began stripping down, tossing our clothes on the pale-green-carpeted floor in the hallway. Sadie slid back the clear sliding glass door, the kind with a pattern etched into it for privacy and turned on the water. One by one, we got in. It was just a normal-sized tub and shower, so there wasn't a ton of room. Somehow the four of us made it work when we stuck our bodies all together, splashing and washing and giggling the whole time. For a split second, I thought, *Wow, we are all naked in the shower together*, but it felt normal, fun, so I just went with it. I had seen Sadie naked dozens of times when we tried on each other's clothes, changed out of wet bathing suits, got ready for bed. Now, in the shower, not only could I look at her body, but I could actually linger a little over her perfect A-cup breasts, her pale Irish complexion, the freckles on her chest, the curly strawberry blond hair between her legs. She was so, so beautiful. But not like the cheerleaders at school with their big hair, flashy fashion, and heavy makeup. She was beautiful in this really understated way, like the star of a Merchant Ivory film, with pristine porcelain skin and blue

Tristan Taormino

eyes that refracted in the light like a celestite geode. She had the confidence of a supermodel without makeup on. We all bumped into each other and casually touched bodies in the shower. Sadie and I hugged and rubbed up against each other briefly. It wasn't awkward, and it wasn't explicitly sexual, but it did turn me on.

I wasn't really ready to dig deep into my relationship with Sadie, which was a romantic friendship that seemed right on the edge of becoming sexual. When I came out to my high school best friend Kathy two years later, she asked point-blank, "So were you and Sadie a thing?"

I was surprised. Maybe not that surprised.

"You were definitely in love, or that's what it looked like from the outside. And your breakup was epic!"

We had, in fact, broken up in some spectacular fashion, as only high school girls can do, and went from spending all our time together to not speaking. I can't remember why.

She turned off the water, and we started to get out, dripping on the floor and scrambling for towels. Ethan made eye contact with me, and I nodded and announced, "We're going to have some one-on-one time."

Sadie and John stood there wrapped in towels, and I wondered if they were going to hook up. I led Ethan to Sadie's bedroom, and we landed on Sadie's sister's bed. Our skin was still damp as we dropped our towels and crawled under the Laura Ashley floral bedspread. Something was different. My body felt pliable and hungry. As we kissed, I reached down and found his cock hard and began stroking it. I slowed down, wanting to really tune in to the way his velvety soft skin stroked the palm of my hand. He moaned, and that got me going even more. He took my hand away so he could move down the bed and put his face between my legs. His mouth teased my opening. I wanted him to bury his nose in my pussy until he couldn't breathe. I finally guided his head up to my face and kissed him. He tasted salty and a little bitter. *Must be all the alcohol.* My desire almost overwhelmed me. I rolled over and reached for a condom, which he'd thoughtfully placed next to the bed. I watched him put it on, looked deeply into his eyes, then straddled him. He reached down and fumbled for a second finding the hole. There was that first burst like I might split in two. It burned for a second. He did slow, short strokes, and soon my pussy began to open up to him. I felt like I was gliding on top of him. He put his hands on my waist. His skin was so warm from the shower, and I was still buzzed from the cocktails. I felt like I was high; my body and his were in another dimension together.

Figure 14.2 In my bedroom surrounded by horse show ribbons, Sayville, New York, 1988

Afterward, I lay very close to him, exposed. He was my true love. I was also still feeling the last gin and tonic. I decided to break the news.

I felt a pit in my stomach. I looked at the ceiling and said, "Ethan, I have something to tell you, but you can't tell anyone else."

"Okay," he said gently. I swallowed. My breath was shallow.

"My dad is gay."

"Oh," he said matter-of-factly. "Yeah."

"Yeah what?" This was not the reaction I was expecting.

"Well, I kind of figured he was gay. He never got remarried. He's an artist. He lives in Provincetown. All signs pointed to gay."

He wasn't being snarky or mean; he was just laying out the facts. I was relieved, like it was clearly not an issue for him whatsoever—it was like telling him my dad was Irish and Italian. But then frustration welled up in me as I relived that moment when Boomer asked me about my gay dad. *Why did everyone know except me????* Later that night, I shared our conversation with Sadie—that way she'd know too.

Tristan Taormino

"Oh, right," she said. "Your dad's gay, that makes sense."

She was loving and sincere and completely nonplussed.

"I really like Ethan. You're very lucky. I just don't think I'm that into John. He's not really my type. But I am still having a really good time. Should we make more gin and tonics?"

Why was everyone acting like this was no big deal?

After we both went to college, Ethan wrote to me:

People like you and me are experiencers. We are interested in life, and we don't just let it pass us by. We take hold of its reins, and we take what we have learned and we create more for others. I love you very much, on several different levels, and I am so pleased our friendship has endured. You mean a lot to me, and don't forget that. And when the rest of the male gender is giving you the signal that ALL MEN ARE FUCKHEADS, remember that there is one fuckhead who really understands you. I need you for the same reasons.

He *saw* me. He was speaking to my soul.

SLUTTY

It's hard to believe that you're starting college. But it's true. Just when I think time has stopped, it tricks me and zooms forward.

I wanted to tell you how proud I am of you. How much I enjoy hanging out with you or talking on the phone. I've been around enough to notice that there is no guarantee that a parent and child will like each other. So I feel very lucky.

And, finally, Tristan, you are one of the few people who inspire me and give me hope.

LETTER FROM DAD, AUGUST 22, 1989

I applied early admission to Yale, was deferred to regular admission, then rejected. I got into all of the other schools I applied to (except Harvard) but had no idea where I wanted to go because I was so upset about Yale. During the application process, I kept a notebook where I listed each school along with copious notes, quotes from *The Insider's Guide to College,* and things I jotted down from my campus visits. I narrowed it down to four and gave each school a score based on my own criteria:

Cornell: diverse student body, Greek life ugh, too big? 9.

Vassar: good student-to-faculty ratio, design your own major, not cliquey, Poughkeepsie sucks, 8.5.

Figure 15.1 Sayville High School graduation with Mom and Dad, 1989

Smith: women, horseback riding program, love Northampton, twelve-college exchange, strong humanities, 8.

Wesleyan: creative individuals, strong English department, diverse, politically active, 8.5+.

I decided to visit them all again, hang out with students, and see if I could picture myself there. I had learned to listen to the inner voice that guided me, and I knew it in my gut: it had to be Wesleyan. I got a generous financial aid package, I had won some local scholarships, and the student loan was reasonable. I found a letter my mom included with my financial aid application that read, "I will do whatever I have to do to make [the parent's] contribution, so strongly do I believe that Tristan will make the most of the intellectual, social, and other resources available to her at your school, earn her degree there, and become an enthusiastic alumna."

"Did you read Nietzsche in tenth or eleventh grade?"

These were the kinds of questions students casually asked each other while scarfing down Lucky Charms in the dining hall. I had never read Nietzsche at all! I quickly realized that a lot of my new classmates came from private schools like Choate or highly competitive city high schools like Stuyvesant in New York City. They had perfect SAT scores, they'd taken every AP class, and their idea of an extracurricular project was raising six figures to feed the homeless or spending a summer building houses in Guatemala. My plaid Tretorns and knockoff IBM desktop felt shabby compared to their BMWs, Apple computers, and Gucci shoes. The best/worst part of the student body: they were brilliant. No wonder no one at my high school knew anything about Wesleyan. Except for class status, the student body was diverse in many other ways: I was surrounded by students of all races, nationalities, ethnicities, religions, sexual orientations, and political affiliations. Every *Breakfast Club* archetype was represented plus serious athletes, frat boys, bold activists, hippie stoners, conservative wannabe pundits, devout vegans, out and proud gays, goths and new wavers (those kids lived in a former fraternity house with big white columns called Eclectic). Unlike in high school, the theater kids were not nerds here, they were really cool. It was a new world with unlimited possibilities. But like in the horse show world and the summer at Cornell, I wasn't sure I belonged there.

All first-year students at Wesleyan had to attend a series of orientation seminars, including one run by a group called BiLeGa. In the workshop we were instructed to go around the room, introduce ourselves, and say, "I'm gay" or "I'm bisexual" or "I'm a lesbian."

"We encourage everyone to participate in a conversation about being gay, lesbian, or bisexual. If you aren't, we encourage you to draw on personal experiences when you've felt different or out of place, when you've faced discrimination or ostracization. You can use those as the basis for relating a story or some general feelings to the group," said Kate, one of the facilitators, who wore tortoiseshell glasses and chunky black shoes.

The idea was that straight students could try out what it might be like to be in a queer person's shoes and relate to them through their own struggles of being an outsider. It was also a safe space for actual queer students to speak freely without *really* coming out if they didn't want to, because we were just role-playing.

A girl named Jessie was in my group; from a small town in upstate New York, she lived in my dorm and was a shy soccer player with icy eyes like

Tristan Taormino

Sadie's. We had calculus together, and neither of us understood our professor's wild handwriting on the blackboard, so we often sat together and rolled our eyes at each other. Back at the dorm after the session, everyone on my floor got together for a meeting with our R.A. Jessie said she had something she wanted to share.

"I'm gay," she announced, a little timid. We all huddled around her, hugging and encouraging her. I pulled her aside and told her, "My dad is gay. I spent a few summers in Provincetown, so, you know, I'm here if you want to talk."

She wrote me a letter thanking me for being so accepting. That year she had a beautiful girlfriend who looked like Natalie Wood, and I loved seeing them together. One thing that wasn't in the brochures and that no one ever mentioned during my campus tour: it seemed like everyone at Wesleyan was queer or at least questioning their sexuality. Everywhere I looked, there were pink-triangle buttons; posters for the Gay, Lesbian, Bisexual Alliance (GLBA) student group; and same-sex couples holding hands. When the GLBA threw a party, it was an event not to be missed. Mocon, the freshman dining hall, was transformed into a colorful paradise, and the hype I'd heard was true: the best music, outrageous outfits, and, by the end of the night, shirtless boys and topless girls on tables bumping and grinding until dawn. No one questioned anyone's sexuality based on that night because it was understood that we all had the freedom to do and be whatever we wanted.

I was still pining for Ethan. We reiterated to each other that we were not in a relationship, and my love for Ethan didn't stop me from slutting around, especially when I had more choices than ever. Sex was a simple, visceral adventure for me. I had a drink or two, I met someone with something interesting about them, there was a physical pull in my body to connect, and we ended up in bed. Sex could bring me to a place where my brain quieted down or even stopped thinking altogether. I could sink into curiosity, into my body, into pleasure, into a different form of communication. It was like riding horses in that way.

I hadn't really processed my relationship with Sadie or my desire for women. It hovered in the background. Plus, men were just easier. Howard was a gorgeous guy who lived off campus and fucked me in his waterbed with his long, thin cock. A junior English major named Scott became my boyfriend, but he was mostly into me because he was obsessed with my uncle. At Wesleyan there was an entire course on one of Uncle Tom's books, *Gravity's Rainbow*, which made me proud and also intimidated me. Scott coerced me to have sex without condoms because I was on the pill. I hooked up with a blond, witty California boy who lived in my dorm and turned out to be gay (we were close friends for many years after). There was some time with a sensitive a cappella singer who was diagnosed with the Epstein-Barr virus. And I won't forget the Jewish musical theater major who had a crying meltdown when I surprised him naked in his bed with a heart-shaped bowl of whipped cream and strawberries for Valentine's Day. I know it seriously lacked imagination, but that's not why he cried. Emo boys, frat boys, theater boys, preppy boys, smart boys, lacrosse boys.

I continued to be clear and assertive when I wanted to fuck someone. Although sex fascinated me, I got the feeling I hadn't unlocked all there was to it. In most cases, I lacked creativity beyond the heteronormative basics. (Notable exception: a rugby player named Danny who, when I gave him the heads-up that I had my period, fucked me with a fresh tampon during our one-night stand.) I didn't have that many orgasms with these boys, regardless of our connection. I didn't ask for what I wanted because I didn't *know* what I wanted. *How am I supposed to figure that out?* The movies I'd seen—*When Harry Met Sally, Say Anything, The Accused*—taught me about fake orgasms, grand romantic gestures, and sexual violence. *Dirty Dancing* turned me on because Baby and Johnny's lust was forbidden, and they had undeniable chemistry. I wanted chemistry like that, physical and emotional fireworks, someone who could match my appetite.

NO PLACE LIKE HOME

"It's just a plane ride away, and of course you have your own bedroom," said my dad.

He'd grown tired of Provincetown and decided to move to Seattle, where he found a condo in a large, old building in the Queen Anne neighborhood with a view of the city.

Shortly after he got there, he scored a job at a popular clothing brand that made busy, graphic sweaters and was known for its T-shirts and jeans that changed color with body heat. The whole thing sounded awesome: a cool new city, a hip new job. I decided I wanted to spend the summer with him again. As I finished my freshman year at Wesleyan, I was eyeing a theater major, so I wrote inquiry letters to all the theaters in Seattle. I landed an internship with New City Theater, working on their summer production of *Pilgrims of the Night* with Len Jenkin, the playwright/director from NYU well known for his avant garde theater.

Pilgrims of the Night is a story about seven strangers stranded overnight at a ferry terminal during a storm. An unexplained ball of fire has appeared in the sky and landed on the banks across the river, and no one knows what it is. As the night progresses, each traveler tells a wild, surreal tale to pass the time. I was in charge of lots of odds and ends, including all the props for the play, and there were a lot of them: a voodoo doll, multiple fresh apple pies, radio-show microphones, and a headless woman kept alive by various machines. At one point in the play, we see a deer appear in the window of the station; his head is bloody and burned like he's been in an accident. I was tasked with finding a real stuffed deer head and applying special-effects makeup to it. I called around to taxidermists in the phone book until I found someone willing to consider my proposition.

"We are looking to rent a deer's head for a play. It makes one brief appearance."

"I don't do rentals. I do custom work for people," said the man on the phone. "But. . . . . . I do have one of my own heads gathering dust on the wall. It's not a big prize or even my best work. I guess you could use that."

One of the actors drove me about an hour outside the city, and we picked up the deer head with the promise to return it two months later no worse for wear. Each night, stage right, I held the deer head as steadily as I could and slowly pushed it through a window on the wall of the set, being careful to stop before the audience could see that it was cut off at the neck. It really did look like a deer walked up to a window and stuck its head inside.

When I got to Seattle, my dad was energetic and excited and wanted to show me *everything*. My dad never owned a car. When he moved somewhere new, it was a requirement that he be able to walk or take public transportation wherever he needed to go. He knew how to drive and sometimes would borrow a car from a friend to pick me up at the airport. But mostly we walked, and he walked at a speed unmatched by anyone I know. To him, walking distance was anywhere from a few blocks to a few miles, so whenever he said we were going somewhere, I prepared for a small trek. We went to Pike Place Market, a cool independent bookstore, *Sunday in the Park with George* at Seattle Rep, and a place that served only coffee called Starbucks. His happiness about this new city was palpable; it felt brimming with possibilities.

I usually had a wonderful time with Dad. He had the advantage of being the part-time/vacation parent. When I visited him, I was usually on a break from school, and we went to the theater, watched movies, got together with his circle of friends. Unlike with my mother, there was little or no arguing about money (he didn't have any), no rules like curfew (I didn't have one), no setting limits (he didn't). His job was just to love and entertain me, and he did both splendidly.

Tristan Taormino

My father loved to hold my hand in public. He loved me and wanted to show the world his affection. When I was young, I was into it—he didn't want to let go of me for a change—but once I was a tween, I thought it was weird. I let him take my hand some of the time because I could tell he really enjoyed it. No one else's father I knew held his daughter's hand so much. Then again, no one else's father I knew dressed so well and owned every single Barbra Streisand album. I wondered what people we passed by thought of us. The only couples holding hands on the street that I saw were obviously lovers. As an adult, I imagine someone thought we could be a May-December romance, but more often people probably noticed that I was his spitting image. Even then, I think we looked like we loved each other, because we did.

One day, my dad announced, "I finished writing my memoir." He had printed a copy of the manuscript and handed it to me with pride. "Lies and Circumstance," by Bill Taormino.

"I can't wait for you to read it, and I want to know what you think."

"This is great! Congratulations!" I said.

I don't know why I didn't dive right in and devour it immediately. I'm not sure why it sat on the dresser untouched for a week or two. I certainly wanted more details about my father's life, especially his experience growing up. All I knew was that he was estranged from his entire family, and that was because he was gay. Sometimes he'd briefly mention his mom being crazy, everyone being homophobic, but I didn't know much else. It was now all there on the page, if I could look past the cover.

One night, after I got home from the theater, he was agitated, really worked up. The minute I walked in the door, he came at me.

"You haven't read my memoir! Why haven't you read my memoir?" he shouted at me. He had a wild look in his eyes.

"I. . . . . . I don't know," I said honestly. "I'm sorry," I followed up. I was sorry. I was confused.

"You are so selfish! I gave you this thing, and you said you would read it, and you didn't! You didn't read it! You didn't read it! You didn't read it!" Now he was shouting. "I think you don't like me, but you're afraid to say it because I'm your dad. I think you have a problem having a gay father!" *No, no, no, that's not true.* His anger was escalating.

I was confused, and his reaction made me a little scared of him, which had never happened before. Plus I had all this guilt and shame (*Why didn't I read it?*). I wasn't yet a writer, so I didn't understand what it was like to create a piece of work that was so important and share it with someone, only to have it ignored. I didn't know how much it meant to him. I wasn't deliberately not reading it; I just hadn't made it a priority, and he could not accept that. Given all the invalidation by his family of origin, he wanted to share his truth, his story, but I didn't see that at the time. I was disappointing my dad, which was a much bigger deal than letting down a friend. I hurt him.

"And while we're at it, you're spoiled. You treat this place like a hotel. You come and go whenever you want. I cook, I clean, you don't lift a finger."

"I. . . . . ." I was just stammering now, trying to figure out what to say to calm him down. I felt bad, but something about the way he was acting was off.

"I want you out of this house *now*," he said. His face was flushed, and he was moving and talking at twice normal speed. "Now now now now now now now!"

"What?" I replied.

"Get out!" he reiterated.

I was totally caught off guard. I'd come to Seattle to stay with him, I was nineteen, I didn't really know anyone except him, and I had no place to go. *What was he talking about?* I burst into tears. He held my gaze and let me know he was serious. I grabbed my backpack and ran out the door. I walked down the hill and called my mom from a pay phone. I didn't know what else to do.

"Mom. . . . . ." I sobbed into the phone.

"What's wrong?" She obviously knew that I was crying.

"Dad kicked me out of the house because I didn't read his book, which I definitely meant to read, but I have been busy, and I am not sure why he is so mad and. . . . . ."

"What? What did he say?" My mom rarely got angry, but I could tell she was definitely pissed off.

"He said, 'Get out.' I am not sure what to do."

"I am going to call him and give him a piece of my mind. Is there somewhere you can go, even just for a few hours, while he cools down?" I thought of Tristan, a blond guy I had met on the bus who had flirted with me and gave me his phone number; we'd been out once for coffee. It would be super weird, but I didn't have many other options.

"Yes, I can call a friend," I said, sniffling and trying to stop crying.

"Okay, just stay away for a few hours, then call me back."

I hung up the phone. I fished around in my backpack and found the piece of paper with Tristan's number. I dialed it.

"Hey, Tristan, it's Tristan. I . . . . . . just had a big fight with my dad, and I need to kill some time away from his place. Any chance you're free to come hang out?"

"Where are you?"

"Queen Anne, near the café we met at."

"Okay, sure, I can be there in a half hour."

Tristan arrived, looking half concerned, half intrigued.

"Thanks for coming."

"Sure. What happened?"

"My dad went a little bit nuts. We had a fight. He kicked me out."

"Kicked you out?"

"Well, my mom's going to talk to him. I think it will be okay."

"Do you want some hot chocolate?"

I eventually called my mother and went back to my dad's that night, but he gave me the silent treatment.

The next day at the theater, I told Susie, one of the actors, what had happened. She was the closest to my age, in her early twenties, and I had heard that she was about to move into the sound designer's place to house-sit for the rest of the summer. She was sympathetic.

"Things are kind of rough with my dad right now. Would you consider me moving into Steve's place with you?" I felt ashamed, but I had to put it out there.

"Yeah, that's cool. Just ask Steve and make sure it's okay. Then we can go over there together after rehearsal, get all the info and the keys from him."

Steve the sound designer had a modest house in a really sketchy neighborhood.

"The most important thing to me is that people know that someone is living here," he declared.

He had put in a high-end alarm system because of the expensive recording equipment in the studio he'd built at the back of the house. I took the bus back to my dad's, packed my stuff, and left my key and a note.

I'd never lived on my own outside of the dorms, but Susie and I took the bus to the theater for rehearsals and performances, and we got into a rhythm. I was so grateful to her for saving my ass, but I also despised her a little. She was self-absorbed, and she wasn't that great an actor, yet her self-confidence was sky-high. But she was beautiful like Cheryl Ladd and had the charm of Molly

Ringwald. I just knew both features had gotten her far in the business. About a week into my new living situation, I got a really bad sore throat and went to an urgent care clinic, where they told me I had strep and gave me antibiotics. I took the meds for a few days and felt a little better. I woke up one morning with a pounding headache, feeling really awful. When I got out of bed to go to the bathroom, I felt very dizzy. I chalked it up to the strep working its way through my body. *Great, now I have a new symptom—a headache too.* A few hours later, I decided something was definitely wrong. The sore throat got worse, and then I had a fever and an even worse headache. I felt really, really disoriented and strange. I took the bus to the closest hospital. It was a busy city ER, and I waited for a while until a nurse came and put me in a curtained room. I told her my symptoms.

"Can you describe the headache?" she asked.

"It's like the worst headache I've ever had in my entire life." Her eyebrows rose a bit. I hoped she didn't think I was being dramatic.

"Okay, wait here." A doctor came back and asked me lots of questions.

"I suspect I know what's going on, and it's serious, young lady. I would like to give you a spinal tap; it's the test that will tell me if I'm right." *A spinal tap? That sounded serious all right and also painful, and God, I wish there was someone to just hold my fucking hand.*

"Okay," I said.

The nurse had me curl up in a fetal position and told me to lie very, very still. The doctor reiterated the still part. Then cold liquid brushed against the skin on my back, and I felt the prick of a needle.

"That will numb the area," he said. "But you are still going to feel the needle go in. Take a deep breath."

I started to inhale, felt some pressure, then the sensation of something in my back crawling around near my spine. It was scary and inescapable. I felt the needle come back out from inside me, then heard the doctor's gloves snap off.

"Okay, now you need to lie really, really still," said the doctor. "As still as you possibly can. Don't move at all. This is important."

"Okay," I said. I was sure I was going to vomit, which would definitely constitute moving. I told the nurse, "I feel like I might throw up."

"I can give you something for that, just lie still." She gave me a shot of something. Seconds later, my arms and legs started flailing uncontrollably. The nurse was still there cleaning things up.

I said, "That's not me moving my body, it's doing it on its own."

Tristan Taormino

"You're probably having an allergic reaction to the Compazine. Have you ever taken it before?"

"No."

She gave me another shot, and my body stopped moving. She touched my arm gently: "It's okay now." Then she grabbed my chart and closed the curtain behind me. I concentrated on being really still. I have no idea how much time passed. The doctor swept the curtain back and walked to my bed.

"So, my suspicion was right. You have meningitis. We are going to admit you to the hospital for some more tests and treatment."

"What is meningitis?"

"It's an inflammation of the tissue around your brain and spinal cord." *Jesus Christ, that did not sound good at all.*

He continued, "There are two types, bacterial and viral. Yours is bacterial, but we caught it early, so you should be okay. We'll get you on track, make sure you're responding to the meds, then send you home with some strong antibiotics. Someone will be back to take you upstairs."

I closed my eyes. I kinda wished Susie had come with me, but I knew she had to work at her waitressing job. I felt alone. Abandoned. My head still hurt a lot, but the nausea was gone. I drifted off.

"Tristan Tara. . . . . . I can't pronounce it. I'm taking you upstairs!"

I tried to muster a smile. She unlocked the sides of the bed and started wheeling me out of my little cubicle.

"Will there be a phone in my room? I need to call. . . . . . work and tell them I won't be in." Stupid. *How did I get meningitis? The crew is going to think I am super weird, and I am letting them down, and who's going to play the deer tomorrow night? I guess I could call the house and leave a message on the answering machine for Susie. She could relay the whole story.* I was really exhausted.

"Is there anyone else I can call for you? Your parents?" the nurse asked. *Right, I needed to figure that out.*

Five days later, my dad picked me up from the hospital, and we took a taxi home.

"I've set you up in my bedroom, where there's more room," he said. "The number-one thing you have to do is drink at least sixty-four ounces of fluid a day. They said you have to stay hydrated."

He bought a pack of a hundred big red plastic SOLO cups, the kind they had at keg parties. Each day he placed a stack of eight on the bedside table.

"This is how much water you have to drink today."

I stayed in bed for two weeks, counting every SOLO cup, drinking water, eating when I could. His manic energy from when I last saw him was gone. He was nurturing, doting, worried about me. I felt his unconditional love and treasured being taken care of by him. We never spoke about that night, the fight, or his memoir. When I was well enough to travel, I flew home.

My mom drove me out to Dee Dee and Gene's beach house for some further convalescing. I wrote in my journal:

> My dad's impossible to live with, that's a given. He has so many neurotic habits that he drives me crazy. And since he claims to be working on his status as the most perfect human being, in his eyes, of course, I'm nowhere near perfect. He is the most viciously articulate fighter I know, and nothing I say is ever right, so I just get beaten down again and again. He also has a list of fears and insecurities that I didn't know about until he blurted them all out the night we fought . . . I think I am resigned to never spending more than one to two weeks with him. One thing he did bring up was that I can't take personal criticism or I don't want to deal with him when it's about something negative with me. Mary said something similar, that I'd freak out if she gave me notes after a performance. I've done it with my mom before also. I think it's a valid point although I haven't admitted it to anyone. It's something I am going to work on . . . I think the root of the problem is his idealistic values. He actually lives by them. I feel pressured when I'm with him. The truth? I must be in denial about my criticism problem. And he's right: everyone in the world lets me get away with it except him.

I was convinced that I was an awful, selfish daughter. Perhaps to reassure me, my mom said, "So he had one of his *episodes* with you. I'm familiar with them because I was once on the receiving end. I am sorry you went through that." He and I still hadn't talked about it, and weeks later there was something new taking up all his energy.

"Something fucked up happened at work," he told me on the phone. "I started getting anonymous letters through the interoffice mail that were sexual and inappropriate. I did some investigation and traced them to a group of five employees in another department, four women and one man. One of the women had made a homophobic comment about me in front of other staffers."

Tristan Taormino

It was pretty clearly sexual harassment. He went to Human Resources, but they weren't much help, and they gave contradictory statements about people being disciplined. Six weeks later, he was let go because of "budget issues." Within a month, four of the five people involved had been promoted. A decade later, I'd find mountains of paperwork and insanely detailed notes about every interaction, every meeting he had, in a file folder labeled "[CLOTHING COMPANY] FIASCO." He railed about sexism and homophobia, the double standard (*If I were a woman in this situation . . .*), and the company as yet another dysfunctional family. Among the notes were other journal entries, reviews of movies he watched, and a pep talk he wrote for himself the day before his exit interview. He wrote that he was having trouble sleeping and was going downhill rapidly. He confessed, with some shame, to going to a bathhouse but didn't say if he had sex. Then he admitted he paid for sex for only the second time in his life (the first was in Okinawa with the female sex worker he lost his virginity to) and called it "enlightening and pleasant." I know about some of my dad's sex life but only from his writing. He would fight for the right of anyone to express their sexuality, but when it came to me, he implied that he'd rather not share or know too much. It was a boundary that neither of us wanted to cross.

He went to the Equal Employment Opportunity Commission and filed a formal complaint. Because he was a meticulous note and record keeper, the company officers knew they were in trouble, so they settled. He announced he had sold the apartment in Queen Anne and was moving south to Portland, Oregon.

"I need a fresh start."

When I visited him for the first time in Portland, I realized the pattern. With each move to a new place, he'd do copious amounts of research beforehand, conclude that it was the perfect city for him, and tell me all the compelling reasons to move there. There was a notable surge of happiness in his voice over the planning, the visiting, even the moving. He sounded full of hope. Then he'd pack his shit and move. He had made a nice little profit on the place he bought in Charlestown, outside Boston, when it gentrified in the 1980s, and he used that money to buy the Provincetown condo, and then that sale paid for the Seattle apartment. For someone who worked "unskilled" and entry-level jobs, he had made a smart decision that kept him housed for the rest of his life. From the sale of the Seattle apartment, he could afford a small house in Portland in another pregentrified neighborhood.

"I found a groovy real estate agent, and she showed me the perfect place," he told me.

My dad was cheap, but he had great taste. He got a new couch with black fabric with a pattern of metallic pink, green, and yellow paint strokes. It was very early nineties, like if Max Headroom was gay and designed a furniture collection. My dad painted each room about the same color, but he made sure to tell me that the living room was Harbor Gray, his bedroom was Timber Wolf, and mine was Silver Lining. (Once in a while, he'd add a splash of daring color, like the time he painted the gypsum fireplace mantle an icy pink. "Fairy Dust," he said with a big grin.) He'd meet new people, make new friends, and get a new job, and he'd be settled, for a little while. Dad couldn't find an administrative position, so he went back to waiting tables, which he'd done on and off. Each time he told me he was moving, it sounded like this was definitely the place, this would be his last move. My dad was searching for the place to call home, but he hadn't found it yet.

Tristan Taormino

MY CLOSET
HAS NO DOOR

I directed my first one-act play in my sophomore year at Wesleyan: *One Person* by Robert Patrick, a story about an affair between two men. About his work, Patrick wrote, "Conformity to the enormity persists, and whereas the straight censors once scathed one for admitting that there were gay people, the political press now chastises one for writing about gay life as it is, instead of as they wish it were."

I cast Jerran, a gay actor I knew who also happened to be one of the most attractive men on campus; opposite him, I picked Leo, a smart straight boy with deep-brown eyes who was ready to fully embrace the kissing scene. Leo's uncle was one of the most famous movie critics in the world, so I thought we might get some name recognition on the poster. *Minor star power couldn't hurt.* They did a beautiful job, and Leo dove into the intimacy with a quiet, sincere dedication. No one questioned, "Tristan's doing a play about gay love? And there's a straight guy in it?" It was Wesleyan, where everyone knew that sexuality was fluid.

I stopped smoking pot because I started to get awful headaches when I did, and I cut way back on drinking. I wasn't interested in getting buzzed that much and decided that hangovers sucked—the next morning, I felt like I'd been poisoned. It wasn't a good-enough trade-off. My interest in sex with men waned.

After the play I reconnected with Jessie, the lesbian from my freshman dorm. Jessie and I had done some mild flirting when we saw each other

Figure 17.1 Wesleyan University, Middletown, Connecticut, 1992; photo by my friend Paul

around, and I finally told her that I was through flirting. I kissed her. I wanted to, so I did. I was intrigued once my lips were on hers and scared about what would happen next. *What happens when two girls kiss?* She became my first girlfriend. Jessie was lots of women's first girlfriend, a one-woman recruiting agent, so genuine and unassuming no one suspected their daughters wouldn't be safe around her. The space between coming to terms with my sexual identity for myself and acting on my feelings was short. I didn't have tremendous

Tristan Taormino

self-doubt because I had the luxury of being in a place where it was not just okay, but great, to be queer. Once Jessie and I became a couple, I was holding her hand around campus just like anyone else I dated.

The way I told my mom was not my finest moment. I was home on a school break, keeping to myself in my room, where I was color-coding some files and poring over the latest issue of the *Advocate* with Urvashi Vaid and Robert Mapplethorpe on the cover, who were named Woman and Man of the Year. I got on the phone with Jessie, and we had been talking for about an hour.

My mom knocked on my door. "Can you get off the phone? I need to make a call," she said. I hung up and stormed into the living room with frustration.

"I don't know who this Jessie is and why you have to be on the phone with her for so long," she said snidely.

"She's my girlfriend! And I'm bisexual!" I shouted angrily. Bisexual seemed to fit me best; I wasn't exclusively drawn to any one gender.

"Okay. Can I have the phone back now?" Later, over dinner, she communicated that she worried that my life would be infinitely more difficult as a bisexual woman, but she loved me no matter what. It was a pretty typical parental response; they probably have a whole session on it at PFLAG.

The next time I spoke to my dad, I told him I was dating a woman at school. I thought he would be jumping for joy over me joining the team. *Your daughter is queer. This is yet another way we are super alike. This is something else we can share, just the two of us.*

"That's good—whatever makes you happy."

It was so uneventful. I thought about how it took him twenty-four years of pain and homophobia to come to terms with his sexuality, and several more years until he could fully live an out, proud life. I, on the other hand, just sashayed out of the closet like I was showing off a new dress to a welcoming band of queers.

Shortly afterward, it hit me like a ton of bricks: I was so much like my dad, but it didn't occur to me how that might affect *my mother.* It was probably an awful reminder to have a little version of her ex-husband running around the house. When I came out, she must have rolled her eyes so hard in private. She never once said, "You're just like your father," or "That reminds me of your dad," but once I became aware of just how similar we were, it was in the air. I thought my coming out might even feel cruel to her in some way, since his coming out had radically altered the course of her life. I was queer, dramatic, creative, organized, and, worst of all, emotional. *God*, I thought, *I must annoy the crap out of her.*

She's good at smoothing out the tablecloth of life, so everything looks in order. My mom doesn't cry all that often. Growing up, she didn't express anxiety about how I was doing in school or about my future, she rarely raised her voice, she barely got mad. Some children would have really appreciated these qualities in a caregiver, and I thought I should, especially considering the abuse my father had experienced from his mother. But my mother rarely expressed *any* intense emotions, and that made me feel like something was wrong with me. During Hurricane Irene, a tree branch crushed the roof of our garage. She sighed, but not dramatically, and said, "Well, now I have to get that taken care of."

Once I flew off Chipper head first while going over a jump at a horse show, and when she arrived at the ER, I had two black eyes, a badly scraped-up face, and a neck brace.

"At least it's not any worse," she declared as she drove us home. "I'll make you some mac and cheese, and you can ice your face."

When the bills were overdue, she'd take any job she could get to keep the lights on. My mom can shut off her emotions like a switch and do what needs to get done.

She can talk to complete strangers with comfort and confidence. With the people she knows, it's a warm, engaging conversation. You cannot tell which of them she likes and whom she actually despises. Watching and learning that skill has come in handy. Because I consider myself so much like my father, it took me years to realize what qualities of my mom I've absorbed. We felt so different from each other.

When I got emotional, my mother often looked like she had no idea what to make of me. I was scrambling to finish a report in tenth grade, and I was panicked and overwhelmed with how much work I had to do. I chastised myself for not starting earlier, which wasn't like me, and got myself really worked up. The anxiety overtook me to the point where I couldn't think clearly, and then I had a complete meltdown. I wandered into my mom's office, sobbing.

"What's wrong?"

"I just really want [short inhale] this project to be perfect. But I don't think I have enough time [short inhale] to [short inhale] make [short inhale] it [short inhale] perfect." I wiped the snot coming out of my nose. I was moments away from hyperventilating.

"Calm down. Don't get so worked up. Crying is not going to fix this problem. You're fine." But I didn't feel fine. I felt out of control. Her words didn't calm me down; they just made the crying worse. As a kid, sometimes it

Tristan Taormino

helps for adults to name and validate your feelings when you can't and help you learn to soothe yourself. In other situations the emotions confused me, felt unmanageable. I believed my mom didn't understand, and, therefore, I couldn't really understand. Sometimes she couldn't read my mood intuitively. She was paying attention, but my inner emotional world truly perplexed her. I wanted her to be attuned to me the way a horse could be, without words. I cried. I yelled. I got scared that the sadness, frustration, and anger would swallow me. She responded evenly and rationally—perhaps in an attempt to counteract the freak-out—but that didn't ground or comfort me. I just felt like a weirdo. I felt like my dad.

I interpreted her reactions to mean that feelings were *bad.* I got the sense I was too emotional, too moody, too intense. Also: too focused, driven, dramatic. I was amazed at how she, and her parents and brothers, could be wired so differently from me. I appreciate that she never screamed or put me down, but this absence in the space that feelings might occupy was unsettling. We sometimes clashed in big ways, but the small things that we couldn't understand about each other were often the most devastating to me.

Decades later, I read in my father's memoir about what attracted him to her: she was calm, level-headed, never let her feelings get away from her. She was the opposite of his mother. Their dynamic was a yin-yang balance he craved. These qualities he loved about Mom were the very qualities that created so much confusion, longing, and resentment between her and me. He was *drawn* to her stoicism, a way of being that left me feeling like I was always too much.

QUEER NATION

don't think people, including me, realized how serious I was about my queerness—this wasn't an experiment or whimsy—until I met Jen. Jen was The. Big. Dyke. On. Campus. She was a senior, super intelligent, opinionated, as out as you could be. She was well known because she was a big-time activist, very outspoken about things like sex, sadomasochism, and lesbian porn. Her curly brown hair was cut short and framed a cute, pale, freckled face; she appeared taller than she actually was. She went to class dressed in men's shirts and ties. This was no friendly, sporty lesbian that most people found charming like Jessie. Jen was a butch dyke, brazen in her gender and style, and I was drawn to her like *Oh. My. God.* She was frantically finishing her sociology thesis about patriarchal representations of women in slasher films, so the first time we kissed was on the steps of Olin Library, a tall, imposing brick behemoth of a building with giant white columns. She was a brilliant flirt, so self-assured, so deliberate and generous with her words, so powerful at casting a spell on me. My desire for her was so intense that it felt like I would explode and shatter into tiny bits of flesh at her feet. And I would be happy in pieces there. She was the fiercest lesbian I knew. And she was *my* girlfriend.

There was no slow burn or ambivalence. I jumped in. Love notes, gifts, inside jokes, and mixtapes. We became intensely close very quickly. She was everything to me. The fire between us fed me on multiple levels—our love was sexual, emotional, intellectual, and political.

Jessie and I had mostly engaged in a lot of humping and grinding, which was very pleasurable, but I knew I had to up my game with a big-time lesbian. When Jen and I had sex for the first time, I went down on her and tried valiantly to figure out how to eat pussy after I'd only done it once, with a woman I knew who looked like Sadie. Jen was a skilled communicator when it came to sex, something she'd eventually teach me.

"That feels good, baby, but more pressure on my clit," she moaned. I made a mental note.

"More clit," she repeated softly. I could hear Cheryl Lynn's "Got to Be Real" playing on her stereo.

When I got back to my room, I searched my bookshelf and found what I was looking for: the 1984 edition of *The New Our Bodies, Ourselves.* Went straight to the index. Clitoris, pages 168, 169–72, 188, 190, 205, 207, 208, 273. Yup, it was important. Then I read: "Learning about the clitoris increased sexual enjoyment for countless women and freed many of us from years of thinking we were 'frigid.' Our ability to give ourselves orgasms and to show our lovers how to please us has been one of the cornerstones of a new self-respect and autonomy, and has therefore been politically as well as personally important for women." That was the day I learned the word *clitoris*. I already knew *what* and *where* my clitoral glans was: the spot on my vulva that gave me an orgasm when I masturbated and, much less frequently, when someone else rubbed it during sex. *Penis-in-vagina intercourse doesn't stimulate the clitoris directly.* But now it had a name. *More clit.* Jen wanted more clitoral stimulation. That made a lot of sense. I read the rest of the pages, studied the anatomy diagram diligently. I carefully reviewed how I got myself off. That wasn't necessarily what Jen's clit wanted, but it was a start. I vowed to learn how to master the clit.

Jen read *On Our Backs* and *Susie Sexpert's Lesbian Sex World* to me at bedtime. (She was even in charge of bringing Susie Bright to speak on campus that spring.) We were so connected, so engaged in the relationship. Every single day, there was something new to learn, share, and discover. Jen was the first girl I ever lived with (for a summer). I experienced the tremors of my first earthquake in bed with Jen and her yellow Lab, Bean. I had my first taste of what now is my all-time favorite food at the hands of Jen: sushi. We used latex gloves and dental dams, something that had been drilled into us and that queers in my generation took very seriously. We tested for STIs, and

I took my first HIV test with her at the student health center. Jen was the first woman to fuck me with a dildo. The first person to fuck me in the ass.

The first time she fucked my ass with her fingers, I went into outer space. I felt pressure at the opening, then her finger sliding into my tight space. It wasn't the same as fingers in my pussy. The pleasure was more concentrated. *We are fucking the patriarchy now for sure. Nice girls did not have anal sex!* She was gentle, used lube and a latex glove, talked to me. I realize this is not a typical first experience with anal penetration, so I consider myself very lucky. I was enthralled. The feeling was so intense I almost didn't know how to react. My body did. When I added clitoral stimulation to the mix, it was transcendent, the best, most explosive orgasm I'd ever had. Seriously. I wanted to do it again. I wanted more fingers. I wanted to do it to her. I had no idea how getting fucked in the ass would change the course of my life. Six years later, I'd write an entire book about it. She stoked the fire first.

I vaguely knew what s/m (sadomasochism) was, and I was curious, but Jen made it very real. Jen topped me for the first time, I bottomed to her for the first time, and we switched. My first safeword was *elephant* because when I looked up from her bed, there was a tall poster with a black-and-white elephant on it. Jen was the first person to tie me up. The first person to spank me. We watched gay porn together. She was the first girl I ever fucked with a strap-on. She was the first girl I ever stripped for. Jen was the first girl I ever bought a tie for. Jen brought me to buy my first pair of Doc Martens. She was so articulate about her desires and her politics, so sex positive that I could tell her anything. She was my lover, my mentor, my dyke teacher, and so much of who I am today came from her. More than a decade later, I would coin a term for myself: a *breakthrough lover* is a person who takes you places you've never been before, including places you thought you'd never go. Once you experience sex with them, your desire and pleasure are forever changed. More possibilities open up. Jen was my first breakthrough lover.

Before Jen, I was confused about my desires and confined by traditional gender roles, normative ideas about love and sex, and slut-shaming narratives. Women were swimming in them all the time, and they seeped in. I knew there was more. I was never miserable with the boys I'd been with; physically, they were fun, although I couldn't connect with most of them on an intellectual or emotional level, and I definitely didn't come the way I came with Jen. While I had sex with a lot of different guys, I never tried new things, experimented, or voiced *my* fantasies. Embracing my new dyke identity gave me my sexual liberation.

Tristan Taormino

My mom met Jen for the first time over brunch when we also broke the news that I was going to Los Angeles with her when she graduated that year. My mother stopped eating her BLT. She rolled her eyes, which is one of her favorite things to say.

"Hmm. Jen, I can see that you are ready to start your career in the entertainment industry. Tristan, Jen has a reason to go. You are running away from home." And run I did. Out, proud, and into the streets.

That was the summer I fully became a queer dyke. We lived with Jen's cousin in his apartment around the corner from Canter's Delicatessen. We quickly became immersed in queer culture, and I felt like I'd come home, found my people and myself. We marched proudly at the San Francisco and LA Gay Pride Parades. Jen took me to my first queer wedding. The femme, Nicole, was a Wesleyan grad in her early twenties. She was fully made up and dressed in a vintage ivory lace dress with matching pumps. She would have made the perfect *Bride Magazine* model, except for the way she carried herself. She was neither blushing nor modest; she was proud and autonomous. She married Tony, a working-class butch with close-cropped hair that was slicked back on top. Tony wore a crisp tuxedo shirt, black leather chaps over black Levis, and a leather bowtie. Nicole composed pages and pages of the most beautiful love poetry to read to Tony through tears of devotion. When she finished, Tony looked deep into her eyes and told Nicole, in about thirty unrehearsed simple words, how much she meant to her. They exchanged rings. Queer love not only was possible but could take my breath away.

We joined Queer Nation LA because that's what you did when you were a fed-up queer in 1991. The *Los Angeles Times* called it "the militant gay rights group," and it was dedicated to radical direct action, much like ACT UP (there was a lot of overlap between the two). The meetings were a revelation. People of all walks of life organized in response to George Bush's refusal to acknowledge the AIDS crisis, the lack of government money and resources for people living with AIDS, conservative Christian antigay rhetoric, police and street violence against queer people. We organized for civil rights, health care, safety on the streets, authentic representation, sexual freedom, and visibility. One of the most active members, a Latina woman with dyed jet-black hair and red lipstick named Judy, took us under her wing and introduced us around. A woman of color named Keiko was only sixteen but so sure of herself and unafraid. She'd already been arrested once. I thought, *This queer high school girl is kicking ass and taking names.* Richard was a tall, round white gay man who was different from many of the men I had met in P-town; he was more interested in planning protests than going to tea dances. Wayne was one of the unofficial leaders of the group who often wore a T-shirt with the word *homo* in all caps.

I was no longer in an awkward padded chair-desk combo listening to a professor lecture about racism, sexism, heteronormativity, homophobia, sex phobia, and classism. I was learning from people doing the work on the ground to combat oppressive systems and injustice. Their vision and practice were intersectional long before I heard or grasped the meaning of the word. During late nights, between bites of cheap veggie burgers at Astro Burger in West Hollywood, they talked about things that were new to baby-dyke Tristan: the playfulness and politics of gender, disability justice, sex workers' rights. Together we protested homophobic churches. We protested a photo lab at the Beverly Center that wouldn't develop pictures of same-sex couples kissing. I marched down LA streets in my Doc Martens, hand in hand with pierced and tattooed perverts in protest.

Jen and I became friends with many of the activists, including a group of radical faeries who lived in a vegan collective. One of them, a skinny guy named Cory, had a shaved head, a pierced septum, a genderqueer wardrobe, and an overwhelming amount of charisma. He boldly identified as an HIV-positive fed-up queer, ready to put his body on the line for real social change. I had a crush—I loved his rage and his spirit, both of which had no bounds. One night, he, Keiko, Jen, and I stayed very late at Kinko's on Highland Boulevard to make Queer Nation's signature stickers: we photocopied hundreds of sheets of fluorescent crack-and-peel paper, then cut them with the industrial-sized paper cutters.

Fuck Your Gender.
We're Here, We're Queer, Get Used to It.
Suck My Lesbian Cock.
Queer Anytime, Anywhere.
Assimilate My Fist.

One of Queer Nation's trademarks was to reclaim—and flaunt—negative terms hurled at us as insults with snark and wit. Cory was copying the zine he made with Wayne, *Infected Faggot*, which had a bright yellow cover. In the first issue, they wrote, "Dedicated to keeping the realities of faggots living with AIDS and HIV disease IN YOUR FACE until the plague is OVER."

As volunteers for the Propaganda Sub Group, Jen and I had a crowning achievement that summer: we helped design and create a safer-sex T-shirt. One side read, CLITLICKER: I'LL BE DAMMED. The other, BUTTFUCKER: TOTAL CONDOM NATION. I still have mine.

When I came back from LA, I played Jen's mixtapes, danced around my room to Monie Love's "It's a Shame," then got to work. I had been radicalized and was ready to bring queer direct action to campus. I was in good company: activism was one of the student body's favorite activities. In the fall of 1991, I recruited a bunch of other queer students who were also sick of the polite politics and activities of the campus Gay, Lesbian, Bisexual Alliance (GLBA). Although there was a general liberal "we accept you" vibe about queer people on campus, there were many incidents of homophobia. We wanted to speak out, be heard. Secretly we formed a group called Queers United in Crushing Homophobia Everywhere, with the super-gay, brunch-y acronym Q.U.I.C.H.E. We vowed to keep the identities of members confidential. We hung six hundred posters all over campus in the middle of the night; they had ten different provocative statements about safer sex, consensual S/M, homophobia, HIV/AIDS, anal sex, pussy licking, fucking... For maximum visibility, we put them up on the weekend that prospective students and their parents came to visit Wesleyan. A public safety officer saw them and had them removed, which of course infuriated us. In a letter we complained to the dean about our free-speech rights, then made more and plastered them everywhere again. We knew our posters would stir things up but had no idea how much they hit a nerve: someone actually filed a complaint with the Middletown Police, and there was talk that the Connecticut district attorney would charge the group with obscenity since one of the posters was on the sidewalk in front of a humanities building that technically was under the state's jurisdiction.

Letters to the editor of the *Wesleyan Argus* poured in for seven months after the initial postering:

We are offended by the posters.

These in-your-face tactics are ineffective.

You shouldn't have slipped them under the doors of professors' offices.

You can't raise awareness or combat homophobia by alienating straight people.

Figure 18.1 With friends at the March on Washington for Lesbian, Gay and Bi Equal Rights, Washington, DC, 1993

Conflict erupted in the GLBA about the incident, which revealed deeper issues within the group. Q.U.I.C.H.E. wrote a response in the *Argus*, but we still remained anonymous. Eventually we had to come out, and we got reprimanded by the dean, a powerful Latina woman I really respected. Privately (and sincerely), she told me she supported our action.

"This thing has taken on a life of its own," she said. "I am under pressure to quash it. Internal politics." It was disappointing but not surprising given all the pushback Queer Nation faced, even from members of the LGBTQIA+ community. We heard what the university was saying: "We love our lesbian, gay, and bisexual students but only if you behave in ways that don't make us too uncomfortable."

Tristan Taormino

FEMME IS MY GENDER

My mother kept all the cards she received when I was born, and as I sift through the pile, one stands out: a Gerber-esque drawing of an infant with a broad forehead and blue eyes holding a blush-colored bunny in its tiny hands in a cloud of pink. Written in script above the illustration: *What Is a Girl?*

At Wesleyan I read everything I could get my hands on about queer sex and gender. In addition to my love of Susie Bright and *On Our Backs*, I discovered *Macho Sluts* by Patrick Califia, who described a world of desire populated by leatherdykes where I wanted to live. Esther Newton schooled me in camp, articulating so much about what I'd learned from the queens in P-town. I diligently read Gayle Rubin, Amber Hollibaugh, and Cherríe Moraga for my undergraduate thesis on butch/femme identities. In her book *A Restricted Country*, Joan Nestle particularly struck a chord: "Does the longevity of butch-femme self-expression reflect the pernicious strength of heterosexual gender polarization—or is it, as I would argue, a lesbian-specific way of deconstructing gender that radically reclaims women's erotic energy?" She wrote about working-class lesbians in the 1960s and 1970s, lesbians who passed as men, women's communities divided over the politics of pleasure. Although they were unfamiliar scenes, desire and power dynamics between differently gendered queers felt—feel—like home. Nestle's writings about what it meant to be a femme spoke directly to my heart.

From an early age, I've been told that I am:
Confident.
Aggressive.
Mouthy.
Blunt.
Bossy.

I speak my mind. I take up too much space. I'm overtly sexual. I'm shameless. These are the opposite of what most people consider ladylike. I knew how a good girl was supposed to behave—be quiet, gentle, deferential, demure, and chaste—and none of that was for me. In elementary school I rushed to do projects on smart white women (my only frame of reference) who lived unapologetic lives, like Amelia Earhart, Eleanor Roosevelt, and Barbra Streisand. I admired my mom for being independent and resilient. I learned an unspoken rule in those early years: there was such a thing as being too smart for boys to like you. Being smart was detrimental to your desirability. *Fuck that.*

I *did* absorb the cultural programming that girl = feminine, and in terms of my appearance, I often felt like a failure. I had acne and a skinny, curveless body. I couldn't quite get my curly hair to look the way hair did in commercials. In the horse show world, I appreciated that we all wore a uniform, regardless of gender. Your hair, however shiny or untamed, was hidden under a riding helmet. I was a late bloomer (the fact that a term exists for me getting my period at sixteen is dumb). I knew I was as smart as Sabrina from *Charlie's Angels*, but her makeup was flawless and her fashion sublime. Even with all those trappings, she was still never an object of desire the way Jill and Kelly were, so what chance did I have?

Gender-bending of any kind seemed most often to be the province of people assigned male at birth: Chickie's fabulous clothes, Jimmy James's glamour, Boy George's makeup, and everything about Prince. I wasn't drawn to the androgyny of Grace Jones or Annie Lennox. I wanted the body consciousness and blatant sexuality of Madonna, Cyndi Lauper, Tina Turner, and Janet Jackson.

On a 1993 cover of *Vanity Fair* is an iconic black-and-white photo: supermodel Cindy Crawford, poured into a black bodysuit and short boots with bows, straddles k.d. lang in a vintage barber chair. k.d. is dressed in men's pinstriped suit pants and a matching vest over a button-down. Foamy cream from a fresh shave lingers on her face. In the inside spread, they look like they are about to fuck. The photo can be critiqued as a co-opted image of a white, middle-class, able-bodied lesbian couple. But it's also unmistakably the iconography of butch and femme, as gender identities, self-expression, desire, and power. I wasn't just interested in looking like Cindy; k.d. needed to be the one in the chair.

Coming out as a dyke readied me to explore my gender identity more fully. I wanted to be a girl, but on my own terms. My real-life role models are drag queens, genderqueers, sex workers, and porn stars. I gravitate to people who can exaggerate traditional femininity and give it a twist. Give me false eyelashes, overdrawn lips, and combat boots all day.

As I explored a queer world, I was ready to experiment with the play of masculine and feminine and what might signify me as queer to other queers. I was particular about my aesthetic. Short, flowery dresses that were popular on *Beverly Hills, 90210* paired with heavy boots. Men's ties with white dress shirts, left open so you could see my push-up bra. Vintage hand-beaded gowns worn with a motorcycle jacket.

My gender presentation began to evolve into a proud, in-your-face, take-no-prisoners, don't-assume-I'm-straight-because-I-wear-lipstick-and-dresses femme dyke. Bold, powerful, overtly sexual but no damsel in distress who courts the male gaze. Femininity with an edge.

Butches, masculine women, and transmasculine and nonbinary folks get a lot of attention for having fascinating, rule-defying, and complex gender identities and expressions (and I love them for it). Femme queer women can be erased, misread, or—in a feat of persistent misogyny—devalued, even within LGBTQIA+ communities. Someone who is assigned female at birth, grows up to identify as a woman, and presents a "feminine" gender expression can be disregarded, like we don't have a thoughtful gender at all, we are just one of the sheep following the rules. Well, I have a fucking gender, and it can have as much nuance as any other gender even if it is supposedly aligned with the sex I was assigned at birth. I am determined to be understood here.

Because femmes are often read as straight by heteronormative society, when I came out, I made sure to wear queer T-shirts and pins, shout the word *homophobic* loudly in conversation, or have a butch on my arm so I'd be read as femme. The boys took one look at me and steered clear. It was as if I was too much of a woman for them to handle, and I was, in fact, a handful. I wanted to attract others who didn't fit in their prescribed gender roles—they were *the* hottest, and in the 1990s they were most often butch women. Butch women love a handful—a handful of tits, a handful of ass, a girl who needs to be handled, and a girl who can handle herself. How I figured out I was a femme had a lot to do with the women I was attracted to and the dynamic between us. Being with a butch, I was valued for my combination of strength and vulnerability. My butches loved me when I took great care to dress up for me and them and wanted an arm to hold on to and hips to wrap my legs around. I wanted someone to give my body over to and say, *I trust you, I'm yours.* Butches loved me in low-cut dresses and appreciated my sexual voraciousness. I reveled in the fact that I could be strong and submissive all at once. Surrender and still be a feminist. Being a femme dyke is not just about who I fuck and love; it's about being a girl who doesn't play by the rules.

Butch women don't play by the rules either. In my coming-out story in *A Woman Like That*, I wrote:

> I love girls with hair so short you can barely slide it between two fingers to hold on. Girls with slick, shiny, barbershop haircuts and shirts that button the other way. Girls that swagger. Girls who have dicks made of flesh and silicone and magic. Girls who get stared at in the ladies room, girls who shop in the boys department, girls who live every moment looking like they weren't supposed to. Girls with hands that touch me like they have been touching my body their entire lives. Girls who have big cocks, love blowjobs, and like to fuck girls hard. Every day, it is the girls that get called Sir that make me catch my breath, the girls with strong jaws that buckle my knees who make me want to lie down for them.

Jen was my first butch, and I fell hard for many more. Like the poet who bought her first strap-on with me and then wanted to sleep with it on. The dyke from Colombia whose brick-solid body and broad shoulders stretched out ACT UP T-shirts. The therapist-in-training who got harassed every time she drove in the South because she looked like a fifteen-year-old boy. The ad exec who had names for her dildos and loved for me to spit-shine her wingtips. The photographer whose face was so mannish, she could pass. The writer who wanted a body like trans man Loren Cameron. The telephone repair woman who drove a truck. The academic who got cruised by gay men on Castro Street. The corn-fed farm boy with arms so hard and strong you'd swear they'd been working the land, not the iron at the gym. I was taken by their James Dean stares, their dandy bowties, their fearlessness in sex and in the world. Butches were (and are) a homecoming for me. These days, the language of gender has expanded greatly, and not all the people I'm into identify as butches or as women, but people with all different kinds of masculine energy have my heart.

My gender reckoning coincided with the release of *Gender Trouble: Feminism and the Subversion of Identity* by scholar Judith Butler. Butler and her book would eventually be considered pivotal to scholarship about gender and sexuality and the formation of what we now call *queer studies*. But back then, it was a new book I read in my women's studies class that broke me open to the possibilities gender held. The first edition of the book sits on my bookshelf today, sandwiched between equally radical works by Kate Bornstein and Leslie Feinberg. These folks articulated gender in all its complexities and spoke to my love of the performativity of gender.

It was a privilege to come out in the 1990s when it was becoming safe for me, as a queer, middle-class, white girl, to explore gender constraints and performance. Today butch/femme is seen as a throwback by younger generations, but femme has both persisted and evolved. People now have language for more gender identities and expressions than ever before, so butch/femme can feel like another binary they want to challenge or discard altogether. But I hold on to my femme identity and honor those who came before me; it marks who I am, when I came out, and what still holds true to this day: I fuck with my gender.

My experience of gender and sexual identity stands in stark contrast to my father's. My father grappled with gender because most of the homophobia that surrounded him growing up was aimed at effeminate men. His parents once detailed a list of ways you could tell someone was a homosexual:

Always wore a hat
Had a goatee
Worshipped Judy Garland
Always had fresh flowers in the bathroom

Dad was comfortable with most of his queerness and his softness and emotionality, but I had the distinct feeling he was uncomfortable acting or being seen as flamboyant, femme, or faggy. He couldn't shake all of the internalized homophobia. I once bought him a T-shirt that said DIVA on it in a bold sans serif font, which he loved to wear. That's about as far as he'd go. In one passage in his memoir that takes place just days before he came out, he recites this list, page 167:

sissy.
fruit.
queer.
fairy.
fem.
mary.
swish.
pansy.
cocksucker.
bent.
queen.
fag.
faggot.
gay.
homo.
homosexual.

These labels were sources of denial, guilt, avoidance, and shame for him.

I have called myself these words, out loud, proudly. I have worn fluorescent stickers and silk-screened T-shirts with these words emblazoned on them. To me, these words are a reclamation, a proclamation, a homecoming, and a warning.

Queer is more than a sexual orientation because it transcends sex: queer is the way I orient myself to the world. Queer is not just about who I love, date, partner with, and fuck—queer is my culture, my community, and my politics. It's the lens I look through every day.

In 2012, four years into living with chronic back pain, I had tried any and all treatments, from physical therapy to herbs to acupuncture. On a trip to Los Angeles, my partner's sister said she could get me in to see a much sought-after intuitive healer. He was impossible to book and wildly expensive, but I'd get the friends-and-family discount. I can't resist a healer or a good deal. I ventured out to his lavish home in Ojai, and something he said has stayed with me.

Tristan Taormino

He was reading me, seeing me in all my complexities, and what he was saying was right on target. I was deeply present in the moment to take in the experience without judgment.

"The masculine and the feminine are at war within you," he said confidently. Then I heard the sound of the record scratch. *Wait, what the actual fuck?*

Later I realized, if he was reading my aura or sensing my energy or whatever his particular process was, he was seeing the masculine and feminine in me. So he got that right. Through his heteronormative, deeply gendered lens, he interpreted what he saw as "war" because, for him, gender was a binary with clear borders. A psychic with a different perspective might have said, "Oh, you have a complicated gender." Or a really good one would say, "You're a femme."

BOMBSHELL

I was strutting back and forth on my parents' bed, having my very own and very intimate fashion show. I was modeling my mother's black half-slip; it was pulled up just above my nipples. The music from the radio was so dreamy, so soothing, that I would stop and stare at myself in the mirror, as if hypnotized.

DAD IN 1954

After my junior year at Wesleyan, I returned to LA for the summer to be with Jen. The long distance had been rough, but we had survived, and I was determined to make the relationship work. Jen had settled into a new apartment of her own and got a job working for a talent agent. My plan was to cover expenses and do research for my senior thesis; my proposal had been accepted, and I was officially writing on lesbian butch/femme identity and representation. I took out ads in *Lesbian News* seeking butches and femmes to interview, and I got a bunch of responses. I landed a crappy day job at a shoe store called Wild Pair at the Century City Mall. The bus commute was long, and the competition cutthroat: we worked on commission, so we fought each other to see who could sell the most shoes, whether garish high heels or cheap metallic sandals.

My weekend job was the one I really wanted: go-go dancing at the Palms, the only lesbian bar in the city. There was no dressing room at the Palms, so it was better to get ready at home than wait in what was usually a long line for the bathroom. That meant I was in high-femme mode as I rode the bus to West Hollywood late on Friday and Saturday nights. I could sense men staring at me, and I had a hint of fear of the ones who didn't look gay because I was sometimes the only woman on the bus. The gay men didn't see me at all.

One night I was nearly late, so I walked past the bouncer and went directly to the back of the club. The bathroom was empty, so I did a once-over in the mirror: crisp white shirt, bright red tie, and a black men's suit I had thrifted at Goodwill. I touched up my Media by MAC lipstick. I could hear voices and music blaring on the other side of the wall, and it sounded like the club was already full. I was still tense from the bus ride, so I massaged my shoulders, stretched a little, and listened to the music. In a flurry, the club manager burst through the door and yelled, "You're on right now!" The DJ announced the arrival of the dancers as I jumped up onto my box. That first moment of nervousness hit me in the stomach . . . I listened for the beat. Prince. "Get Off." *Here I am.* I grabbed the thick metal chains that hung from a beam in the ceiling, spun around, and peeked at myself in the mirror. *I can feel their eyes all over my body. Is that man clutching his girlfriend just like those creepy men on the bus would have clutched me? Are they going to go home and have really good sex tonight? Am I part of their fantasy?*

I had only ever seen images of women stripping for men; for me, the mechanics can be the same, but the difference is who's looking. It's all about the tease. You shimmy your pants or shorts or skirt ever so slowly. You bend over and display your ass. You take each piece of outer covering off slowly until you're wearing a push-up bra and red satin shorts. You make eye contact. You shake your ass. You make them part with their sticky dollar bills. You make them beg for it. You grind up against the sweaty body of the other dancer. She has close-cropped jet-black hair and a perfectly muscled body poured into a boy's wrestling singlet. She gets on her knees in front of you and shoves her face between your legs. You throw your head back and thrust your hips. You move in a way that says *Look at me, worship me,* PAY ME.

I took a break to get a bottle of water from the bar. Sharon the bartender wasn't really my type, no tomboy with big puppy dog eyes. She had medium-length bleach-blond hair fried from all the dyeing, full lips coated with bright fuchsia lipstick, piercing black-brown eyes, and a pierced pink tongue. She was thirty-five, and her body was covered in tattoos that represented a life of wild adventures. She was a chain smoker. She was in an all-girl punk rock band. She'd been through some things. There was no chance in hell this woman would ever be interested in *me*. But she flirted—well, she flirted with every-

Figure 20.1 In Prospect Park, Brooklyn, New York, 1996; photo by Lisa Graziano

one, she was a bartender—and my overeducated, upwardly mobile white girl sensibilities were transparent to her.

The first time she took me home, she got behind me and whispered, "I knew the moment I saw you—that energy, the connection. You couldn't control yourself. You had this air of innocence about you, but I knew you weren't innocent at all. I could hear all these nasty thoughts running through your head. Nasty thoughts I really liked the sound of." She snatched my neck and sank her teeth into it. She lifted up my dress and ripped my fishnet stockings roughly.

"I love this dress. You look like such a little girl in it, and I really love that."

Her fingers slid into my pussy, and I was throbbing, swollen, dripping wet.

She whispered, "I wish I had a dick right about now," as she pushed harder into me. *Why is it that all the women I end up in bed with say they want cocks when they already have them?*

She purred, "I want to feel what it would be like to be inside you. I'd fuck you harder than you've ever been fucked, and I would come inside you..." (She was inside me.) She eventually did get her cock, then told me I was a good little girl and bent me over her kitchen table; I felt the cold glass push against my clit. She fucked me furiously, then slowed down until I could feel every movement, every inch. I screamed in ecstasy. The noise just came from somewhere else, deep, guttural. It didn't sound like me. It sounded like a girl on the edge of a cliff.

Later I found out she had a girlfriend named Karma.

"We have never talked about monogamy or nonmonogamy, and Karma knows me."

Jen and I did talk about that stuff and had agreed to be exclusive once I got to LA, so I was cheating. It felt like I couldn't resist.

No matter how many hot dykes I saw at the club, I was under Sharon's spell. The bruises on my tender ass, her lipstick smudges all over my underwear, and memories of our nights together left me ravaged and satisfied. Sharon fucked me in a kind of I'm-in-charge-this-is-as-rough-as-I-like-it-angry way. I got wetter and hotter, and all I wanted to do was come all over her hands. Just as my insides opened up, she pulled her fingers out of me. She blindfolded me and cuffed me, took me into the bathroom, and laid me on the cold floor. Her metal piercing was on my tongue. She slid my dress up my thigh and pulled my panties down to rub her fingers against my wetness. I heard her move around, and then I felt the sharp points of scissors on my cunt. I must have jumped a little because she slapped me in the face and told me to stay still, then began hacking away my pussy hair. I heard buzzing, and something thick and warm vibrated against my clit. She pulled the clippers away, jerked me off a little bit, and then warm liquid ran down between my legs. The feeling was sharp again, but not so pointy, as she scraped away the hair, until the abrasive razor became her pointy metallic tongue flirting with my clit and lapping at my cunt, reminding me of the power between my legs and her absolute possession of it.

"If you are very, very good, one day you will get to do the same to me . . . One day you will get to touch me and make love to me. But not yet. Don't get ahead of yourself. I'll tell you when I want to, when I'm ready."

Not only was she dominant, she was also stone at the beginning. The women I knew who identified as stone were butches; they got off on giving pleasure to their partner but preferred not to be done in return. For Sharon, it may have been protective, but it was also a power move. I left her place with a shaved pussy and a deeply bruised ass. The next morning in the bathroom, as Jen finished getting ready for work, I slipped into the shower in my underwear to avoid detection. I was soaked in guilt. I had to tell Jen.

She was devastated. My desire had steered my decision-making, and instead of telling Jen and being honest, I had opted to deceive. I regret it. I told myself I was a bad girlfriend. I started sleeping on the couch in the living room. Eventually she asked me to find another place to stay; she said it was just too painful to see me every day. I had my obsession with Sharon to keep me from thinking too deeply about how much pain *I* was in. Jen was my first everything. She guided and nurtured me. In some ways, she created me. She helped me find *me* and introduce myself to the world. And she loved me fiercely—powerful, passionate, unconditional love that my twenty-one-year-old self couldn't fully recognize or hold. We can joke a little about it all these years later. I tell her she turned me out. She says I took to queerness like a fish to water.

I kept moving to try to put distance between me and my grief. I didn't have the skills to be in an adult relationship. I didn't want to process it. At that point, loss felt familiar and inevitable. I kept dancing at the Palms, which was my refuge from my shitty job at the mall and the relationship ending with Jen.

Sharon didn't have a lot of time for me; she was rehearsing with her band or silk-screening T-shirts that said "Stay out of my uterus you fuckhead." One

Tristan Taormino

night I managed to catch the eye of Jo, a Mexican butch who wore a backward baseball hat, a bomber jacket, and a flannel shirt. She looked like a teenage boy to other people, and her energy was undeniably boy to me. The ones who knew exactly who and what she was would kill her for such clarity. Around 4 a.m., after the bar closed, we sat in her truck in a deserted West Hollywood parking lot. I told her I didn't have time, and I wasn't interested. Pat Benatar was playing on the tape deck. She slid her hand up my polka-dot dress and teased my thighs. I reminded her I probably wouldn't call her. She fucked me slowly, like we had all the time in the world, and I felt a little delirious. She drove me back to my friend's place and said, "I'll see you at the bar."

On my final night dancing at the Palms, Jo was leaning against the wall near my box, the place she liked to occupy. She couldn't take her eyes off me, and the way she watched me made me shiver. One seductive sex-kitten look from me plus my painted nails dragged across my bra, and I got her where I wanted her to be, where I wanted them all to be. They couldn't stop watching, and I couldn't stop being watched. I took off my shirt to reveal a red satin bra, a vintage style that pushed my breasts into torpedoes, like Madonna's pink Gaultier bra-corset from the Blond Ambition tour.

The waitress handed me bottled water with a note from Sharon: "I hope you're pacing yourself. I've got plans for you after work. I want to blindfold you and lick you behind the knees and . . ." An unfinished sentence written on a damp white bar napkin. The icy water ran down my throat, and the hot pink lights beat down on my face. Jo casually rubbed her hard cock through her pants. I danced in the sharp, shiny mirrors of her eyes.

I realized the evening would end soon because the club was getting uncomfortably stuffy and crowded. I wondered where I was going once I finished for the night and who was going to take me there. As the lights came up, I jumped down and made my way toward the bar. Exhausted, sweaty, charged up, I guzzled the last of the water and looked at myself in the mirror again. I spotted Sharon's girlfriend by the bar; she had arrived to pick her up. *Guess there won't be any blindfolding tonight as promised.*

Jo made her way over to me and slipped me a piece of paper.

"I'm going to an after-hours club with my friends. You were great tonight! Here's my number . . . for when you can call me."

Women poured into the street, and I went with them. I was thirsty and hungry, and one of my knees was starting to ache. As I made my way down the sidewalk, a pickup truck passed by and slowed down. It was one of the bar's bouncers, a real old-school butch who had been flirting for weeks.

"Need a ride?"

There was nowhere I called my real home in the city anymore, so where she was going was as good a place as any. But I shook my head and smiled at her as the bus rolled up to a stop. I tossed my backpack over my shoulder and climbed the stairs.

Tristan Taormino

RILEY

briefly dated a basketball player from Yale named Christine whom I met at a women's night at the gay bar in Hartford. She dumped me quite abruptly. A year later, she began secretly seeing one of my best friends. Classic dyke drama. But Christine introduced me to her friend Riley, and when we broke up, I was ready for Riley to sweep me off my feet. She also went to Yale but had graduated a year before and stayed in New Haven to work in the photo archive department of a local company. We fell madly in love in the beginning of April as graduation approached at the end of May. I can accomplish a lot in two months.

Riley was so butch that she could easily pass as a man in certain situations. She was very tall and had pale skin like mine and dark brown hair cut short, but not too short. She played basketball and volleyball, so she had a thick, strong jock body, with the tiniest tits. She was smart, interested in history, anthropology, archaeology, and I love a smart butch. Weeks after we met, she was quoting poetry by Adrienne Rich, *Leaves of Grass* by Walt Whitman, *The Passion* by Jeanette Winterson: "And if anyone had said this was the price I would have paid it. That surprises me; that with the hurt and the mess comes a shaft of recognition. It is worth it. Love is worth it." Words have always seduced me.

Her passion was photography, and she thought I was the most beautiful woman in the world. She took pictures of me all the time. We were so wrapped up in each other, and we couldn't spend a moment apart without tremendous pain and longing.

Ry was from a tiny town in South Dakota. We went there together once, and it was very close to what I expected. Long, winding roads that seemingly lead nowhere, an endless sky of stars. That small-town vibe where everyone knows everyone's business. We visited a friend's family, and there was an entire deer carcass on a tarp on a big wooden table in their kitchen. They had dismantled most of it and were using an electric knife to cut smaller pieces for homemade jerky. Lots of her peers had remained close to home after they graduated high school. She was a big volleyball star at her high school, and she remained closeted to most people in the town.

Although I read her as butch, when I got to know her, I quickly realized she had not yet fully explored her gender or her desires. Early on, I thought I might have fallen in love with a really vanilla lesbian, but no, she wanted to try everything. She only required permission and encouragement, which I freely gave her. She loved to get fucked and had the most sopping wet pussy I've ever had my hand inside, then or now. She found her butch top with me, and it was so powerful to see this part of her come out, to see her discover and embrace it. She knew she was safe with me, and I adored this part of her, so she ran with it. She became a fantastic top, dirty talker, and pervert. I was the first to be able to hold both her Midwest wholesomeness and her dirty deviant side. Two years after Jen, there I was teaching another dyke a thing or two. *I'm the breakthrough lover.* A letter she composed opened with:

> How do I write to the woman who, from the first moment I saw her and without a word, forced me to start challenging nearly every imaginable boundary I've erected in my 24 years? I've changed with you, and I want to continue to change with you—always.

When she tied me to the bed with leather restraints and strapped on a cock, she made me watch us in the mirror; she pushed me around; she told me to beg her to fuck me. When I rode that cock, she said filthy things to me. She'd slide three fingers in my ass. She'd lift me up above her like she was bench-pressing me. When I flogged her back until it was streaked with red, I rubbed her skin and slapped it hard. When I felt her clit get hard beneath my fingers, I'd stop moving to tease her. When she finally surrendered, I made her get herself off in front of me.

She gave me a silver necklace with interlocking pieces. At one end was an open ring, and at the other, a T; the T slipped into the circle and turned, and that's how the necklace stayed on. It had a sort of collar feel to it, like if you didn't know, you didn't see, but if you were kinky, you did. Our power-drenched love hiding in plain sight. We wrote letters to each other about going to graduate school at the same university, traveling the world together, getting married. So many plans. I was twenty-three, and the possibilities for my life felt absolutely endless. I wanted to share all those things with her. I wrote her poetry:

> *The car windows were steamed up*
> *I was on top of you*
> *and you were inside me*
> *first in my cunt*
>
> *then in my ass*
> *Then your arms were tied behind your back*
> *the seat was all the way back*
> *I had the knife at your throat*
> *and the dick inside you*
> *your tears terrified me*
> *I was elated*

Our connection was as fast and easy, as obvious and predestined as a hook and eye. We fused together, the adhesion was sturdy, and we never came apart. Until we did. She pops into my head now during a mundane task. When she got out of the shower, she used to turn off the faucet but stay in. She'd wick away water with her hands first, then reach for a towel. I clearly picture her large hands swiping the pale, taut skin of her rib cage, her hips, her generous ass. When I twist the dial to turn off the shower, I see the water flying away from her body.

CHANGE OF PLANS

I love a plan. At Wesleyan I had a firm one for after I graduated: I wanted to be an activist dyke lawyer—a lawyer in public service to underserved communities helping people who were marginalized and didn't have the same access to the system as the privileged. By the fall of my senior year, my applications to twelve top law schools reflected my success: top 10 percent of my class, sterling recommendations, an active extracurricular life, and a compelling essay. I read a few books and did some practice tests, then took the LSATs; my score was dead middle on the bell curve.

"They will look at the complete picture, and you'll be fine." Everyone told me not to worry. Spring came, and I was rejected from eleven of the schools and wait-listed at Boston University. I was devastated. My plan had evaporated in the span of a few days. All my color-coded files, meticulous note taking, research, careful consideration for . . . what? I went to see Claire Potter, my professor and thesis adviser, and I sobbed in the chair across from her desk.

"I had a plan! I had a plan! What am I supposed to do now?"

"Well, you can see if you get off the waitlist at BU."

"I don't even want to go to BU!"

Claire was brave. She was junior faculty and an out, proud dyke. She worked among other queer professors, many of them tenured, who were closeted or very discreet. She was not. Her sandy brown hair was short, her mind was on fire, and that little space between her front teeth made all the baby queers swoon.

She looked in my eyes and, in her matter-of-fact tone, said, "Listen, I don't think you want to go to law school, and I don't think you want to be a lawyer. I think you want to write about sex. From what I've seen, you love it, and you're good at it. My advice? If you do get in, defer for a year. Continue writing and see what happens. You can always go to law school."

I had been working with Claire for a year and a half on my honors thesis. I brought together memoir, postmodern gender theory, lesbian porn, s/m, and the interviews I did with real butches and femmes from LA. I absolutely loved every aspect of the project, and here was Claire telling me this might be my future. *But law school was the plan! That's the plan! What the hell is she talking about? Writing about sex isn't an actual job.* I looked up to Betty Dodson, Carol Queen, and Patrick Califia, but I didn't think they were making a living being sex writers. There was Dr. Ruth Westheimer, America's sex therapist, but she was grandmotherly, and I couldn't see myself in her. Nope, I needed a new plan and fast. No matter how much I loved writing about sex, it wasn't going to pay my bills.

I went to the Career Counseling Center and found a listing from an alumna: "San Francisco Bay Area Political Consulting Firm Seeks Research Assistant." The firm was owned by women and dedicated to grassroots political organizing. San Francisco, the queer mecca. Working with a nearly all-female, feminist staff. Progressive politics: check. Land the job: check.

A year earlier, my father had made another big move: from Portland, Oregon, to Portland, Maine. I was prepared for his pattern to repeat, for it to only last for so long, but held out hope that this was it, that maybe he would finally hit his stride. He cleaned offices and worked part-time at a restaurant called the Mad Apple Café, run by a husband-and-wife duo whom he adored. He was writing a lot and submitting his stuff to magazines and journals.

Soon he met someone named Ted, and they fell in love. Ted was warm and grounded, and I could tell my dad was head over heels. This was the first partner he could introduce to me *as his partner.* It was a big deal. Ted moved in, and when I visited them at their condo in a cool historic building, I could see how it was all coming together.

Ted was smart and sarcastic; he had a biting, bitchy sense of humor. He had a big, nearly bald head, and the remainder of his hair and his neatly trimmed mustache and goatee were salt and pepper. He was an ordained pastor in the Lutheran Church who left pastoral work to become a social worker, which all made sense: he was a listener and a problem-solver with an open heart. He belonged to Alcoholics Anonymous, which was a good fit since my dad didn't drink, and they loved to make snide comments about people who did (including my mother). Given that my dad and I had such an intensely close relationship and this was his first serious, live-in partner since I was about ten, I expected I might feel jealous. But I genuinely liked Ted and saw that they complemented each other well. In Portland my dad was the happiest he'd ever been. I knew this is what he had wanted his whole life: a place and a person to call home.

Mom, Dad, Ted, Uncle Tom, and Riley came to Wesleyan to watch me graduate. The day before, we were at a reception, and I gave bound copies of my senior thesis to my dad and my mom. By the next morning, he was already talking about it.

"You are just so smart—the way you've processed all these theories about gender. And your writing is clear and commanding. You see and write about what others wouldn't even touch. The way you live your life, the things you are passionate about . . . I think you will make a difference in this world. Sometimes I can't believe you are my daughter! You're brave. Braver than me. I'm so proud of you."

Riley walked over and exclaimed, "Let's do a picture!"

We were in front of the auditorium in the performing arts section of campus, a cluster of tall, stark modern cement buildings, which contrasted with the classic architecture around them. I was wearing my combat boots with a black suit I borrowed from my friend Ruth. My dad grabbed my hand, and our fingers intertwined. He started to move his hips and dance playfully, and he twirled me around. I savored the moment. We turned to face the camera, and he cocked his head to rest it on my shoulder. I smiled widely, and my lip got caught on one of my teeth.

"I couldn't have dreamed up a better dad. You mean so much to me."

"You are becoming a remarkable woman," he said softly as he looked deeply into my eyes. "And I can't wait to see what you do next."

The next day, I stepped on the stage to accept my diploma in combat boots and the same red polyester gown that my classmates were all wearing. I wore my Phi Beta Kappa key on a gold chain, pinned three buttons to the front of the gown (a pink triangle, a black triangle, and one that said "femme butch") and stuck on two fluorescent stickers from Queer Nation that read:

Tristan Taormino

Figure 22.1 Wesleyan graduation, with Dad, Middletown, Connecticut, 1993

PROMOTE DYKE VISIBILITY and FUCK YOUR GENDER. There were more stickers on the back:

ACTION=LIFE

FIGHT HETEROSEXISM

PROMOTE LESBIANISM

DYKES TAKE OVER THE WORLD

QUEERIFY AMERICA

Riley shot pictures of me with my friends, and we all look downright giddy. I felt seen and accomplished, surrounded by queers and allies. When the ceremony ended, I began to look for my family, but it was hectic and crowded. Suddenly, the sea of red parted, and a man I didn't recognize was making a beeline for me. He was dressed in a neat seersucker suit.

"Hello!" he said to me. He was fit and confident, and I could see perspiration on his tanned brow under the rim of his boater hat. "I just had to come

Figure 22.2 My graduation gown with Queer Nation stickers, Wesleyan University, 1993

Figure 22.3 Winston Wilde, Hollywood, California, circa 1996

over and meet you. Girlfriend, I saw your stickers and thought, *yes*. Queer visibility!"

"Oh, thanks," I replied. "Gotta represent."

"Frankly, I expected to see more of this here. I'm Winston Wilde." He held out his hand. "Paul Monette's husband."

Paul Monette had received an honorary degree that day, along with Cornel West and several others, and had given a rousing speech that really moved me.

I introduced myself.

"I read your name in the program. You won all sorts of prizes, including the gay, lesbian, and sexuality studies prize."

"You read the program?"

"It was a long day."

"Yeah, I wrote my thesis on butch/femme."

"Well, that's very interesting. I'd love to read it and stay in touch. Can you give me your address?" He pulled out a small notepad and pen, and I wrote down my mom's address.

"Come meet Paul!" He took me by the hand and walked me over to Paul, who was clearly sweltering in a long black robe under the bright sun. *I am meeting Paul Monette.* Borrowed Time, *his memoir about AIDS, was beautiful and devastating.* I tried to sound smart but definitely fangirled. Then I left to find my people.

Later that day, as I packed my stuff, I worked on a scrapbook for Ry; on the first page, I wrote:

> You are strong and sure, and I will never lose my faith in you because the power, the energy, and the connection between us is too intense and too important to me. I may be going to the other side of the country, but you're not getting rid of me. I want you ... I need you in my life. It's taken some adjusting on the part of this self-centered and oh-so-independent woman, but I can finally admit that. I miss you already. This present is about memories and the past, about that which we can never escape but which we sometimes forget. I hope it will help both of us get through the rough times that are ahead. In creating it with my hands and heart, I have come to realize the clarity of my love for you.

I moved to San Francisco a few weeks later, where I scored a sublet in Noe Valley through a friend of a friend. Ruth was planning to start grad school in Northern California in the fall, so she had her car shipped out to the Bay and told me I could drive it for the summer. Everything was falling into place.

Riley and I decided we'd be long-distance and nonmonogamous as she figured out whether to move, and my heart was with her. But I was also in queer heaven in San Francisco, with a hot, sexy butch around every corner. I became a regular at Josie's Cabaret and Juice Joint in the Castro, a cool café that featured celesbians like Marga Gomez doing comedy at night. The usual counter person wasn't there one day, so the cook came out from behind the line. She had sandy blond-brown hair, kind of greasy, cut very short, and a crooked smile. She wore a sweaty tank top hanging off her skinny frame; there was no bra in sight, barely noticeable tits, and a thick leather belt through the loops of her jeans. Very rough around the edges. She was definitely older than me, judging by the lines in her face, and she look like she lived *hard*. I looked up at the blackboard with a hand-lettered menu and ordered my usual. She was abrupt, barely saw me as I told her what I wanted. The next time I went, I looked for her behind the line and saw her stacking meat on soft wheat bread, then pushing carrots through the juicer. One day, she was outside smoking a cigarette.

"Hi." *Casual.*

"Hey. You really like that avocado veggie sandwich, don't you?" *She knows my order.*

"It's delicious," I replied, turning on the femme charm. I still didn't like to be coy, but I wanted to remain cool.

She put out her cigarette. "I'm Maddie," she said, holding out her hand.

"Tristan."

"How old are you, Tristan?"

She invited me to the Eagle, a leather bar south of Market. That night, she told me she had this other name she went by, an alter ego of sorts. His name was Al. Al was a kinky Daddy type who did whatever he wanted. *Cue swoon.*

After a month of dating, I used nearly my entire paycheck to buy a long single-tail whip at Mr. S. Leather. I'd never been single-tailed before, but I wanted the meanest thing in the store. I coiled it in tissue paper in one of those rectangular boxes that long-stem roses come in, complete with a big red bow. I convinced some guy on Sixteenth Street to play deliveryman and walk into Josie's. A few minutes later, Maddie came out of the restaurant holding the box and looked both ways. I was there, waiting.

Maddie hung out with lots of musicians, people who were tattooed, smoked weed, and didn't work during the day. They all smirked when she introduced me. I wanted to make a good impression, but I'd given up pot in college, and I was so clearly not one of *them*. I was high on Maddie.

But there was Riley, waiting patiently for me on the East Coast; she had finally decided to move to San Francisco. Ry was thoughtful, caring, generous, one of the nicest people I'd ever met. She was so good to me. Unbelievably, really. Sometimes it bugged me that she was so kind to me. I thought it was because she lacked an edge that I had been looking for (which I believed I had found in Maddie). I realized much later that I got annoyed when she was so giving of herself because deep down, I didn't believe I deserved so much unconditional love. I believed I needed what was in front of me, which was exciting and dangerous, everything I thought Ry wasn't. I didn't tell her about what was going on with Maddie; I just kept asking her for space. I was playing both sides. I wasn't honest with her. It unraveled in a messy way. Her gorgeous love letters turned angry and hurt, spilling out her confusion, pain, and—still—her enduring love for me.

I'd been in San Francisco for a little over a month when, unexpectedly, the woman whose room I was subletting in Noe Valley came back to town. Her plan of a year backpacking around the country had fallen apart. She started sleeping on the couch while I lived in her bedroom. It was awkward, so I figured I ought to find another place to live, but I didn't have that many options because my salary wasn't very impressive. *I am doing it for the cause!* In 1993 the Mission was mostly Latinx businesses and families, so it was considered a rough area by middle-class white people. Queers, especially dykes, who couldn't afford to live in the Castro found their way to the neighborhood, which had a BART station, dive bars, delicious burritos, and the famous sex shop Good Vibrations. I got a railroad apartment in a peach building with picture windows that popped out in the front on a small, narrow street that ran between Valencia and Guerrero, right down the block from the Women's Building. It was the city's first center for battered women, and ACT UP, social justice artists and groups met there, so there was activism and community right outside my door. Maddie told me she could move in and pay half the rent. I was already caught up in her, so that made perfect sense to me. Before we were fully unpacked, folks starting coming by the apartment at all hours of the day and night. She knew a lot of people. And she always had drugs. She introduced me to speed, which I loved, but my gut told me I shouldn't do it again.

The first time I tripped on acid, it started out fun. We went at each other like crazy on the futon for what seemed like hours. She strapped on the biggest dick she had. *This is the hardest I've ever been fucked.* Whenever we had sex, she never hesitated. I was free and uninhibited, like I could take all of her and still want more. I saw rainbows of colors and felt both deeply connected to my body and completely absent from it. Then she started to come down a little, but I was just getting started. My horniness and wonder turned into a bottomless darkness. I felt overwhelming sadness and loss I couldn't understand. I wept for what seemed like a very long time, and then I panicked.

Maddie tried to calm me, but I couldn't be consoled. I just continued wailing; my mind and body felt beyond my control.

She took my face in her hands, stared right into my eyes very seriously, and firmly said, "Are we going to have to go to the hospital now, little girl?" That completely jolted me. Panicked me more. *I do not want to go to the hospital.* I did not want to go to the hospital. So I lay down in her lap, and she stroked my hair and spoke softly to try and soothe me. She did this for hours while I continued to trip. Eventually I fell asleep. When I woke up, I had a headache, a dry mouth, and a painful bruise along my spine. It didn't make a lot of sense, but there it was: a deep, dark purple cloud on my back. That cotton futon was no match for her; she'd rammed me so hard that it was as if the wooden frame had dug into my flesh somehow. Very *The Princess and the Pea.* The next day, someone sketchy came by the house, and I was so out of it, Maddie didn't take her into the other room to give her what she came for. My brain was foggy, but a single clear thought popped into my head. I finally put it all together: Maddie was a drug dealer. And my life was not going as planned.

"Daddy."

Her fingers were inside me when the word first came out of my mouth, and it was a revelation. Daddy is a revered archetype first used by gay leathermen to signify sex and relationship roles. Now it's a very elastic category that transcends gender, sexual orientation, age, ability, and personality type. There are strict daddies, nurturing daddies, daddies who punish, and daddies who please. Maddie/Al and I defined these roles on our own terms, and I slipped easily into a young, submissive girl under her control because it was hot. It is a powerful acknowledgment of consent, desire, and power. Having an actual queer dad whom I was devoted to and being into Daddy play is supercharged. Her dyke Daddy, and the daddies I am drawn to, have qualities of my father—nurturance, adoration, pride—and others I don't associate with him: control, dominance, danger. My sexual Daddy is assertive and a little selfish, he's got swagger; he protects me; he sometimes makes me feel good, and other times he hurts me. Maddie/Al had her own magic ways, sucking me into her world, making my skin and soul pliant under her. All with that sexy mix of hard and soft. *Daddy.* My protector, my lover.

DADDY'S GIRL

A few months after I moved to San Francisco, I picked up the phone at work, and it was my dad's partner Ted.

"Tristan, your dad got really sick and has ended up in the hospital. It's..." Worrying pause.

"He's very ill." Another pause. My dad never got sick, not even a cold, so this was very strange news.

"Is it serious, like I-should-come-to-Maine serious?" I asked.

"Yes." He didn't really have to say much more. I got on a plane to Boston, then took a puddle jumper to Portland and a cab directly to the hospital.

I went to the front desk because Ted had forgotten to tell me my dad's room number.

"Hi, I am looking for my dad's room. His name is Bill Taormino," I said to the woman sitting at the desk.

"That's an interesting necklace," she said, noticing the metal dog collar around my neck that Maddie had given me. "Where are you from?"

I touched my neck, and my fingers followed the metal links down to the small brass lock. Maddie hadn't given me the key.

"San Francisco," I replied.

"San Francisco, that's really the fast lane out there, isn't it?" she said.

I looked at her impatiently.

"Room 152," she said. "Elevator's right there."

When I got out of the elevator, Ted was in the hallway, and he hugged me.

"Sorry I didn't explain more on the phone, but I do want to bring you up to speed."

"Yes, please, what is going on?"

"Back in the spring, I got hepatitis B. A few people at the YMCA did; they think it was from our work with the homeless folks. I had it when we were at your graduation, but I was on medication and doing well, and we didn't tell you because we didn't want to worry you. I finished the meds, and I got better. Well, apparently I gave it to your dad. But he is much, much sicker than I was, and the doctors are perplexed. They're running tests, and we're waiting."

I walked into his room, and my dad looked pale and tired in his hospital bed. Not only had I never seen my dad ill, I hadn't seen him so weak and vulnerable. It was startling. His face was gaunt, and he looked a little scared.

"Hey, Dad," I said. I sat down on the edge of his bed, picked up his hand, and intertwined it with mine. "I heard you needed a visit all the way from San Francisco."

"Thanks for coming," he said.

"Can I do anything?"

"I'm just glad you're here."

A while later, a young guy appeared in a white coat with Dr. Paul Farnsworth embroidered on it. He looked like he was a little older than me, definitely in his twenties. He had reddish-brown hair, pale skin, and a wide mouth. *He cannot be a doctor. How old is he?*

"Hello," he said, making eye contact with my dad, Ted, and then me.

"This is my daughter, Tristan," said my dad.

He shook my hand. "Nice to meet you." He paused. "So, I have some news."

I could see it all over his face. Now it was he who looked scared; it was obvious he'd given himself some kind of pep talk in the doctors' lounge before he came in, one that failed to steady his nerves.

"Mr. Taormino..."

"Bill," said my dad.

"Bill." He smiled weakly and inhaled. "You have AIDS."

I froze. No one said anything else. I looked at my dad. His eyes were welling up. I felt the tears come for me too. I tried to keep it together.

Finally, Ted broke the silence in his calm therapist voice: "AIDS or HIV?"

"AIDS, I'm afraid," said the doctor. "His..." He hesitated, then looked down at the papers in his hand. "His T-cell count is fifteen. Because of this, I assume you have probably been positive but asymptomatic for as much as ten years."

1983. Where was he in 1983? Who did he fuck in 1983? His T-cell count is fifteen. Fifteen? That's really, really low.

"Um. I know this is a lot, and I can leave you alone right now with your family... Then, obviously, we should talk about a treatment plan. We don't have to do that right this minute. But I would like to get you on the meds as soon as possible. I'll be back in a little bit."

He looked down at his shoes as he left. I leaned over and put my head on Dad's chest and sobbed. Ted was on the other side of him, and we stayed like that for a while. My brain was short-circuiting.

"You... you've never been tested before?" I asked him. *For God's sakes, he worked at the Provincetown AIDS Support Group.* Then immediately regretted it. *Not the right time.* But he coordinated testing; he drove people to doctors' appointments; he wrote a whole play about it. He had dozens of friends who had AIDS. Christ, what percentage of the population of P-town had died of AIDS? I assumed he knew his status and was negative. AIDS was very stigmatized, and I think the shame must have driven him to denial. He was lying to himself.

"No." He shook his head.

I just couldn't... I didn't...

"Why don't you go outside and get some air and let me and your father talk?" said Ted.

I just did as he said. I walked one floor down to the pay phone, dialed, then punched in my calling card number. Maddie picked up on the first ring.

"Josie's," she said. I could hear the sounds of the busy café in the background.

"I..." I started sobbing into the phone. I couldn't keep it together.

"Hang on a second," she said. I knew she was making her way out from behind the line.

"He..." I tried again, but the tears kept coming.

"It's okay," she said, her voice in full Daddy mode, trying to soothe me. "It's okay. He's in a better place, he's at peace, he's got good karma, he's—"

"Maddie..."

"What, baby, what? I'm here for you, honey, I am right here."

"He's not dead!" I blurted out. "He has AIDS. My father has AIDS." There was silence on the other end of the phone. Maddie was a dyke who lived in San Francisco. She knew everything this meant. I didn't have to explain it.

"I'm so sorry, Tristan," she said sincerely. "I'm sorry."

"I don't know anything, they just told us … Will he go on AZT, I don't know … His doctor is like Doogie Howser, he's so young! Has he ever even treated someone with AIDS?"

"Just take it easy. I am sure your dad is glad you're there. Take it easy, baby."

My sobbing turned into a low wailing sound. Snot ran out of my nose. I wished I had taken the Xanax she offered me on the way to the airport.

"I need to go back in to be with him. Can I call you later?"

"Of course," she said. "I get off at six." I hung up the phone.

I was crushed. *This cannot be happening. Not to him. Why wasn't he tested? This isn't fair. Why is this happening? We are a queer family. He was doing great. Not now. Not now. What will my mom say? How was he infected? What do I even know about my dad's sex life? He cried so much when the doctor told us. He's going to fall apart. But I might need to fall apart. Will I have to be the parent now? Remain calm and keep it together? I don't know if I can do that. When do I get to be Daddy's little girl? Fuck.*

I bolted out the front door and ran across the lawn, looking for the exact place where the street began. I wanted to run into traffic, be rendered unconscious for a while, get heavy pain meds, have my own hospital bed. I stopped short when I got to the curb.

SAILOR'S BERTH

When I got back to San Francisco, I slept for two days. I didn't want to get out of bed, not even to eat. Maddie was sweet and gentle with me, but her care had a weird undertone as if she wouldn't indulge this mood for very long. She spanked me and made me suck her off, and that helped my brain shut off for a little while. I felt both numb and on edge, with a constant pang of dread in my stomach. My heartbeat sped up whenever I thought of my dad. I finally got out of bed because I had to. I covered the dark circles under my eyes with concealer, put on some blush, and took the bus over the Golden Gate Bridge to work at the political consulting firm. I poured that buzzing, nervous energy into being hyperproductive at work. I held my pen in a vise grip, and my knee bounced up and down under my desk all day. I felt like I was losing control of my body. And maybe my mind.

I didn't feel like I could call Riley. I reached out to my friend Ruth, who would arrive in the Bay Area shortly to start grad school. She was my closest friend from Wesleyan, and in senior year we had lived in a big gray colonial called Womanist House, dedicated to a cooperative feminist living experience. We threw really fun parties. Ruth was movie-star gorgeous with light olive skin and long, wavy auburn hair with perfect, tasteful highlights. Her brown eyes were deep sparkling pools, her perfectly shaped lips coated in expensive lipstick; when she got dressed up to go out somewhere, she picked something delicious for her curvy frame. Her sense of style was impeccable, and her politics were radical. Whether she was brilliantly breaking down critical theory, the LA riots, or a Sir Mix-a-Lot song, Ruth opened her mouth and blew my mind every time. Her senior thesis was a manifesto on the clitoris. She was also emotional, affectionate, and generous. When I needed her, she was there to solve a problem or take me into her arms for a good cry. I knew she'd be my rock as I unpacked this devastating news about my dad.

One day at the office, I got a call from Justin, one of Ruth's close friends from the prestigious private school she had gone to; we'd hung out a few times.

"Ruth asked me to call you," he said, not in his usual jovial tone.

"Unfortunately, I have some awful news. Ruth's sister, Danya, has died. She committed suicide. Ruth is in Chicago, and she wanted you to know."

"What?" I couldn't believe what I was hearing. Danya was just a few years older than Ruth, and just as beautiful and bubbly. I'd only met her a few times, but she was full of life, with the same sparkling eyes as Ruth. They looked so much alike. My heart broke for Ruth.

"I . . . don't know what to say."

"Of course," he said in a soothing tone. "None of us do. Their mom found her. Everyone is devastated."

"Please tell Ruth I love her. I just don't . . . If there is anything I can do . . . Will there be a funeral?"

"They are sitting shiva, and then there will be a service. Maybe leave Ruth a message at her mom's house. I don't think she can talk to anyone right now. Take good care of yourself."

"Okay." Frankly, I couldn't fully process it. I didn't know anyone who had killed themselves. I wrote a letter to Ruth and sent it to her in Chicago, and she called when she got it. We couldn't make sense of it. Nothing made sense.

I cried every day. I couldn't stop crying. I couldn't do the most basic tasks at work, so I quit. I had failed at my first full-time job as a college graduate. They were understanding. Everything started to move at a snail's pace. I didn't know what to do. I needed a job to support myself, but it had to be easy. Something to pay the bills and get me out of the house that wouldn't require too much thinking or emotional energy.

I applied to work at the Gap on Market Street. Khakis and button-down shirts seemed simple enough. Since I was overqualified, I decided to be vaguely honest with the person who interviewed me.

"I'm going through . . . something very difficult in my personal life, and I want something steady without a lot of worry. I just want to show up, do a good job, and go home."

The manager bought my story, and I became a sales associate the next day. This location was the flagship store of the Gap empire, so it had particularly high standards, but it caused me zero stress to help people find jeans in their size and make casual suggestions about what belt might look good. I was not yet qualified to work the register, so I handed customers off to someone more senior to ring them up. It was what I needed at the time: I could put a fake smile on my face for a six-hour shift, and the hardest thing about my job was folding sweaters on a clear Lucite board. They really are hard to fold neatly.

Maddie had become increasingly erratic, and I suspected she was doing more speed more often. She was on edge all the time and started to bully me. Sometimes I didn't feel safe around her. I wanted her to soothe me in her arms or fuck me into delirium, but she just yelled over stupid stuff. She couldn't tolerate my crying and sadness. I talked to my dad on the phone, but he felt a million miles away. He had started AZT, and it was making him sick. Nothing was right.

Maddie came home from work with my favorite veggie sandwich wrapped in tinfoil. I was skipping meals because my appetite had disappeared, but I unwrapped it and bit into the edge of the sourdough bread. I wanted to be honest with her about what I was feeling.

"Thanks for this. I know I'm kind of a mess. I don't know what to do," I told her.

"It's okay. We're going to get through this together, babe."

"I was thinking: maybe I should move to Portland to take care of my dad since they have no idea how long he will live, it could be months…" I had talked about it with him the last time he and I spoke, but I didn't tell her that.

Her eyes flared for a second, and her smile turned to anger.

"I don't think you've thought this through. Move all the way across the country? That's kind of dramatic! You're just going to leave?" Her voice got louder. I felt so small.

"I don't know how much longer he will be in my life. I don't want to regret anything. I need to seriously consider it. He needs me. I need him…" I said, my voice trailing off.

"I think it's super fucked up for you to just leave me."

"But he's my father!"

"And I'm your Daddy."

That stopped me in my tracks. *What did that even mean?* I turned to go into our bedroom, and she grabbed my arm roughly. I pulled away, and she let me go.

Tristan Taormino

The next day, she left the apartment before I woke up. *She'll cool off, and I will go sell more polo shirts.* We had several more tense discussions, and I told her I would make a final decision in a week. A few days later, I came home from a shift, and a few of Maddie's friends were standing in the kitchen with their arms crossed, surrounded by a stack of boxes with stuff thrown in them randomly. My stuff.

"Maddie didn't want to make a scene. But she thinks it's a good idea if you leave. You were gonna move east, right? Well, we started packing for you," said her friend Nancy, the one with the bleached pixie cut and thick black eyeliner. She wanted me to be intimidated, and I was.

I am being kicked out of an apartment when I am the one whose name is on the lease? Was she serious? I guess this makes the choice easy. I felt messy and lost and unable to think clearly.

"I . . . at least need a few days to get my shit together," I said to Nancy, who rolled her eyes at me. She handed me the key to my collar. The crew left. I called my dad.

I didn't go into the details because it would just stress him out, and that was the last thing he needed.

When he was seeing the Marine during his army days, they had an awful breakup. Page 76 of his memoir:

I was going back to the States in two days. The Marine and I had spent the weekend together. I had been afraid of him for months. He continued to make nocturnal visits to my barracks. He was manipulative and possessive. I did not know how to deal with him, or the implications of our relationship. I had no skills when it came to being honest with myself, so how could I be honest with another person? I had given him control of the relationship because I did not want to take any responsibility for it.

We were sitting up on our hill. We were both drunk.

"I've made you my beneficiary," he said.

"Whoa, what?"

"My life insurance policy. You're the new and improved beneficiary."

"Oh?"

I was playing dumb; he had talked about this several times.

"It used to be my aunt. She raised me. She's fine. All she cares about is *Wagon Train* and Lipton tea. She doesn't need it. I hope I spelled your name right."

I said nothing.

"I'll be back home in Boston in a few months. I'll come see you."

He reached out and squeezed my dick.

"Stop!"

"I think you're funny!"

"Stop it!"

I realized I wanted to leave it all behind, here on the hill. I didn't want to take it to my real life.

"Willy, you are funny! Such a funny queer!"

I shoved his hand away, and he smacked my arm, and suddenly we were rolling around on the damp grass . . .

punching

kicking

biting

skidding down the hill, screaming under the Latin cross

motherfucker

asshole

cocksucker

I managed to get up, and I ran down the hill—bleeding, frightened, and relieved.

I spent the next few hours in a dark emergency room getting my lip stitched. I thought again of how much I wanted to leave it all behind, start over. What real life? Back home? Okinawa was real. Not only was it real, it had become just like home—fear, dishonesty, and violence prevailed.

Things ended with Maddie so abruptly that I couldn't catch my breath. She turned the power she had over me into a weapon. I left feeling empty and abandoned by her, especially the Daddy part of her, but I knew that being in Portland was what I wanted.

"We created a sailor's berth for you," said Ted with a smile. He was referring to the single bed in their home office, which was nestled in one corner between two walls; there was a tall bookshelf at the end of the bed, and the setup was meant to evoke a cabin on a ship and give me more privacy since there wasn't a door on the room. It was super cozy. There was a dresser for my clothes, and I could share the closet, which was behind an entire wall full of mirrored sliding doors. I was drained of every ounce of energy. I chalked it up to the frantic scene just before I left San Francisco, jet lag, and the big change I'd just made.

Tristan Taormino

Over dinner Ted said, "So let's talk about the rules. We want you to know that this household should function around making sure your dad takes his meds, stays on his schedule, and especially gets enough sleep."

I soon learned the routine. Ted went to work, and my dad rested in the morning. I made him lunch so he could take his pills, we'd watch movies or TV or listen to music, Ted came home, we had dinner, and we retired to the couch. My dad went to bed early, and Ted made clear that the house should be quiet by 10 p.m. Because he was a therapist and a dedicated member of AA, Ted liked to talk a lot about *boundaries* and *expectations*.

Although my dad was not a party person, he agreed that his fiftieth birthday (also his first birthday postdiagnosis) was worthy of a celebration. We ate antipasto, spinach lasagna, chicken with basil and lemon, and homemade cheesecake for dessert. My dad knew a lot of people from a lot of different places, and many of them flew in to reminisce, tell stories, and toast him. I knew it was probably the last time he would see some of them. We laughed a lot, and he was full of the vibrant energy that I hadn't felt from him since his diagnosis.

I had trouble sleeping when I first got to Portland, but it was a new bed in a new place, so I cut myself some slack. Some days, I woke up and wanted to go right back to bed. Ted was at work, and my dad was puttering around the house, so I'd wander into the kitchen to get something to eat or drink, although I still didn't have much of an appetite. My dad and I would check in about how he was feeling, and if he didn't need me to do anything for him, I'd go back to bed. I stayed in my pajamas all day.

I pored over the pages of *On Our Backs*, read an article titled "Lesbian Sex Clubs: The Agony and the Ecstasy," and perused a pictorial of a four-way of hot dykes jacking off. Some of the photos were too dark because the mag wasn't printed on very good paper, but it still inspired me. I missed Riley. I combed through the personal ads: *GWF, 30, trains thoroughbred racehorses in Maryland.* And: *Don't understand butch/femme but will do anything Susie Bright says.* Sometimes I put the magazine down and just cried. I didn't know what I was crying about. Ted would come home after 6, or later if he worked at his private practice, and then the routine started all over again.

I decided I should get a therapist. I'd seen one at college, and it was nice to talk to someone. *I mean, my dad is going to die, I should probably be in therapy, right?* I looked in the local newspaper and found a small ad for WomenSpace: A Healing Center. *There will be a lesbian feminist therapist there.* It was a long walk from my dad's place, down near the water on the other side of town, but I could do it. The office occupied half of a traditional-style house with a porch. I walked into a waiting room with soothing music playing, soft furniture in shades of pink and red, a large selection of tea with teacups, and a kettle on a hot plate. My therapist's name was Genevieve; she asked right away how I felt about dogs because she often brought hers to sessions. I knew I would enjoy having him there. I told her what was happening in my life, and she said something like, "That *is* a lot." We agreed I would see her every other week, which is all I could afford.

Getting into therapy felt like a very big accomplishment. I planned to get a job in Portland, but I wasn't looking very diligently. The warmth of my comforter and the solitude in the sailor's berth called to me, and most of the time I just wanted to sit quietly in my bed or take a nap. I was mopey and unmotivated. Every other week, I'd shower, make myself look presentable, and take the long walk to WomenSpace to talk to Genevieve and pet her black Lab. Otherwise, I didn't do much. I didn't feel inspired to explore the city or make new friends or even go to a movie. My dad was tired a lot, and I was tired too.

THE LESBIANS UPSTAIRS

The lesbians who lived upstairs in my dad's building, Susan and Jamie, invited me out to the local gay bar. I needed an excuse to shower and a break from what felt like a slow march toward death. One of Dad's closest friends was a woman named Lucy, a no-nonsense Maine woman with short hair and practical L.L.Bean shoes who looked like she could shovel enough snow to clear an entire Target parking lot. At Dad's birthday party, I met her oldest daughter, Tonya, who had just graduated from Hampshire College with a degree in fine arts. She took photos that night; when she printed some as a gift for Dad, they were all very high contrast with more black than white. There was something moody and dark about her that intrigued me. I invited her to come with us. *Maybe some alcohol would help take the edge off, and I can try flirting with her even though she's not my type.*

The bar was as I imagined it would be: small, dark except for several neon signs, filled with an assortment of local gay guys, a smattering of dykes, a drag queen or two. It was clear everyone knew everyone else, and the atmosphere was friendly. A remix of Janet Jackson's "That's the Way Love Goes" played a little too loud, and there were a few enthusiastic queers on the small dance floor. Tonya and I chatted about how utterly predictable the bar was. It was just nice to be with other queer people. I was not a big drinker—a glass of wine would get me very buzzed—but we decided to do what I did when I wanted to let loose: shots of tequila. As the liquid burned its way down my throat, I was reminded how much my father disapproved of drinking.

Tonya was androgynous with pale skin and circles under her eyes that matched mine. She had long, pin-straight, dyed black hair, and her wardrobe reminded me of the new wave kids in high school. She had icy green eyes and didn't wear makeup. She wasn't butch, but she was interesting, so we flirted. Hooking up with her felt like it might be pretty straightforward. I could use simple for a change. The tequila took the edge off, and I stopped thinking of how long I'd be in Portland, which depended on how long my dad might live. My sadness didn't fully retreat, but it moved to the background of my brain. My world revolved around his illness, things like making sure he got food down to take his meds and enough calories so he wouldn't lose too much weight. Ted ran a tight ship, so it was nice to be out from under the routine for just a night—to get lost in the warm familiarity of an average gay bar where Madonna blasted on the speakers and well drinks were $2.

By the time we left the bar, it was past midnight. As we drove home, I realized that I didn't have a key to the condo. Ted and my dad had said they would give me one, but it had only been a few weeks, and it wasn't like I was going out all that often. When my dad had first moved into his place, he had installed a vintage silver doorbell with a key-like switch that you manually turned to trigger the round bell on the other side of the door. It made a sound somewhere between an old-fashioned doorbell and an old rotary phone ring. It was kitschy but definitely not subtle.

"Shit. I don't have a key to my dad's place. And he has been having trouble sleeping lately. They really stressed to me that he needs sleep. If I ring the bell, it will definitely wake him up. What do you think I should do?"

"Why don't you just stay with us?" said Susan. "Your dad knows we went out together, we're right upstairs, and you'll be down in the morning." Then she added, "And Tonya, you can stay over too," winking at me. They obviously knew we wanted to hook up. My dad and Ted would wake up and assume I was upstairs, call or come up, and it would be fine. *Where else would I be?* We pulled into the gravel parking lot, and I was still feeling good from the tequila as we walked up the staircase to their place. Jamie pointed us to the first bedroom off the hallway and told us to settle ourselves. *So I guess this is happening.*

We shuffled around in the room for a while, and then we heard Jamie and Susan's door shut.

"I'll be right back," I said. We had talked about kink at the bar, and I wanted to surprise Tonya, so I headed into the kitchen to find something, anything,

Tristan Taormino

that I could use to fuck with her a little. I wanted to run the show. I settled on an ordinary steak knife from the butcher block on the counter. *This will have to do*, I thought. I put it behind my back and returned to the room.

"Lie on your back," I instructed, and she did it. I slipped the knife under a pillow so she couldn't see it, and I lay on top of her. We kissed, and her lips were soft against mine. I sat up and pulled her shirt over her head and took off her bra. I was used to being the one who got seduced and undressed, but I tried on this role, and I liked it. She straddled me, and we kissed some more, and I grabbed one of her breasts—they were big and bottom heavy; I traced her nipple with my finger, then with my tongue. She got goosebumps. I laid her back down and undid her jeans and slid them and her underwear over her hips, which were narrower than mine. I climbed back on top of her, slid my right leg between her legs, and applied pressure on her vulva. She moaned softly. I reached under the pillow and produced the knife. I showed it to her. "I want you to be good for me," I said. Her eyes got big for a moment, and then she smiled and nodded. I traced the back of the knife down the front of her chest, between her breasts, then curved off down her right thigh. I went slowly and looked into her eyes to gauge where she was. She was going there with me.

"I'm not going to cut you, but you've got to be good," I said. She moaned.

The next morning, I heard some noise in the kitchen and woke up lying butt to butt with Tonya, naked. My head hurt. I pulled on my clothes and wandered out to the living room. Susan was making coffee in the kitchen, and Jamie was washing dishes. I didn't know what time it was.

"Your dad called already. You should go down there," she said with a little edge in her voice, and I knew immediately. *I'm in trouble.* I looked back at the bedroom.

"Just go," Jamie said. "We will take care of things up here."

I walked down the staircase to the back door of my dad's place. The door was still locked. I turned the silver handle on the doorbell and heard it chirp loudly. Ted came to the door with a pissed-off look on his face. He didn't say a word, just let me in. I followed him down the short hallway to the living room, where my dad was on the couch.

"Have a seat," said Ted. I did.

"You didn't come home last night," he said.

"I'm really sorry. It was late, and I realized I didn't have a key, and I didn't want to wake up Dad—"

"Let me stop you right there," said Ted. "We were worried and had no idea where you were. You could have called earlier in the night or left a note on the door." *A note on the door: that was a good idea.* I just hadn't thought of it last night, and the tequila hadn't helped my decision-making.

"I'm sorry I didn't leave a note."

"Sorry?!" my dad chimed in, his voice raised in anger. "This is so fucked up. What were you thinking?" It was sinking in to my pounding head. They were both really mad.

"Did you drink last night? Were you drunk?" Ted asked in an accusing tone. The look of shame on my face answered his question.

"And what the fuck were Susan and Jamie thinking? Oh, they were probably drunk too. A bunch of drunk dykes!" yelled my father. "In fact, I'm mad at them too. I am going to go up there right now and give them a piece of my mind."

"Dad, it's not their fault. They let me crash at their place, but don't blame them."

He was already on the move, headed toward the front vestibule and the staircase that led to their apartment upstairs.

"Dad!" I called, but there was no stopping him. I panicked. Things were already heated, and I didn't want them to escalate. I knew how my dad could cause a scene. But most prominent on my mind was: he's going to walk upstairs to Tonya lounging in the living room, and it will be obvious she slept over too. There was no time to warn her he was coming. I trotted after him and got to the middle stair as he was knocking on their front door.

Jamie opened the door, and he started right in.

"What the fuck were you thinking..." I heard him say to her.

"Bill, calm down, she was just letting off some steam. It was late, and we didn't—"

He interrupted her train of thought. "What?"

Then I got to the top stair and looked over his shoulder. He spotted Tonya and just lost it. She looked panicked.

"What the—" his anger stopped him from using complete sentences. I froze. He flew into a rage and turned to me. "You lying bitch!" he shouted. "So this was about more than a late night... So fucked up. Can't believe. Stupid fucking dykes..."

Tristan Taormino

He stormed down the stairs. Tonya's eyes got wide. I stood there in the doorway unsure of what to do.

"Come in, Tristan," said Susan. "Just give him a minute to cool off." She walked over to me and guided me to the couch. "We'll make some breakfast. This is all going to be fine." I wasn't sure.

"You can stay up here all day if you need to, that's no problem," said Jamie.

Bacon began to sizzle in a pan, but it didn't cover the sound of my dad screaming and things crashing around downstairs. Ted's voice was raised too. I didn't know what to do. There was more stomping around, more yelling, and then we heard the front door to the building open and slam shut. I looked out the window and saw my dad running into the street. I was terrified. He was shouting at the top of his lungs. I heard "Drunk fucking dykes! Drunk fucking dykes!" He was making a scene all right, a really big scene. Ted went to him, tried to calm him down, but it was no use. My father was in a full-on rage. I'd seen it before. It was terrifying. They were standing in the middle of the street. Now cars were coming, and traffic was stopping. It became chaotic.

"Oh shit!" said Susan as she looked over my shoulder out the window. "He's lost his mind!"

"What do we do?" I said, turned to her, and began sobbing.

"Ted will calm him down," said Jamie as she put her arms around me.

"I think you should just come away from the window and let him handle it." Susan coaxed me to sit down, but I didn't feel like I could eat.

"I don't think I can . . ." I felt dizzy and confused. "I think I need to lie down."

"That's okay. Go back to the bedroom. Try to get some rest." My heart was racing, my thoughts coming quickly one after the other, I was so freaked out. *Rest? I cannot possibly fall asleep.*

I heard the phone ring and opened my eyes. The bright sunlight in the windows was gone. I had dozed off after all. I heard Susan talking, and then she knocked on my door.

"Come in," I said, still sleepy.

"That was Ted."

"My dad?"

"It's been a long day for everyone. Your dad is okay, he needs some rest. You're going to stay here tonight. Would you like some dinner?" I declined, so she made me some toast. I ate it in bed, and I drifted back to sleep.

I woke up the next morning and knew I had to face the music. I put my clothes on, and then I climbed down the staircase and opened the door to the vestibule. There were five or six boxes sitting near the front door. I recognized them right away because I had just finished unpacking them. I wasn't sure what to do. I knocked on the front door, and Ted answered it.

"Come in," he said in his annoyingly calm therapist voice. He led me to the living room, where, once again, my dad was sitting on the couch. He looked frail, exhausted.

"Your father's illness is very serious, and his health has to be our top priority," said Ted. He was talking to me like I was a child. I listened.

"We have decided that we need to live with adults, and you're just not an adult. You're incapable of making good decisions, so you have to leave." I looked over at my dad, disbelieving what I was hearing.

"You do," he echoed.

"What do you mean?" I said, my voice shaking.

"Listen, this isn't working. You stay in bed and sleep all day, you haven't found a job. You're not *doing* anything. It just isn't working. We can't have you in our house," said Ted.

In hindsight, I was living with a mental health professional who either couldn't or didn't want to see the classic signs of depression in me. I don't know why. I felt like he blamed me for my depression and couched it as a personality defect: I was lazy. All these years later, I fear he will try to discredit me by calling me crazy. He will use his expertise to label and shame me. Decades earlier, somehow he couldn't use that expertise to see me or care for me.

He gestured toward the front door. "I've packed your things for you. You need to go."

"Right now?" I asked, incredulous but already knowing the answer.

"Yes," said my dad, his voice hoarse, probably from the screaming.

"But I don't have anywhere to go! I just got here! I don't know anyone. I don't have any money, I don't have a car, I—" I locked eyes with my dad and pleaded.

"You'll need to figure that out," Ted said calmly as a satisfied look came over his face. It wasn't really a conversation, and I wasn't being offered any

Tristan Taormino

options. My father's partner of less than a year was telling me what to do. And my dad was not stopping him.

The next few days were a blur. I went to stay with the lesbians upstairs. I was in bed mostly, except when Jamie or Susan made something to eat and got me to come to the living room. They were both at work during the day, and I was walking around in a daze. I was in so much pain. I couldn't believe what had happened, and I kept replaying it over and over in my mind. *It's my fault. I fucked it up. Ted said so. Dad agreed with him. I shouldn't have gone to the bar; I shouldn't have had a few drinks; I shouldn't have slept at Jamie and Susan's; I shouldn't have had sex with Tonya; I shouldn't have hidden several facts of the story from my father. I am an irresponsible, immature slut who doesn't think of anyone but herself.* The lesson was definitive: I was bad. I had internalized everything Ted said to me, and there was no alternative narrative. I had ruined everything.

I felt lost. And unlovable. My father was dying, and I was an awful daughter. The negative talk in my head continued, unrelenting. *What was going to happen now? Would I ever speak to my father again? Would he forgive me? Would he disown me like he did close friends in the past, like the rest of his family?* Plus none of these questions felt that open-ended. The clock was ticking. *If I stayed in Portland, where would I live? What would I do for work? If I left, where would I go?* Everything was closing in around me. My brain was foggy.

You did this to yourself.

It's your fault.

You're never going to see him again.

The one person in this world who was so important to me, whom I loved so much, was done with me. There wasn't anything left. And it was all because of my carelessness and selfishness. My dad couldn't love me because I couldn't be loved. His home was not my home, and I didn't belong there. I was terrified and alone.

I pushed the comforter off me and dragged myself to the kitchen. I eyed the butcher block where I had gotten the steak knife to tease Tonya when we fucked. I pulled out the biggest knife in the block and just stared at it for a few minutes. Looked at the distorted light bands on the blade. I held it in my right hand and pressed the sharp side against my left wrist and stayed still. Then I dragged it to the right against my flesh. The knife was not that sharp. I went back to the original position, went over the same spot, this time applying more pressure until it sliced the skin. It felt like a scrape. *I cannot even do this the right way. This is parallel. Aren't I supposed to go the other way? I'll just cut a little. This feels right. This will accomplish something.* I pulled the knife away and saw tiny beads of blood begin to form. *Blood. Okay, I am getting somewhere. Do I want to die? Yes. Yes, I do. It will show my dad how sorry I am, that I took my transgression and his disappointment seriously.* I was willing to die to apologize and make it right. *It's the only play here, there are no others.* I dug the knife deeper into my skin. I was expecting some big release, but it didn't come. *Keep going.* Then the voice inside my head changed course. *This is not your best idea, Tristan. Stop.* I put down the knife and picked up a dish towel from the counter, pressed it to my wrist.

I went to the phone, dialed the WomenSpace counseling center, and pushed 2 for Genevieve's extension. She picked up right away.

"This is Tristan. Um, I think I am in trouble, and I need your help. My dad . . . he kicked me out . . . I have a knife . . ." I started to cry.

"Can you come here right now?" she asked. "Promise me you will come straight here."

"Yes," I said.

I wrapped the thick dish towel around my wrist, and there was no blood seeping through. Genevieve's black Lab greeted me with his wagging tail, and that immediately calmed me down. She brought me into the bathroom, assessed the cut, then put some hydrogen peroxide on it.

"I don't have any gauze," she said. She used several Band-Aids, laying them vertically until the wound was covered.

"It's not that deep," she said. We went back into the office, and I sat on the couch. She asked me a series of questions, and I answered them as best I could. She was calm but serious.

"I would like to call your mom, tell her what's going on, and make a plan. Is that okay with you?" she asked.

"Okay."

I recall telling this story to therapists (so many therapists), but it took me twenty years to share it with anyone else in my life. I carried the shame of it with me for two decades. One of my closest friends, Wyndi, was visiting me from DC. Wyndi and I have a remarkable friendship, and she is the person I

Tristan Taormino

would call if I was in any kind of trouble because I know she would show up for me. She inspires honesty and vulnerability in me always. We were sitting at the kitchen table eating blueberry pancakes one morning with my partner Calvin. Wyndi asked me something about my dad. A strong feeling came over me, and I burst into tears. I needed to tell them both the story, so I blurted it out. Wyndi and Calvin looked stunned.

"I didn't know that happened. You never told me," said Calvin. There was sympathy and also some betrayal in his voice.

Wyndi looked at me directly and asked, "So, when that happened, what did you think? What was your takeaway from the whole thing?"

"That I was a horrible person," I responded confidently. "That I *was* lazy, that I wasn't an adult, and that I deserved to be kicked out of the house. And I guess in hindsight now, I was being punished for being a slut, because everything escalated once my dad found out Tonya was there."

They both shook their heads adamantly.

"You've been carrying that around all this time?" Wyndi looked empathetic but also pissed off. She never shied away from her anger.

"That was totally shitty, unacceptable parenting," she said, evenly.

"You were young. You were acting *your age.* They were the adults, and it was their job to step back from the situation and not react in the dramatic way they did. You did not deserve any of that."

Tears rolled down my cheeks. No one had ever said anything like that to me before, not even a therapist.

She continued, "Did it ever occur to you that there were other things going on that contributed to what happened? You want my guess? I think Ted wasn't happy about you moving in with them in the first place but went along with it to appease your father, and he was just waiting for an excuse to get you out." Her take was baffling to me. I'd never questioned the narrative about what happened. To me there was no alternate interpretation: I did something unforgivable, and Ted and my dad responded appropriately.

"Yeah," said Calvin. "That makes a lot of sense to me. There was conflict between them about you that you didn't know about."

"After it happened . . . down the road, did they apologize to you?" asked Wyndi.

"No," I said, trying to keep up with their analysis of the situation.

"But I wasn't expecting an apology because I was the one who was 100 percent to blame."

"No. You weren't," she said gently.

THE PRICE OF OUR REDEMPTION

Faith is that grace of the spirit whereby a sinner is enabled to apprehend and receive the Father's merciful atonement by which their sins are forgiven, covered, and not imputed.

WILLIAM PYNCHON, *THE MERITORIOUS PRICE OF OUR REDEMPTION* (1650),
DEEMED HERETICAL AND BANNED BECAUSE IT DEFIED PURITANICAL
CALVINIST CHURCH DOCTRINE

Genevieve hung up the phone.

"Your mother is going to drive here from New York. I recommended that you go to the hospital for your own safety. She is making arrangements. Do you have a safe place to go while you wait for your mom?"

"I can stay with the lesbians upstairs."

"Okay, but can we make an agreement? If you have any more thoughts of harming yourself, I want you to call me immediately." I promised her.

I walked back to my dad's building, climbed the stairs, and knocked. I didn't even know if anyone would be home. Susan answered the door. She looked me over, and her face softened.

"I got blood on your dish towel, and you need to wash a knife . . ."

"Just come in."

"My mother is driving to pick me up. I think it will take her about six or seven hours."

Susan wrapped me in a blanket, and Jamie offered me food. They had already gone above and beyond what they needed to do for their gay neighbor's daughter whom they barely knew. We didn't know at the time that in return for this kindness, my dad would cut them out of his life and never speak to them again.

There was some noise in the vestibule downstairs, and I knew my mother had arrived. I heard the voices of Ted, my dad, and my mom, and their conversation was short and tense. Then there were footsteps, and my mother was at Susan and Jamie's door along with her friend Carol. Carol was a therapist at an in-patient drug treatment program at the hospital where my mom worked. Carol had thick, beautiful blond hair in a shoulder-length bob, and she was made up and dressed impeccably. She had a round face, blue eyes, and that upper-class therapist vibe. My mom looked worried. Carol looked prepared. They had driven up in her car, which was nice, because it meant I got to ride the seven hours in a Mercedes with a leather interior. They packed the trunk with my boxes and luggage. I didn't see Ted or my dad.

When we got on the road, my mom explained that Carol had secured a bed for me at a mental health unit at Long Island Jewish Medical Center, and it would be best to just drive directly there since it would be late when we arrived. They didn't ask me a lot of questions about what happened. My face was red and puffy from crying, and I was exhausted. I took my coat off and balled it up to make a pillow. I laid down across the backseat with my knees bent toward my chest and fell asleep. It was dark when the car slowed down, and I started to wake up.

I had no idea what to expect. Long Island Jewish was a sprawling campus with lots of buildings and parking lots. They took me into one of the buildings, and Carol approached a woman standing in front of a desk holding a bunch of papers. My mother started filling out paperwork as Carol gestured with her hands as she talked. Another woman with dark hair approached and joined in. They all nodded.

I tried to hear what they were talking about.

The dark-haired woman said to Carol, "They didn't have any open beds on the young adult unit, so this is the best we can do."

Carol replied, "I understand and appreciate you getting her *any* bed."

I was standing in the common area, where people were seated at tables playing games, talking, staring into space. Some of them were in street clothes and some in hospital gowns. One person was pacing around and talking to herself. Another sat in a corner and looked catatonic. I was the youngest person there by at least fifteen years. The staff member took my suitcase and asked me to take off my Doc Martens. Then it was time to say goodbye to my mother and Carol. I thanked them both for coming to get me and made sure my mom had the pay phone number to the unit. The staffer brought me to another room and shut the door. Yet another woman walked in with a clipboard and a file folder and introduced herself as a social worker. She asked me a lot of questions.

"Hi. Can you tell me what brought you here?"

"Have you ever been treated for depression before?"

"Are you currently on any medication?"

"Have you ever been on medication for depression or anxiety?"

"Any previous suicide attempts?"

"Are you having thoughts of suicide right now?"

"Do you have a plan about how you would do it?"

Then she introduced me to the woman with the dark hair, who was a nurse, and the nurse showed me to a small room with two beds and a window.

A twitchy woman with thinning brown hair and big, tired eyes who I guessed was forty-five or fifty was lying in one of the twin beds and looked up from reading a paperback.

"Hello," she said, a look of pity coming over her face. "I'm Jean."

I sat down on the other bed.

"Is this your first time, honey?"

"First time . . . ?"

"In a mental hospital?"

"Yes," I said.

"Well, I've been in and out of these places for years—I'm a regular. This time, I am just here to get my meds adjusted. Don't worry, it's going to be okay. As soon as I get my meds right, I am out of here. You want my advice? Don't ever come back to a place like this. Make this your first and last visit. You do not want to be around all these nutso people."

I took her words seriously. *Of course I'm never coming back here. This is just a special situation.* Our conversation was interrupted by yelling and commotion in the hallway. There were raised voices; then things quieted down. I didn't like it. *There are actual insane people in here.* That felt really scary to me. They were so much older, and I couldn't relate to them. If I was in here with them, that meant I was crazy. And I didn't want to be crazy. I would,

Tristan Taormino

in fact, come back to places like this. I would confront the shame I felt about my mental illness. But not for a long time.

"They'll probably bring you a tray because you missed dinner. Avoid the meat," said Jean. That night I barely slept. It never quieted down, and the noise outside our door kept me awake.

In the morning I headed straight to the pay phone in the hallway, which patients were allowed to use if they were given free time. I had nothing but free time, although some people did seem to be on some sort of schedule. I dialed my mom.

"Mom, I am freaking out. This is *not* the place for me. There are schizophrenic people here, psychotic people. They are all way older than me. I don't think this place is going to help me get better. Is there anywhere else? Can you ask Carol or other people you know?"

She sighed. *I am being too much for her again, I'm sure of it. Too much for Mom, not enough for Dad.* If I felt overwhelmed, she probably felt overwhelmed too.

"You knew it would be rough. You probably need time to acclimate. I will see what I can do. Don't worry. I know it's hard. Let me see what I can do."

A short woman under five feet tall with a sandy blond bob approached me. She was wearing a tunic-style shirt with embroidery on it. She said she was my assigned social worker, as opposed to the intake social worker I had met the night before. I recognized her right away. She was Sammie's mother. Sammie was one of my housemates in Womanist House at Wesleyan. I had met Sammie's mother, the woman standing in front of me with a clipboard, during graduation weekend. That was a little more than six months ago, but it felt like years had passed. *Maybe it's nice to see a vaguely familiar face?* That thought didn't linger, and I panicked.

Will she tell her daughter about seeing me? My stomach tightened. *It's probably against their code of ethics, and she respects privacy.* I tried not to focus on it. She asked me all the same questions that the last one did and took notes.

"I don't think I am in the right place," I told her. "I'm not as bad as a lot of these people. And I am a lot younger than anyone else. I called my mom this morning and asked her if she could find another place for me."

"May I talk to your mother? Perhaps I can help?"

Months later, I nearly collided with Sammie getting onto the 1 train to Penn Station.

"Hey, Sammie. Fancy meeting you here." She looked at me with very serious eyes filled with worry.

"How *are* you?" she asked in a sympathetic voice. She knew. It was disconcerting to me; it was exactly what I feared. Or maybe I was just paranoid. I was glad I only had two stops to go.

My mom somehow worked it out to have me transferred and picked me up two days later to drive me into Manhattan.

"We're going to Regent Hospital. This place is supposed to be much better," she said. "Carol says people will be high functioning, and it's geared toward teens and young adults."

I was just so relieved to be out of Long Island Jewish. *Regent has to be better than where I was. It's in the city; it's bound to be.* We got off the FDR highway, turned onto Sixty-First Street, and pulled into the parking garage of a high-rise building with mirrored glass that looked like insurance companies and law firms had offices there. We took the elevator to the third floor. We approached the door and heard a long buzz. My mother pushed the door, and we stepped in. It locked behind us.

With its richly colored mahogany furniture, plush pale gray carpet, and wallpaper dotted with framed prints of old-fashioned drawings and maps, the place looked like what the exterior promised: a law firm, not a hospital. Nothing was white and sterile. No one was wearing uniforms, just name tags. *It already feels different.*

The nurse asked me some questions, then looked through my small suitcase, taking out my razor and vitamins and putting them into a clear bag.

"You can keep your boots, but please remove the laces and give them to me. Procedure. Mom, you may want to bring some other slip-on shoes for her to wear."

My mom hugged me goodbye. "You're going to be fine," she said. Then the nurse led me down a short, curved hallway to an empty, stuffy room that belonged in a dollhouse: two beds neatly made, two dressers, two lamps; everything painted Pepto Bismol pink.

"You can get situated, and someone will come get you. Door open at all times, that's a rule." There was no one else's stuff in the room, so I assumed I didn't have a roommate this time. I wandered into the bathroom, flicked the light on, and was confronted with my face in the mirror. I brushed back the wisps of dark brown hair that had slipped out of my ponytail. My black roll-neck sweater brought out the shadows under my eyes. I looked ten years

Tristan Taormino

older than I was. I pushed my sweater over my head and headed to the bed closest to the door, then saw someone walk by. She poked her head in.

"Hey," said a woman who looked my age. She had brown frizzy hair in a ponytail and wore red sweatpants.

"Hi," I returned. We introduced ourselves. Her name was Dorothy.

"How are you?" Kind of a weird question to ask someone who was institutionalized.

I just shrugged.

"I've been here like a week. You'll settle in."

"Yeah."

I wondered what she was there for, until I looked at her wrists. The healed incision on the right one was longer and darker and looked more painful than the left one, although they both looked like they still hurt her. She was bolder than me. Her body, which at first had appeared strong, now seemed to sag under some invisible weight.

"Is the . . . food okay here?" I was trying to make small talk.

A worker in a green sweater came by and announced, "It's time for group, ladies," and I followed both of them down the hall. *The hall keeps curving around. It's just a circle. No matter where you go, there you are.* I couldn't get away from anything, but I couldn't actually get anywhere either.

People were sitting in a circle on dark wood chairs with square blue cushions. It looked like the common room in a dorm.

The facilitator was wearing soft gray pants and a flowy layered top with a beige cardigan. She introduced herself as Lily. "Who would like to start and tell us about something they learned today?" Pause. "Shirley, it looks like you're having some feelings."

I looked over at a young woman with jet-black hair who was starting to cry.

"I had a good talk with Lisa," she said, sounding congested. "I'm still trying to understand boundaries and realizing no one in my family has them." There were murmurs of agreement.

"Same," said a blond girl. "But how do you straight up tell people *no* without freaking them out?"

"Who would you like to say no to?" asked Lily.

"My boyfriend," she replied. "Like, no, it's not okay to say those shitty things to me. No, I won't have sex whenever *you* want to."

"Yeah," a guy chimed in. "Now that I am clean, I don't know how to act. I feel awkward as hell."

"So let's explore saying no . . ."

I just listened. Each person took their turn.

I wondered who was on medication since that's all anyone talked about at Long Island Jewish; later that night, they all lined up to get their pills—Prozac, lithium, Xanax—except for me.

My first few days at Regent, I met with a lot of different people, who each began our meeting with "What brought you to us?"

"My dad kicked me out of the house, and I got really freaked out, and my mom came and got me . . ." It sounded stupid, especially because by then I knew my fellow patients had experienced sexual abuse, domestic violence, and drug addiction.

"Have you had suicidal thoughts in the past?" *No.*

"Do you hear voices that aren't really there?" *No.*

"What causes you the most distress?" *Thinking about my dad and what got me here.*

I was invested in the social workers understanding the details of what happened, but they were more interested in how I *felt* about all of it. I felt tired. I felt crushed by hopelessness. I felt numb. I felt confused about how I got to this point. I felt tremendous shame because I had set all of it in motion. I also wondered how my mom was going to pay for this place.

"Is there anything that makes you feel better?" *No.*

It's difficult to sleep in a mental hospital because they wake you up a lot. They do it at a regular hospital as well, but here checking on you was actually part of the program. My file was marked for suicide watch. So a nurse made an hourly visit to me. If I did fall asleep, the creak of my bedroom door, the jingle of keys, and the bright glare from the end of the nurse's arm roused me back to consciousness. All I wanted to do was sleep.

The psychiatrist wanted to start me on antidepressants; that appeared to be what you did in a mental hospital. You got meds.

"Let's try Paxil," he said. At least I could get in line when it was time for meds like everybody else. I wasn't sure I wanted to be taking pills, but I was feeling so hopeless, I was willing to try whatever anyone remotely competent recommended. He seemed competent.

I listened in group and continued to feel like everyone had it worse than me. I went to art therapy, where I made a mosaic trivet with small white, green, and maroon square tiles. My mother came to visit me every other day. One day, a letter arrived for me, and I immediately recognized the handwriting. *Dad.* My mother had given him the address, so that meant he knew where

Tristan Taormino

I was. She told me that several days after she picked me up at his house, he had had some kind of episode. He was shouting and ranting and ran out into the middle of the street. Ted took him to Maine Medical Center, this time to the in-patient mental health floor, where he was admitted. So both my father and I were in psychiatric facilities at the same time. *We had a deep psychic connection, but this is just weird*, I thought. Looking back, what happened had triggered us both for different reasons. I was anxious and worried about getting a letter from him: Was this an apology or a kiss-off? I went back to my room and opened it.

Tristan:

So we are now at this terrible moment. I think we both need to get better. I think it would be a mistake for you to focus on the events of this past weekend and how they may have impacted on my AIDS diagnosis. I also think it would be a mistake for me to focus on the events of this past weekend and the pain that you are now in. You have to take care of yourself. I love you.

Dad

He didn't offer an apology, just referred to "the events of this past weekend." He instructed me in mistakes neither of us *should* make. I interpreted the last line not as one of empathy or encouragement to focus on my healing but more one of brutal truth: *You're on your own, darling*. It was disappointing. But it was something? An acknowledgment that this horrible thing happened. A clue that he might not disown me after all. He reached out to me but wasn't willing to actually comfort me or hold my hand. I wondered if Ted had dictated it to him, but when I went through his files decades later, there was a draft in his handwriting (my father often wrote and kept drafts of his letters to me). It was not what I needed from him, but it was what I got. He was not coming to New York to visit me; he was not dropping everything to make things right. He was in the hospital; I was in the hospital. We were both broken.

I tried to open up to people, but when you're in crisis, processing your feelings can be terrifying, and attempting to reflect on their roots impossible. My fellow patients validated that the whole thing was a lot for me—or anyone—to handle. That made me feel less crazy. It was nice to be in a place where the only expectation people had of me was that I wouldn't kill myself. I could achieve that. I started to come down from the adrenaline-fueled panic, the everything-is-closing-in-around-me feeling. But then it was replaced with a drowning feeling, the grief pulling me under. I expected I might get some deep therapy there, but my days were filled with lots of short meetings with lots of different people who spent lots of time writing things down. I got into the routine: eat, take meds, go to group, go to art therapy, meet with social worker, eat, go to group, take meds, go to bed . . . Then I started to feel off. I had a constant headache, my face was flushed, and I felt like I had a fever. I definitely didn't feel *better*. When I met with the doctor again, I asked him if these were side effects of the Paxil.

"They could be."

"I don't think I want to be on it."

"Well, we don't want you to do anything you're not comfortable with. I really think that this medication can help you, but it's up to you."

"I don't want to take it anymore."

We made a pact that when I left Regent, I would reconsider antidepressants.

I called my mother every day. There was little to no privacy, but that was part of the deal there. She told me a guy named Charlie had called.

"I said you were out of town, and I'd pass the message along." I know she was convincing because she had this smooth way of making things seem very normal. I had interned for Charlie in Los Angeles the first summer I lived with Jen, when he was the interim executive director for the Gay and Lesbian Alliance Against Defamation (GLAAD). I worked with Charlie doing a lot of administrative tasks in a small office in a dingy building on Sunset Boulevard off La Brea with two strip malls on the corner. At that time GLAAD was very small, probably fewer than a dozen employees total in both LA and New York. Charlie and I had an easy rapport, and I really liked working for him.

I'm not sure what possessed me, but I decided to return his call. From the pay phone in the common room at a mental hospital. I didn't know what I might do if someone had a psychotic break nearby or how I could explain it. I just hoped for the best. He was his energetic, bubbly self when he picked up the phone. I put on my best "I am perfectly fine!" voice. He told me that he was living in New York City; his boyfriend, John, was the executive director of the Gay Games; and John was looking for a really sharp executive assistant.

"You'd be so perfect," he said, sincerely.

"So, do you, um . . . want my current résumé?"

"I know you're amazing, and I told John all about you. Why don't you just come for an interview with him and bring one with you then?"

"Um, I am . . . away and not sure when I will be back. It might be more than a week," I said, hoping for some leeway.

"Sure, just call John and make a plan when you're home. Here's his number." I grabbed a Crayola marker that was on the couch and wrote it on my arm. I was job hunting while institutionalized; no one would ever believe me, and I certainly wasn't going to share this shameful secret with Charlie.

When Regent discharged me, I had the name of a psychologist to start therapy, a psychiatrist (someone my mom worked with at the hospital), and some tiny measure of hope. And one other thing: I did end up interviewing with John about two weeks later, and I got the job.

UNITY

After I got out of the hospital, I called and told Riley everything. She sent me a blue-and-gold woven blanket with the sun on one side and the moon on the other and a love letter. I wrapped the blanket around myself day and night. She was so supportive, nonjudgmental, and fully present in the aftermath of my breakdown. I wanted those strong arms back in my life. We reconciled and decided we'd move in together in Manhattan. I was living with my mom in her small apartment in Port Washington on Long Island and commuting into the city daily. Finding a place to live in New York City is the ultimate scavenger hunt. A guy at the Gay Games connected me to another guy, and I found a sweet deal subletting a place on Twenty-First Street between First and Second Avenues, around the corner from one of my favorite places, Ess-a-Bagel. We found a couch at a secondhand store and used the blanket Riley gave me to cover the one noticeable stain. Riley and I could start over.

Both my parents were self-employed and underemployed for most of their adult lives. They worked at home, in retail, or in restaurants and did a bunch of small jobs for a lot of people. They were both hustlers. My big dream was that I would go to the same job every single day at the same time and same place with the same people. I'd have a steady paycheck, health insurance, and retirement. Financial stability had eluded both my parents (and therefore me), so I yearned for it. Until I got into the working world, especially corporate America, I had no idea what the trade-offs for that stability were.

The job of assistant to the executive director at the Gay Games was as demanding as the massive event sounds: over ten thousand athletes competing in more than twenty-five venues scattered across all five boroughs. It was 1994, the dawn of the LGBTQIA+ nonprofit, when most organizations operated with one paid staff member and volunteers, and only a few major players like the National Gay and Lesbian Task Force had the funding to run a real operation. It was before an LGBTQIA+ nonprofit-industrial complex existed, before people built their entire careers around being professional gays. The idea of working at an organization by and for queer folks was downright dreamy. I'd have an instant queer family after moving back to New York. My expectations were high: no closet, no heteronormativity, no problems.

In April our sweet living situation turned sour. We were subletting from Roger, a gay man who had AIDS, and his friend James was often the go-between because Roger was beginning to show signs of dementia. James told Ry and me to keep a low profile and, if anyone in the building asked, to say we were staying with our friend Roger. This was typical for a sublet in New York, so we were on board. It turned out the apartment was subsidized by the city specifically for people living with AIDS. Roger's rent was being paid by the Department of Social Services, and we were paying about four times that amount to Roger. It was pretty enterprising, actually, but illegal. The landlord discovered the scam, sent him an eviction notice, and threatened us. Then James called to say that Roger had gotten worse and was at St. Vincent's Hospital in the West Village, which played host to most of the gay men with AIDS in New York City; he told us to stay put—Roger needed our money. Roger started leaving angry, frantic, jumbled messages on our answering machine every day. When he got discharged from St. Vincent's, he came to the Games office and made a big scene. None of my coworkers appeared that alarmed; they recognized the dementia and the desperation. We found a house-sitting job in Chelsea taking care of Albert, a dog low to the ground like a corgi but smaller, with a bug-eyed Chihuahua face. I wondered about Roger, but I knew how his story ended.

Unity was selected as the theme of the Games, but it served another purpose: to remain acceptable to donors and sponsors. The ideals I'd imagined—a workplace where you could be comfortable and 100 percent yourself—were, in reality, available only to a certain group of gay people. If anyone wanted to critique the whitewashing and homophobia, they got excluded and, in some cases, fucked over. As long as there were enough women and people of color on staff to appear diverse, white directors made little effort to listen to them or put them in positions of power. I was a firsthand witness to the contradictions and compromises the mainstream LGBTQIA+ movement would go on to make over and over again (and still makes today).

I became a liaison to the mayor's office and was told repeatedly to dress in a suit, cover my one tattoo, and never hand staffers anything with the word *gay* on it. I wasn't the only one who noticed these contradictions, and things came to a head at a much-anticipated reception for the Gay Games staff at the home of Mayor Rudy Giuliani. As Giuliani delivered some banal remarks about tolerance, six people ripped off their tops to reveal ACT UP T-shirts and began shouting (they snuck in despite tight security). ACT UP was doing amazing, creative actions all over the country. I wanted to lie in the streets with them. There was anxiety, annoyance, anger, then yelling and threats of violence, but they came from the *guests*, rich white gay men in three-piece summer suits sipping complimentary Hiram Walker cocktails. A short, heavyset man pushed right into a woman protester who was half his size and shouted in her face, "You cunt! Get the fuck out of here!" Unity.

My dad hung up the phone first. We'd only spoken a few times since I got out of the hospital, and the call had taken a bitter turn. He often expressed his softness, gentleness, and affection alongside reactivity, rage, and intolerance. He saw and understood me in a way other people didn't, yet sometimes his own suffering blinded him to mine. His love for other people was deeply felt and expressed, but it came with conditions—strict, unspoken, impossible conditions. Inside, I dreaded I could be the next to be banished. It was a terrifying thought.

Riley walked out of the bedroom. I just stood there.

"You both love each other very much," she said softly. We sat on the couch in our new apartment on Twelfth Street. I wanted to shut down or bolt, but I knew I needed to talk about it.

"And you don't know how much time you have left with him." She looked me directly in the eyes. She was reading my mind again. There was so much I didn't need to explain to her. She knew me, really knew me. She understood me.

"I don't know what to do." I sighed. "Do I apologize again?"

"Do you want to apologize? Apologize for what? It was a fucked-up thing that happened."

Tristan Taormino

"But it was my fault, I shouldn't have . . ." The tears came fast, and my chin quivered.

She handed me a tissue, then moved closer, so I could lean into her arms. She was my soft place to land. I was sobbing.

"You have one of the most special father-daughter relationships I've witnessed. You're family. Don't walk away from yours the way he did. That's not good for either of you."

"I just don't know how to begin again, where to start . . ." I blew my nose and needed another tissue. Ry had already reached for the box and was holding it in front of me. She was not afraid of my emotions, so I let them seep out.

"I'm not sure what to say when we talk."

"Not that much time has passed, and you were traumatized. You almost . . ." She paused, didn't want to finish the sentence.

"I think you're being really hard on yourself." I was. Of course I was. I blamed myself. It was a well-worn path in my brain. I have a set of cards called Affirmations for Cynics, and the one that resonates most is: "Since no one else seems to be willing to take responsibility for anything, it is best for me to take responsibility for everything." It was such an old, deep wound. Not even a scar yet, still weeping. I'd been in therapy for only six months, and it would take a lot longer to untangle my feelings of unworthiness. I don't know if it was with Therapist #3 or Therapist #5 when I realized that I had internalized the blame for my father leaving me and my mom. This explanation wasn't one I had language to name at the time, I didn't even have a fully formed brain, but it bored into my soul and had so much time to grow there. He left because I wasn't enough for him to stay. This time he couldn't leave, so he made me do it. Reconciliation felt elusive, and our connection fragile.

"You will get through this," said Riley, one hand holding the tissues, the other stroking my face. "You have already survived a lot. It would be awful to see you give up on each other."

"*He* will give up on *me*." I dropped my head down and continued to sob.

A few days later, I wrote him a note asking that we steer clear of the phone, at least for a while, and write to each other instead. He wrote back updating me. Before he was diagnosed, he and Ted had begun a crusade to get Ted's employer, the United Way, to fund same-sex domestic partner benefits. Once my dad needed all this medical treatment, the fight became more urgent. Things were getting more serious, and they got a lawyer. He attached an op-ed he wrote about it. Doctors took him off Mycobutin because he had some eye problem. He needed to get on another new drug to thwart an infection that caused wasting syndrome. He had returned to reading my senior thesis and commented, "My respect and admiration for great writing is immense, and when it comes from someone you love, it's even more thrilling." Later in the letter:

After our last phone conversation, I had this strange feeling that we were somehow competing. My illness, your recovery, my drugs, your drugs. It seemed so crazy and off. This mixture of love and anger (for me) is lethal. But here it is . . . when the dust settles (I hate clichés, but it applies here), I am always left with this other thing, much stronger, overwhelming actually. This thing I'm left with does not always appear with all my relationships once that dust is on the floor or out the window. But with you . . . it is always the same. My intense love for you. In my face. In my cells. And so, I think, well, now what? What's to be done? What can I do? What do I need to work on? What needs to be repaired, changed? Because it would be nice if there was less dust. It blocks the view, the love.

Competing? How could a parent and child compete for anything? I chose to focus on the other parts. My worst fear was not coming true. He wasn't cutting me off. It was so clear, so precise, so moving: I was in his cells. I wrote him back. The bottom line was that I wanted him in my life.

The night before the opening ceremonies of the Games, Ry and I were in the Hotel Pennsylvania, where the staff was staying. It was across the street from Madison Square Garden; it was game five of the NBA Finals, and Midtown was swarming with people. Our room was filled with half-unpacked suitcases, rubber-banded stacks of yellow-and-white tickets, glossy brochures filled with beefy men in skimpy swimsuits. We invited Roxxie—a hot dyke with long, brown curly hair and a year-round California tan—to stay in our room so she could cover the Games for her popular zine *Girljock.* No surprise, we ended up in a playful three-way where she and Ry immobilized me with athletic tape and Ace bandages and "hazed" me with their fingers and mouths. I love staying on theme. Naked and satisfied, I went into the bathroom and saw big splotches of bruises on my skin from the tape; it turns out I am allergic to the adhesive. I came out, and the two of them were setting up a rollaway bed for Roxxie. I got into bed, and Ry turned on CNN. There was an aerial shot of a white SUV driving on a highway. The headline read "Police Pursue O.J.

Tristan Taormino

Simpson's Bronco on Highway." We stayed up late, transfixed by the action on the screen as the story unfolded. Now *that* was dramatic.

Days later, Dad and Ted arrived in the city—it was the first time we'd seen each other since I left Portland. I felt very anxious, but that all transformed into excitement when I saw his face. *This is what we need, a return to the before times when everything was lovely.* My queer friends thought it was the coolest that I had a gay dad. We got together for a group dinner in Chelsea where every table was filled with gay people. We all spoke the same language, got the inside jokes, and could be our authentic selves. Everyone was family. A far cry from when I was a teenager and didn't know what to do when I found out he was gay.

I was allowed to attend only one Gay Games event as a spectator, and I timed Dad's visit with what we both wanted to see most: figure skating. We used to spend hours on the phone talking about skating competitions on TV: Tonya Harding's take-no-shit attitude, Surya Bonaly's history-making wins, which sequined costumes worked and which were just tacky.

My dad, Ted, and I took the subway to a rink in Queens, where we watched a few hours of magic. The *Advocate* wrote an article about how one of the competing pairs was kicked out of the rink where they practiced because they were a same-sex couple. They were two beautiful men about the same size, quite tall and muscular, wearing full bodysuits that were beige with a black print of branches, leaves, and shapes. They did this one move where the first man lifted the second, who split his legs and rested on the first one's knees with his arms straight out, and then the lifter let go and put his arms out to his sides. It was breathtaking. Another male couple skated in military fatigues with their mouths taped shut, unafraid to say that politics will always be a part of queer lives.

The day after the closing ceremonies was Stonewall 25 to commemorate the twenty-fifth anniversary of the Stonewall Riots (which replaced the yearly Gay Pride March). Ry and I met up in Midtown with my friend Alan, who was dressed in a plaid kilt and an ACT UP T-shirt for the *other* march, the one to demand more resources for AIDS and protest the corporatization of pride and the depoliticizing of our identities. We took over Fifth Avenue, a fast-moving crowd carrying confrontational signs, a mass of neon-glowing bodies stickered with phrases like QUEER: A MOVEMENT, NOT A MARKET. The adrenaline was invigorating, probably similar to what many of the athletes felt in the previous ten days. I needed a dose of anger and militancy to help me recover from the Games. I felt queer and free again.

REGGIE LOVE

Love is hard, demanding, exhausting, exciting, but so is writing, but we get clues to who we are, we get to express ourselves hopefully freely. It's like writing with the reader in the room. Exhilarating and scary.

A LETTER FROM DAD

Riley and I had an unbreakable thing. It felt special. It felt like Ethan, it felt like Jen. Riley knew all the parts of me—I cheated, I lied, I was depressed, I went to a mental institution—and she loved me without conditions. Desire thrived in that relationship, until it didn't. Two summers with Jen didn't prepare me for what it would be like to really live with a partner and navigate the realities of adulthood: rental applications, security deposits, grocery budgets, cleaning the toilet. I couldn't be domesticated. I still can't. We managed the mundane, but our resilient emotional bond began to override our sex life. The ache between us was gone. At twenty-three, sex was so important to my identity and my politics that losing it felt like losing a part of myself. A missing limb. Neither of us had the skills to understand it or work through it. I took off her silver necklace. She went back to South Dakota.

I have a thick black binder of more than a hundred notes, cards, and letters from Riley, each one carefully placed in a plastic sleeve to protect it. To protect the memory of her. When I read the letters now, the language is beautiful, and she paints a portrait of a once-in-a-lifetime kind of love. I had forgotten how devoted we were to one another, to love itself, and it was startling to see it in her handwriting. Now I can't access the feelings I had for her; the emotions are somehow out of my reach. When I put myself back there, nothing moves or changes in my body as it does with memories of other ex-lovers. I don't know why. Or maybe I do feel something. Something like sadness mixed with some guilt, a little regret—like a heavy heart.

Riley and I lost track of each other entirely. Unlike other exes, we don't have a friend or a place or a thing that drew us back to each other, so I never heard her name come out of someone's mouth. I'm left to wonder. When I last looked at her Facebook profile, she was working to bring clean drinking water to remote parts of Africa. I hope she has someone who worships her and has all the faith in the world in their love—and who believes in forever.

Before she left, Ry and I adopted a dog together from a shelter. We originally went to North Shore Animal League on Long Island *just to look*. I dreamed that a Labrador puppy would be a good match, something affable and reliable. When we walked into the room designated for puppies, the most crowded and popular, all of the furry, squirming creatures were in the arms of prospective owners. I spotted a small girl holding a black pup headed back toward the cages, presumably because she wasn't interested.

I made a beeline for her and asked, "Do you want that puppy?" She shook her head no and handed it over to me. I could see why this tiny black dog with a few small white markings hadn't wooed her. She was quiet, cautious, not overflowing with enthusiasm and irresistible tongue baths like the others. She looked a little shell-shocked. I lied on the application and said I worked from home, and the nice woman who checked my references called my employer to confirm. My mom played the role perfectly, and that black puppy was ours. I was really into Susan Sarandon at the time, so I wanted to pick a name that paid homage to her. Louise was too on the nose for a feminist dyke. So instead it was Sarandon as a feisty, take-no-shit lawyer in her latest movie, *The Client*. We named her Reggie Love. It didn't occur to me that I'd repeatedly have to explain to people I wasn't a John Grisham superfan.

While she was shy and slightly sullen at the shelter, as soon as Reggie Love came home with us, she showed her true self: a ball of fire. She picked up the first thing she found on the floor, a sock, and tore around the apartment with it in her mouth, then jumped up on the couch and started chewing it. She was so delighted with herself. She turned out not to be a black Lab at all; she grew up to be much longer and leaner, like a whippet but with a bigger head. She looked exactly like Santa's Little Helper on *The Simpsons*.

Reggie Love and I needed somewhere new to live after the breakup, but most apartments in the city were too expensive for me. Greg, a friend of mine from the Gay Games, suggested I check out Williamsburg, a neighborhood in Brooklyn that I'd never heard of.

"A lot of Polish people live on the North Side and Puerto Ricans and Dominicans on the South Side. Farther east there's an enclave of Hasidic Jews. It's super cheap," he told me. "Young artists are starting to move there. It's really funky, and there's a cool park for Reggie Love."

I took the L train to the first stop in Brooklyn. When I came up from the subway, I walked south on Bedford Avenue past a bodega, a restaurant with a Polish name, the L Café, and then a bunch of ugly row houses and old factories, some of which had been converted to artist live/work lofts. I walked several blocks and turned right on Metropolitan, then two blocks to Wythe Avenue. There was enough dog poop on the sidewalk to confirm what Greg said about everyone having dogs. I saw a handwritten apartment-for-rent flyer taped to a telephone pole, and I ripped off one of the tabs. Greg lived in one of the converted buildings, and you had to climb the fire escape to get inside his apartment because the staircase inside the building wasn't safe to use. His apartment was the epitome of funky artist chic, with painted murals and homemade tile mosaic on the wall.

Greg and I walked about eight blocks to McCarren Park with his dog, a white pit bull mix with scattered black dots all over her body. It wasn't an official dog park; around dusk, people gathered and let their dogs off leash, and no one said anything. We walked up to a group of mostly white, eccentric twenty-somethings with fluorescent hair and piercings dressed in thrift store clothes put together in creative ways. They were straight out of the casting call for *Rent* ("New York City artist types") before *Rent* actually made its off-Broadway debut. Greg introduced me to a woman with dreadlocks in an oversized sweater coat who had a Doberman with floppy ears.

Later that week, I called the number from the poster and showed up to look at a one-bedroom apartment on the top floor of a brick row house on Berry Street.

"I live here with my family, my husband and our two young daughters," said Isabella, a short, friendly woman in her early forties with lush black hair and a Spanish accent. "You have to walk through our home to get to the apartment upstairs. So it needs to be the right person. It can't be just anyone."

The apartment had a big kitchen, a light-filled living room, and a tiny room that fit a double-sized mattress and not much more. It was five blocks to the subway, and she said they would consider a dog. There was no formal application. The rent was $300. My femmeness meant I passed as a normal-looking young woman just out of college, plus I was polite and employed. I had recently secured a new job (and my pay stub didn't give away that I actually worked for a smut peddler). Two weeks later, I found a couch on the street in a bright floral fabric with several substantial rips in the cushions but no signs of animal piss or bug infestation. Greg helped me carry it up two flights of winding stairs to the top floor of Isabella's house. Reggie Love and I had a new home.

Reggie Love kept me company, which I desperately needed to fill the space that Riley left behind. She was affectionate and very high strung. Because I worked a nine-to-five job with a forty-five-minute commute to Midtown, there was no way for her to get enough exercise to burn all that energy. When she was bored, she ate—not chewed, but actually ingested—stuff she wasn't supposed to. Couch-cushion foam, plastic bottles, a remote control. There was a lot of vomiting. I started keeping Reggie Love in the bathroom of my apartment to help confine her and keep her out of trouble.

One day after work, I came up from the L train, and the smell of pierogi and oil filled the air. As I headed south, I passed a group of Latino men in front of the laundromat playing checkers on a small card table and drinking Café Bustamante. I stopped at the only place to buy food besides the bodegas, which were dusty, understocked, and overpriced. It was a big warehouse where you had to walk through a thick yellowing plastic curtain with slits that brought you to one entire room that was refrigerated.

I met Isabella in the hallway, and she offered me some of the family's dinner: rice and beans, avocado, and carnitas. It turned out Isabella was a devout evangelical Christian, the kind that recruited and gave you the hard sell; the rest of the family went to church and prayed, but it was Isabella who read the Bible daily and talked to me about it any chance she got. I wasn't in the mood to hear scripture even though the food smelled delicious. I gently declined, anxious to get upstairs. I opened the bathroom door, which had been painted so many times it stuck to the frame. Reggie Love greeted me, wagging her tail furiously, but my eyes were focused behind her, where I saw that a big swatch of my shower curtain was missing. I expected the vomiting would come soon, but it didn't. Later, when we went on a long walk in the park, she pooped. I bent down to scoop, and there it was: a long, coiled piece of leopard-print fabric covered with shit.

Reggie Love got me out of the house on a regular basis, which was good because my depression, despite therapy and Zoloft, had not abated. Somehow I managed to get out of bed each morning, take the train to Grand Central Station, and keep it together enough to be an executive assistant at my new job at Masquerade Books, a mass-market publisher of erotic novels. My boss was the head of it all, Richard Kasak, infamous for publishing a book called *Becoming a Sensuous Homosexual* in the 1960s with Grove Press. He had a reputation in the publishing world as both a veteran and a pervert. His taste ran the gamut: he loved anonymous or trashy novels of yesteryear like *My Secret Life* but also valued cutting-edge and kinky work no one else would publish, by outsiders like John Preston, Larry Townsend, Samuel Delany, Laura Antoniou, and Patrick Califia.

Notoriously finicky, Richard would draft a contract for a book in the morning and burn its manuscript and the author's Filofax card by the end of the day. He wanted to know every single detail about every single thing I was doing at all times. He did give me free rein to read as many unsolicited manuscripts as I could carry on the subway and make recommendations if I found any gems. This job was one my college adviser might have envisioned for me when she encouraged me to make sex writing my career. I was there to soak up everything.

One Masquerade author, David Aaron Clark, and I made an easy, fast connection. David was a big guy with pasty white skin covered in tattoos and scars from deliberate cuttings. He looked terrifying, but I could see the kindness in his squinty eyes. When you talked to him, he was so clearly genius-level smart, you just had to get past the darkness surrounding him to see it. Not brooding-bad-boy-with-a-skull-on-his-black-T-shirt dark. More like thinking-about-blood-pain-and-death-seriously-and-often dark. To my young self, he was living a coveted life on the edge filled with debauched sex and BDSM with his dominatrix girlfriend. We went on to edit an anthology together titled *Ritual Sex*, about the intersections of sex, religion, and spirituality.

Masquerade was part of a larger parent company that published porn magazines, including *Cheri* and *Playgirl*, and the corporate Christmas party predictably featured strippers in sexy Santa outfits. There I met Mario, a short, cheeky editor from Bensonhurst with a thick Brooklyn accent and an old-school ducktail haircut and goatee. Mario was crass but in the best possible way. He said, "You have a great ass." I appreciate that kind of direct communication. We had all sorts of adventures watching German fetish porn at his big apartment in Morningside Heights, taking naked Polaroids, and fucking with abandon.

Work, sex, and the city itself acted as external momentum that kept my brain occupied and pushed me forward. But when I was by myself, sadness enveloped me, and thoughts of my father dying, thoughts of me dying, crept in. I got lonely living above the nice Christian family. My dad visited me in my new place and bought me a green patterned duvet from Urban Outfitters to cover the old ripped-up couch, but it was often disheveled, so the muted, soothing pattern was interrupted by the garish red floral print poking through. When I had a crying jag, Reggie Love would curl up behind me on the couch and not leave my side; she gazed into my eyes with a never-ending love. She was too loyal and kind for me to leave her. There were days I got so sad that I was frozen, and I couldn't even brush my teeth. Reggie Love wiggled and wagged and got me up and out of the house to walk her. Sometimes I couldn't muster the energy, and she peed on a section of newspaper I laid down on the kitchen floor. Dogs need consistency, and it was hard for me to stick to a schedule. As a dog parent, your thoughts are reduced to feed her, keep her hydrated, take her out to pee, when did she last poop? I had trouble taking care of those things for myself. I felt dragged down. I never told anyone I was in therapy or on medication, or had been hospitalized. I was ashamed. If I had nothing to do on the weekends, I just slept. When I got so sad, the idea of making something to eat or getting takeout felt like it took so much energy. I read the *Village Voice* cover to cover, then put fresh pages down for Reggie Love.

PARIS

"I don't know what to expect of Paris at this point. I believe we will go, but it is apt to be a good deal of work for me and you," said Ted. "I'm sure you agree that it is worth the effort for your dad to be able to see Paris again, however limited that might be."

In October at his fiftieth birthday party, my dad had announced that he and Ted were taking me on a trip to Paris in the spring of 1995. Paris! It was high on my dream list of places to visit, and of course I would love to go with my dad. It was bittersweet, though, because he was obviously checking things off a list that he wanted to do. Before he died.

One day in the spring, I received a letter from Ted telling me that Dad's HIV had infected his brain fluid, and he was experiencing some symptoms of dementia. He wrote it in a formal way, as if reciting his case file: loss of verbal and motor skills, pathology, psychological symptoms of depression with mixed mood and mild paranoid ideation. He admitted that he'd seen the signs for weeks but was in denial about it. Dad was losing his balance, falling, and the cane they got him wasn't helping. Ted had to get up with him at night and worried for his safety during the day while he was at work. Dad was in therapy, and his doctor had changed his antidepressant, but he sometimes said he wanted to give up on both of them. Ted wrote, "He knows, however, that if therapy stopped, I would be out the door the next day. That ole fear of abandonment comes in handy sometimes!"

I had just spoken to my father a few days before, but Ted explained that Dad was on the bed, curled into a fetal position, relatively unresponsive, before he got on the phone with me, when he became more animated and alert. Ted feared I didn't have an accurate picture of what was really going on. Ted expressed his anger, resentment, isolation, and exhaustion—all signs of caregiver burnout. It was a reality check that I didn't want. The situation sounded awful, and also familiar, like so many stories I'd heard. A week later, my dad broke the news: he was not well enough to go to Paris. I told him I totally understood.

"I've told Ted he should go anyway. We made all the plans, the hotel is booked, and the tickets are nonrefundable. Besides, he needs a break. So he's going. And we're wondering if you might come spend those twelve days with me."

"Of course, Dad." I didn't really even have a minute to digest the news or process it, but obviously I would take care of my dad while Ted went to Paris. He did need a break. I knew how difficult it was when the partner of the person with AIDS bore the brunt of the care work. How draining. I flew to Portland to be with my dad.

I had taken Ted's letter seriously and prepared myself, but I was not ready for the changes in my father to be so drastic. He was very thin, quite frail, and definitely out of it. He was less mobile, shuffling much slower and needing to steady himself on the wall or a piece of furniture as he moved (he had abandoned the cane). His brain and speech, once sharp and cutting, seemed dulled and fuzzy. Things were actually worse than what Ted described. I suppose he couldn't see it because he was in it, but to me Dad needed full-time care and supervision. Ted stood in the kitchen and took me through the medication schedule.

"You know your father has trouble swallowing big pills, so, for those, we're crushing them up and putting them in smoothies or juice." Ted reviewed what he was eating, how often he took a bath. All the doctors' numbers were on the fridge.

"This is a new prescription lotion for his skin, which is severely dry and is really bothering him. Remind him to put it on, especially his legs."

"We got a walker." He pointed to it in the hallway, standing at the ready. "But he hasn't used it that much. He can be wobbly on his feet, so you see if you can get him to use it more."

"He shouldn't get up by himself at night because he is so unsteady. You will have to help him to the bathroom. Lucy will bring over a meal one day this week for you. Seth's around to visit and help. He's going to run out of Elavil this week; you can call for a refill and walk to the pharmacy to pick it up. He is drinking tea before bed to help him fall asleep."

And then: "Thank you for this."

Our days together were quiet, and we stayed on a schedule. He needed a lot of rest. I crushed the pills with a mortar and pestle, mixed them into banana-strawberry or Citrus C Odwalla smoothies. I offered him food, but many times he was too nauseous to eat it. I could always get him to eat scrambled eggs, though, so I made those a lot. We watched movies from his VHS collection. *The Godfather. Do the Right Thing. The Piano. Dead Poets Society. Kramer vs. Kramer. The Crying Game. Bette Midler: Art or Bust*, a recording of one of her live shows. My dad and I both liked to escape into other people's stories, real and imagined. He had a lot of history to turn away from—abuse, homophobia, mental illness. I just wanted to be in someone's else's shoes and a story that was different from my own. *Anywhere but here.*

We never tired of rewatching *The Wizard of Oz*. I identified with Dorothy building a crew of misfits and having the courage to stand up to powerful forces. Like the young girl in one of my favorite childhood stories, "Mrs. Gertrude," Dorothy could see things about people that no one else could: their true, best selves. That yellow-brick road was a metaphor for finding oneself but also a real haul. Dorothy wanted what most of us want: to be home. Also, you can't go wrong in a movie with witches, ridiculous levels of camp, red sparkly shoes, and a cute dog. Dad worshipped Judy Garland, so we had a mini marathon. His love of her, of old Hollywood, held this dual image for me: the height of glamour, style, and sophistication clashed with the real-life stories of beautiful starlets strung out on booze and drugs and closeted gay men fiercely protecting their careers by any means necessary.

I played CDs every morning, and he picked which ones he wanted to hear. Donna Summer. Jennifer Warnes. Dionne Warwick. One morning, he selected Barbra Streisand, *The Broadway Album*. This was the time of the day where, before he got sick, he'd normally be dancing in the kitchen while he cooked breakfast, bright eyed and ready to plan our day. Now he hummed along sometimes from his bed. I brought him his drinks and meds. I really wanted to crawl in bed with him, so after he ate a little lunch, I put the dishes in the sink and came back. I sat on the edge of the bed and swung my legs around and rolled onto my side so I was facing him. The wolf was in the bed. It was a beautiful stuffed wolf puppet with layers of different shades of gray fur and a red tongue; you could nestle your hand inside and open the mouth

Figure 29.1 My dad in Portland, Maine, 1994

wide to show the teeth. He was holding it gently, and it obviously brought him comfort. I remembered that he had a stuffed Bambi when he was young. Page 15 of his memoir:

When I was bad, or, more accurately, whenever my mother decided I was bad, she would threaten me with "I guess we're going to have to put you in a home for bad boys."

She had often described this home to me. It was a dark, crowded place with double-decker metal cots. At the foot of each cot, a miniature blackboard dangled, upon which each bad boy's name was printed. As she forced me to imagine this place with her, I watched her storming along the cots, bitterly shouting each bad boy's name. And always, always, no matter how crowded the darkness, she would find one empty, waiting cot, and she would stoop down and print Billy Boy on a tiny blackboard. Then she would rise and walk off into the blackness, leaving me behind forever.

"So . . . I guess we're going to have to put you in a home for bad boys."

Once this threat had been made, my mother would pack a small carpetbag and place it in front of the door. Then she would dress me and say goodbye to my room. It was usually here that she would improvise something — "I'll give your toys to your cousin Teddy Boy!" Or: "If you take your stuffed Bambi with you, they'll burn it!" Then we would slowly walk to the subway station.

Throughout this Gothic tap dance, I would cry and beg for her forgiveness.

"I'll be good! I swear I'll be good! I promise I'll be a good boy! I will! I will! Don't send me! Please don't send me there! Please!"

"I love you," I said, which seemed redundant. *What is left to say?* I knew he loved me; there was never a doubt in my mind; he said it, he showed it, I felt it. He knew how much I loved him.

"Can we just lie here for a while together?"

"I . . ." he hesitated. "I just want to make sure this isn't . . . wrong. A father lying in bed with his daughter." Maybe it was confusion from the dementia, but it also made sense that he was thinking about his role as a father, my father, and what was right. He didn't exactly have good role models. But he wanted to be good.

"It's not inappropriate, Dad. It's not."

He relaxed, and I recounted some of my favorite experiences with him. Dad had a very particular sense of style that revolved around wearing oversized clothes. He was an average-sized guy, lean and strong from walking

Tristan Taormino

everywhere and doing manual labor. Yet he never bought anything smaller than an extra large.

"You drilled it into my head: if you're going to get me a shirt, it's gotta be XL. XL only!"

He wanted to be swimming in his clothes. He often experimented with bold patterns and colors. Canary yellow knit top! Geometric prints and primary colors! Baby-blue-and-purple striped hoodie!

When I visited him at his place in Portland, Oregon, I was newly out, getting more comfortable with my femme identity and interested in making bolder choices. We strolled into a store that sold Doc Martens and club wear, and I made a beeline to something, grabbed it, and headed toward the dressing room. The store was small, so I knew he was in earshot when I emerged.

"Dad? What do you think?" I asked. He turned to look, as did a few other customers, naturally curious. There I stood in my jeans with my bare midriff and my B-cup boobs pushed up in a black bra covered in large, round royal blue sequins. It reminded me of a drag queen's dress. It was campy. I thought it would make a perfect addition to my wardrobe.

"It's gorgeous," he said, and I could tell the onlookers weren't quite sure what to make of us. "You should definitely get it."

We both giggled at the memory. Then we lay there for a while, not speaking. I breathed deeply. He had a faint smell of his favorite face lotion, Oil of Olay. *He doesn't smell sick, although I don't know what that would smell like.* Finally, I heard the sound of his breathing, slightly congested. He'd fallen asleep.

Throughout that week I slept restlessly in the sailor's berth, or I didn't sleep at all, on alert in case he needed me. One morning I had actually dozed off when I heard his voice calling me. That was the routine: he'd call me from his bedroom. I'd get up. Help him to the bathroom or get him something.

I was exhausted, wanted a little more time in the warmth of the covers. My limbs felt heavy. I wasn't ready to face the day. He called to me again. I shut my eyes and rolled over. *He can wait.* But his voice didn't stop. He kept calling my name. He sounded weak, defeated. I just wanted five more minutes. He'd take short breaks, I'd be thankful for the silence, and then I'd hear him again. Finally, I called to him, "I'm coming, Dad."

I shuffled out and saw him lying on the ground in the doorway between the living room and kitchen. He was still saying my name. He had a big gash on his head, and it was bleeding. He was clearly in pain. I rushed to him.

"Oh my God, Dad, what happened???"

"I got up . . . to get a glass of water . . . I got dizzy. Did I hit my head on something?"

I looked down and saw a smear of blood on the newly painted light gray molding.

"I was calling you . . ."

How long had he been lying here? I am an awful, awful daughter. I am horrible. Why didn't I get up when he first started calling me? Oh my God, how could I let this happen? Ted's going to kill me.

"Let me help you sit up." I surveyed the gash. "I think we should go to the hospital to get that looked at."

Ted's car was in the parking lot, but I was awful at driving stick shift. Plus, I was shaking and freaking out, so I decided to call Seth. Seth was briefly my dad's lover when he first got to Maine. He was a white guy with a thick head of dark hair, a heavy five-o'clock shadow, and full, rosy lips, an aspiring artist and filmmaker who was enrolled in Maine College of Art. He was the same age as me. That bit felt a little awkward at first, but when I got to know Seth, I realized how smart and thoughtful he was, so I saw what my father saw in him. Eventually he became one of my dad's closest friends.

He picked up on the second ring.

"My dad fell, and his head is bleeding. Could you please come here and help me take him to the ER?"

I remembered a story my father told me about when his mother broke his arm and drilled him about what to say when they got to the hospital. *He slipped on the wet grass.* Seth was there in ten minutes, and we drove to Maine Medical Center emergency room. It was early on a Saturday morning, so we didn't wait long. When they took us back to a bed in a curtained area, Seth said he was going to move the car.

The triage nurse asked a few questions, and I explained what happened. She took his blood pressure, his temperature.

"How much does he weigh?"

"About 110 pounds." She made notes. She gave me a nod, and there was kindness in her eyes.

"Okay, let's see if we can get that cut fixed up."

Tristan Taormino

He was slightly agitated but also confused, so he didn't resist anything. Another nurse came in and asked most of the same questions. "A doctor will be in soon to see you."

A young guy in a white coat slid back the curtain, then closed it behind him. "So I understand you've had a little fall, Mr.—"

"Tah-ruh-meen-o," I interjected. "It's hard for people to pronounce."

He approached my dad and turned to me. "And what's the...underlying condition here?" Apparently he had not read the two sets of notes.

"AIDS. He has AIDS, and he's having some confusion."

He examined the wound on my dad's head, made him follow the penlight with his eyes, asked him some questions, looked down at the chart, wrote something.

"He is a little dehydrated, so we will give him some fluids. I don't think he has a concussion," he said to me.

Then to my dad: "Okay, well, this could have been much worse. We're going to get you stitches and some antibiotics, then you can get home and take it easy."

My dad was just kind of staring into space.

"Can I talk to you privately for a second?" I asked the doctor.

We stepped outside the curtain, and I lowered my voice. "You're not going to admit him?"

"Well, there is nothing to admit him for. He just needs fluids and stitches. I can't justify admitting him."

"What about for, like, a suspected concussion? Look...I am alone, his partner is in Paris, and I am taking care of him by myself. I feel really overwhelmed. I am afraid something like this will happen again, and I won't know what to do. I don't feel like I can take proper care of him. Can't you just admit him overnight for observation?" I hoped I sounded as desperate as I felt.

"I'm sorry, I really can't. Maybe you can get someone in, a home nurse? I'll be back to do the stitches." He walked away.

I went behind the curtain and again explained to my dad what was happening. I held his hand.

"Don't get up by yourself anymore. I will help you. Call me from the bed. You can use the walker." They stitched his forehead and waited for the bag of fluids to empty. I signed the discharge papers.

"I'll be right back. I am going to find Seth."

I went back to the waiting room and updated Seth. Tears welled up in my eyes. It was all too much. He hugged me.

"I'll get the car," he said.

I wiped the tears and went back in. I helped my dad get out of the blue hospital gown and back into the plaid pajama pants I brought him in. There was blood down the front of his off-white Henley shirt. A nurse put him in a wheelchair and pushed him out to the parking circle. Seth helped Dad into the front seat. I put his seatbelt on, then got in the backseat. We drove home. Ted returned a few days later, and he looked refreshed. I went back to Brooklyn feeling heavy.

About two months later, I got the call from Ted that Dad was moving to hospice. Reggie Love and I packed up and got on a plane to Portland.

SCRAMBLED EGGS WITH BETTE MIDLER

The Peabody House was a sprawling yellow three-story house on Orchard Street in a historic part of Portland. In 1995 it had just opened and was the only residential hospice care facility for AIDS patients in Maine. It was founded by Frannie Peabody, a ninety-two-year-old woman who became a leading activist in the state after her grandchild was diagnosed with AIDS. My dad's room on the first floor had walls that were painted a happy but subdued yellow. The staff was a small team of warm, compassionate folks. I found myself relieved that my father was in hospice because Ted wouldn't have to do all his care work; he could concentrate on just being his partner. I was also terrified because hospice means you're dying. My father was dying.

My father's commitment to honesty and direct communication meant that he had made his wishes abundantly clear to Ted and me about what he wanted when things got to this point. So, thankfully, we didn't need to agonize over what to do.

"I want the morphine drip at the end," he used to say over and over with morbid humor. "Give me that morphine drip!"

When I first saw him in hospice, it was dramatic: he was a shell. He had wasting syndrome, a common stage in the disease where a person loses about 10 percent of their body weight. He was frail, gaunt, incredibly weak; his pale white skin had turned an ashy gray color. He smiled when he saw me. The attendant helped him sit up by arranging a series of pillows to give him support. He had no muscle tone left and couldn't hold himself up.

"He's still semilucid and can stay awake and alert for short periods of time," said Ted. "He hasn't been eating very much. I thought maybe you could whip up some scrambled eggs. There's a full kitchen. He loves your scrambled eggs."

So I made him scrambled eggs, taking care to add milk and whisk them aggressively to make them fluffy. You have to keep the burner low. Turn it up to high, and everything gets flat and overcooked. I brought a plate to him, sat on the edge of the bed, and offered up a spoonful.

"I made these for you and hope they are up to your standards," I said. I was concentrating hard on not crying. That wouldn't help matters.

He opened his mouth and took a small bite.

"We brought some of his favorite tapes. Bill?"

"Bette," he said in a gravelly whisper. *Bette Midler: Art or Bust.*

His eyes lit up and followed Bette as she moved across the stage. He ate a few bites of the eggs, then shook his head at me, so I took the plate away. We got to the classic part of the concert where Bette and her backup singers appear dressed as mermaids. She has on a bright green feather headpiece and blue sequined bra and tail. They do wacky choreography in motorized wheelchairs and sing a medley of "We Are Family," "In the Mood," and "I Will Survive." It's high camp, it's drag, it's fabulous.

Dad began to nod off, and Ted made eye contact with me. We headed out to let him sleep.

"He'll be asleep for a while," said Ted outside his room. He told me there was a sort of dog park within walking distance of the hospice. Reggie Love was in the car, so I leashed her up. I didn't want to see anyone, especially new people, but Reggie needed the exercise. I followed Ted's small handwritten map until I came to a sign: Western Cemetery. I wasn't sure I was in the right place, but then I saw a small group of dogs in an empty field behind gravestones in neat rows. I let Reggie off the leash, and she immediately ran full speed toward the group. I caught up with her and nodded to the folks there. A black Lab drifted too far and was getting near the graves, but the owner quickly and firmly called it back. This happened several times with different dogs. I didn't want to be disrespectful to the dead, to their relatives. I certainly didn't want Reggie Love to poop near someone's resting place, so I kept a close eye on her. I was standing in a place full of bodies and spirits and a handful of living people. It was all a little too on the nose.

I walked back to the condo, and Ted announced we would be returning to Peabody House, so I put Reggie in her crate and got in the car. This dynamic,

Tristan Taormino

of Ted running the show, of never speaking about, let alone negotiating, what we did, was set in motion and continued. We would be sitting vigil at the house, I learned. No one actually asked me what I wanted or needed. My dad's friends and adopted family would come by at various points in the day: Seth, Bill, and Andrea from the café where Dad once worked, Lucy and her family. Their visits with Dad would be short, and then they would sit with us in the small living room just outside his room.

My dad was a man with so much vitality and energy; his will to live was powered equally by his exuberance for life and a middle finger to homophobes everywhere. *Not that long ago, he was racing down High Street in a fit of mania. But here he is now, lying in a bed, not even his own, with all that energy so thoroughly drained from his being.* I held his hand at his bedside; sometimes I read to him, or I'd press play on Barbra Streisand's concert in New York City, and he'd smile ever so slightly. She closed the show with "Somewhere" from *West Side Story.*

> *There's a place for us*
> *A time and a place for us*
> *Hold my hand and we're halfway there*
> *Hold my hand and I'll take you there*

He was often barely conscious and incoherent. Within days, he couldn't talk anymore, only wrinkle his face together like a cringe to tell me—his only child—that the pain was getting unbearable. I'd press the button, and when the morphine kicked in, we'd go back to watching.

Sometimes when the one nurse he didn't like showed up in his room, he gave me a look. Rolling his eyes without actually rolling his eyes. I knew what he was telling me. Once, he squeezed my hand, and I thought for sure he was totally out of it, but when I looked at him, he winked at me.

As the days passed, when Dad was awake, he was agitated and uncomfortable. "The morphine drip!" his voice echoed in my head. Ted and I met with the doctor and the staff and decided it was appropriate to increase his dose.

"He will become less lucid, less present," said the nurse. "I want you to be prepared for that." *Who is prepared for any of this?*

The next day, Frannie Peabody herself, a slight but powerful woman with short white curls of hair and wire-framed glasses, arrived at the house. She visited each and every resident at Peabody House, and when she came, you

Scrambled Eggs with Bette Midler

195

could see how dearly she was loved by the staff. She'd become an activist at eighty years old, so I already respected her.

In the hallway one of the nurses said to me quietly, "Sometimes when Frannie comes and lays hands on someone, they are ready to finally let go." I think it was meant to be comforting.

At the next meeting with the nurse and doctor, they told us we could make the decision to withdraw water and nourishment.

"Then it should be just a few days, so we will do it when you are ready." Ted said we were ready. At that point he had infantilized me to such a point that I was being treated like a preteen, incapable of making any decision. I didn't have the energy to fight it. I was told what to do, and I did it. Days went by, and then it had been an entire week. Dad was unconscious but alive. When I was with him by myself, I watched him breathe. Intrusive thoughts came into my head. *Should I just cover his face with a pillow?* I considered this on several occasions, to put him out of what must be misery. *Will anyone know? That will end it for sure. Why am I thinking such horrible thoughts? This is my father. I am clearly a monster. Why won't he just let go?*

"He's got strong lungs and a strong heart," said one of the nurses, but it didn't make any sense given the way he looked . . . so emaciated, so sick.

"You have no idea how right you are," I told her.

Several times, I thought he stopped breathing. I would hold my breath and stare. *No, no, there goes his chest. It's subtle, but it's still moving.*

Eleven years before his death, my dad wrote and directed a play in Provincetown called AIDS: *The Writing on the Wall.* From a monologue:

Ralph is twenty-nine. He used to live in Atlanta, and I am just holding his hand, and the lights keep going dimmer and dimmer on him. It's incredibly lonely—for both of us, and I can't even imagine what is going on for him. His eyes are vacant and bloodshot and teary, and his breathing is erratic, and sometimes he is peaceful and sometimes he looks so frightened behind the green oxygen mask. A few times he has made eye contact with me, and his stare just holds me intently, and I think he is acknowledging my presence, or maybe he could be desperately trying to determine if he is alive, here or there or where, or what is going on, or who I am. But I don't know, and it's frustrating. He never completely closes his eyes, even when he is sleeping, and possibly dreaming—as if, if he did, he would never be able to open them again. I sense he is not quite ready.

Tristan Taormino

"Love is like writing with the reader in the room," Dad wrote in a letter to me once. It was about lovers, but still. I couldn't imagine what it must be like for him to be in the room but not really be there. *How aware was he of what was happening? Was he in pain? Was he sad? Was he scared?* I was scared. I had never seen a dying person or sat with them for long periods. All of my grandparents were still alive, although I never met my dad's parents. I began to feel really overwhelmed, so I left his room and told Ted and Seth, who were in the sitting room, that I was going to get some air. It had all gotten to be too much, and I thought that's what people do in movies; when they get overwhelmed, they go outside for air. As I walked out the kitchen door into the garage, a woman with dark hair was walking in, and I recognized her; she was one of the social workers. She could see I was upset.

"Are you okay?" she said. She was genuinely concerned.

"Oh, um, my father's dying and . . . That's really hard. I just . . ." I was stammering. "Everyone is just waiting in the house . . . they said just a few days . . . and it feels like it's been two weeks. It's become too much, and I don't know what to do, and his partner says we should go in there, but when I do, it's so clear that he's not there, not totally conscious . . . so it's like he's not there . . ." I began sobbing, couldn't put words together anymore.

"All the things you are feeling right now are totally valid. And you have a right to feel them. And you can feel differently than other people." She continued, "You don't have to go back into that room again if you don't want to."

"I don't?" I was confused. "But Ted . . ."

"No. You can say goodbye to your dad in whatever way *you* want to. You don't have to stare at him, watching him wither away. What do you feel like doing?"

No one had asked me that in a long time.

"You get to choose how you honor him and do what's right for you and not anyone else."

Wait, what? I was twenty-four years old, my father was dying, and this was the first time anyone said that to me. Or it was the first time I listened. *Your feelings are totally valid.* I'm sure at least my therapist had said something like it before, but I was hearing it for the first time. Life-changing, really. It hit me like a ton of bricks. My sobbing turned to wailing. It was so incredibly profound. I was trying to wrap my head around it. I could have feelings. I could have feelings. I could have feelings. What I wanted mattered and was totally valid. I didn't have to do what everyone said I had to do. And I wasn't disrespecting my dad or anything like that. He knew I loved him. I knew he loved me. Sitting next to him as he lay barely conscious was not going to change any of that.

I walked back into the house to the living room. Ted was standing, and his face said it all.

"One of the workers was in there, turning him to change his diaper," he said, his voice cracking. "He took his last breath. He's gone." I walked over to hug him. He told me to go in and say goodbye. Even with my epiphany, I didn't question this directive. I just went in.

I walked over to my dad's bed, and his skin had turned an entirely different shade of gray, like a cement wall. I did not want this to be my last image of him. No life. But his eyes were open. Looking up at the ceiling. Far, far away. He had this red dot on the white of his left eye; it was the color of Judy Garland's lipstick. I drew my fingers over his eyelids to close them, like I have seen people do on TV. But it didn't work; they stayed open. Stubborn. For the first time in my life, I couldn't see into him. And he couldn't see my green eyes filled with tears.

Tristan Taormino

THE WOLF

The day my father died is both crystal clear in my mind and a complete blur. I felt sad, tired, numb, devastated. I felt relieved, then felt bad for feeling relieved. The hospice staff made arrangements for his body to go to the crematorium, which is what he wanted. I woke up the next morning in a daze. What do you do the day, or days, after your father dies? In the movies people go to their favorite restaurant, sit across from an empty seat, and make a toast. They wander down beaches, piers, trails, alone with their thoughts. They sit shiva. They have a wake. They go through the parent's belongings, find something that has tremendous meaning, look up and smile at the ceiling. They walk into an ordinary place, a gift shop or an ice cream parlor, notice something that reminds them of the parent, and they take it as a sign. They gather with the rest of their family members in the living room and bicker and laugh. I didn't want to get out of bed, but I did. Ted toasted me an English muffin. I ate it. I had no idea what to do.

Before the death certificate had been signed and recorded, Ted bought my friend Gabrielle an airline ticket to Portland with my father's credit card. "It will be good for you to have some support," he told me. "And when someone dies, the credit card company will forgive their debt."

I went into the bedroom to tell Ted that Seth was going to pick me up so we could go to the airport together. He was standing over the bed, looking lost.

"I. . . . . ." He paused. "I think I will go through some of your father's things, to. . . . . . get it done."

"Okay."

"Are there any pieces of clothing in particular that you want to keep?"

There were.

"You can grab them before you go."

I went back into the room where I slept in the sailor's berth and opened the mirrored sliding doors of the closet. My dad's clothes were a big part of how he expressed himself, bold and bright; they just screamed *him* to me, and I wanted to keep him with me. I found the black T-shirt with the word DIVA screen-printed in white on it that I had gifted him. A cement-colored Generra sweatshirt with a geometric pattern. The pair of plaid pajama pants he wore to the ER. A T-shirt of William Wegman's Weimaraner posed like a person sitting in a chair. A beautiful silk kimono. I laid them on the single bed.

A shower was too daunting, so I went to the bathroom and brushed my teeth. I changed out of my pajamas into sweatpants and a T-shirt. Seth let himself in the back door and walked into the kitchen.

"Hi," he said.

"Hi."

"We can leave whenever you are ready."

It was easy to spot Gabrielle at the airport with her wild, curly long hair dyed the color of an Irish setter. Gabrielle was my friend from high school who had kept my secret about my affair with the student teacher. We'd been through a lot together. I picked her because she was one of the most nurturing people my age that I knew. She would hug me. She would ground me. She was exactly what I needed. I made a list of folks for her to call to let them know my father had died. We went back to Seth's studio apartment, and I asked him if I could get in his bed. I just wanted the comfort of blankets and pillows. Gabrielle sat at the kitchen table and used Seth's phone, and I could see and hear her as she made the calls. She spoke in a quiet, respectful, understanding way; answered some people's questions; then hung up and did it again. Occasionally, after a call she'd relay a message to me of condolences or comfort from someone. *Now they know.*

We got Chinese takeout and ate quietly, and then Seth drove Gabrielle and me back to my father's place. When we came in, I introduced Gabrielle to Ted, and she gave him one of her warm smiles. "I am so sorry for your loss," she told him, and she meant it.

"Gabrielle made all the phone calls for me today," I said.

"I'm going to go home unless anyone needs me," said Seth. He and Ted exchanged a look, and he was off.

I walked back to the guest room to put my purse down, and the doors to the closet were open. Half the clothes were gone, and a series of empty hangers remained. Gabrielle saw it on my face right away: I was shocked.

I walked back out to the living room, shaken.

"Where are all his clothes?" I asked, not quite sure what was going on.

"I took them to Goodwill. Just the clothes and some other stuff," said Ted, matter-of-factly.

I had assumed when he said he was going to go through some things, he was going to go through them, not *get rid of them all that day*. I was confused and pissed off.

"Um. . . . . ." I wasn't sure exactly what to say. "I guess I thought it would be a process, like a few days or something." I looked back at my bed to make sure the things I had picked were still there, and I saw immediately what was missing: the wolf. The night before, I'd grabbed the wolf from their room and slept with it like a child.

"Where is the wolf???" I knew I sounded panicked and really fucking irrational.

"Oh," he replied, "I didn't know you wanted that, I thought it was just the clothes. The wolf went to Goodwill too."

I burst into tears. Gabrielle looked really uncomfortable. "I—I—" No other words formed. I couldn't believe it.

"I really want the wolf. I *need* the wolf."

"But I already gave it to Goodwill."

"Then. Get. It. Back," I said with some force. Again, irrational.

"Oh. . . . . . kay?" he said like it was a question. "I will try to do that." He looked inconvenienced as he left the room.

Gabrielle walked over and hugged me tightly. She didn't judge me or try to talk me out of it, she just held me.

"We will work it out," she said, reassuringly. I heard the back door open. *Ted better get me that goddamned wolf.*

"What the fuck?" I yelled as I pulled away from her, wiping the tears with my sleeve. "Who just donates shit the day after someone dies? Am I being unreasonable here? He didn't tell me he was going to just round up whatever and get rid of it today."

"It does seem kinda fast," said Gabrielle. "I'm not sure why—"

I interrupted her thought. "I wanted to go through his clothes one more time. I did it this morning, but I didn't know that was like my last chance ever to go through them!"

"Yeah" was all she said. "Well, show me what you did keep."

About an hour later, Ted returned with the wolf; he said they hadn't processed the donation yet, so it was in one of the garbage bags he'd dropped off. I had the wolf. It would all be okay. Then the phone rang. No one moved right away to get it. Gabrielle asked if she should. Ted went to the wall, picked it up, and said hello.

"Hi, Judy," he said. It was my mother.

"Of course," he said, then handed the phone to me and walked out.

"Hi, Mom," I said.

"Hi, sweetie." She sounded sort of muffled. "How are you?"

"I'm okay."

"So, honey, I have some bad news that I have to tell you." She paused, and I thought I heard her voice crack like she was crying. I didn't completely recognize it because she so rarely cried.

"Poppie has died."

Poppie, my grandfather, her father.

"What?" My head shook in disbelief.

"The independent living facility called. He didn't go to breakfast, so they knocked on his door at lunchtime. He didn't answer. They got the key and found him. It appears that he just died naturally in his sleep. Probably his heart."

She paused and waited for me to say something. I didn't, so she continued.

"I'm not sure what to say. This is a lot, I realize. The funeral is on Friday. I think you should come home for it."

Friday was two days away.

"Right," I said.

"I am making all the arrangements because, of course, your uncles are completely useless in the situation. They'll show up, they just won't do anything to make it happen. There will be a church service, and he will be buried at St. John's Cemetery in Syosset. He and Grammy already have plots there. You can bring someone if you'd like, a friend or something."

"Right," I said again, nodding but still in disbelief.

"The reception. . . . . . well, I am still trying to figure out the reception," she said, slightly exasperated. I didn't think to offer *her* condolences.

"Okay," I said. "I will call you with my flight info." I hung up.

Gabrielle said, "Tristan? What's wrong?"

My grandfather was one of those tough-as-nails WASPs, in near-perfect health at eighty-eight. A year after my grandmother went into a full-time care home because of her Alzheimer's, the family worried about him all alone in the house, so my mom and uncles pitched the idea of moving him to assisted living. The kind where folks are pretty independent but if something happens there is a nurse on duty. He really didn't want to part with his beloved rose garden, which he tended every day, but he understood. Forever the pragmatist, he didn't put up a fight. My mom visited him regularly there. In fact, she had just had lunch with him four days before he died. The day before he died, he did his favorite thing: played nine holes of golf. He ate dinner and went to bed and never woke up. It sounded like a wonderful death. No struggle, no pain.

"My grandfather died," I said to Gabrielle. She looked stunned. "The funeral is Friday. I have to go home."

POPPIE

I would be taking my father's ashes, so the crematorium put a rush on his remains (a weird request we had to make), and the next morning I got on a plane to New York carrying a small cardboard box with his ashes in a thick plastic bag inside. Greg picked me up at JFK in his beat-up Volvo and took me home to drop my stuff off and get changed. A few people were available last minute to go with me, so Greg; his boyfriend, also Greg; and a newish friend, Coral, drove out to Long Island. We got out of the car at the cemetery like the ragtag bunch we were. I was the tin man in our foursome, empty and armored. Coral, who stood out with her flaming Manic Panic red hair and black vintage crepe dress, grabbed my hand as we walked to the grave. I saw my mom. She looked awful. She caught my eye but then turned her attention elsewhere: there was a photographer behind a tree attempting to get a photo of Uncle Tom (who not only is famous but famously eludes the media). She dealt with that guy summarily, then walked back and hugged me.

"Well, there was bound to be at least one asshole trying to get a photo of Tom. Tom is, of course, oblivious, but I took care of it. Hi, hon. I'm so sorry," she said. "Thank you for coming." Her eyes welled up, and we hugged.

My small family had assembled, something we usually did only for holidays. On Thanksgiving, Christmas, Easter, Mother's Day, and Father's Day, we would all get together at Gram and Poppie's house in East Norwich to eat a meal and exchange gifts. The family tradition was to go to a nice restaurant right around the corner called Rothmann's. It was founded in the early 1900s, and big stars like Elizabeth Taylor, Bob Hope, and Jackie O were said to have dined there. My grandfather picked up the tab.

There was a fancy dining room with beautiful goldenrod linens on the tables and brocade curtains, but we ate there only once or twice. Most often, they sat the ten of us in the dark bar at a long table where people carved their initials and messages into the wood. There was a giant stuffed moose head on the wall that I was terrified of as a child. The menu never changed from year to year: roasted turkey with stuffing, prime rib, glazed ham with pineapple, lamb accompanied by mint jelly, Dover sole. I loved the way the hunter green mint jelly glistened, but I never wanted to eat a lamb. At Rothmann's, we were treated like family since my grandparents were regulars, and the staff was attentive and gracious. (After I worked in food service at an expensive restaurant in my hometown, I knew what hell it was to work on a holiday with big parties and a packed house.)

Family members were warm enough and pleasant at these get-togethers, but we weren't connected in any real way except by my grandparents. We caught each other up on recent events, gave each other gifts without the slightest hint of what anyone might actually want (I am looking at you, baby-pink acrylic sweater). There wasn't necessarily arguing, teasing, or other things I saw families do on TV. No one was having deep conversations like on *This Is Us*. There were no challenges where we all pulled together and triumphed. No tearful lessons that ended in us all feeling closer. I always drank a Shirley Temple. My grandmother and Uncle John had a few too many scotches and would often fight near the end of the meal. We came, we departed, we returned for the next holiday.

I did have a connection with my cousin Kara, who was only a year older than me, and when we were young, we used to go off by ourselves to play "Skate," our own made-up game about a pair of tough detective ladies in shiny pants on roller skates; think *Cagney and Lacey* street smarts with the glamor of *Charlie's Angels*. We investigated, followed bad guys, and triumphed by solving the crime. The only other person whom I felt related to was Uncle Tom.

At Poppie's funeral, the fact that my grandmother was alive but not there was strange. When she was well, she was still cranky most of the time and never afraid to say what was on her mind. She was not afraid of expressing her anger. She lost her edge as she grew older. She spent her days sitting in her favorite place—an old-fashioned chair with flowery upholstery and a squishy cushion—watching soap operas. She was really into them, never missed an episode, but whenever you'd ask her about what was happening on *Days of*

Our Lives, she couldn't tell you anything. Or she wouldn't. I wondered what she would say if she gave a eulogy.

Poppie was the foil to my grandmother's fussiness and ill temper: he was steady, reserved, almost presidential, actually. He looked you in the eye when you spoke, and he was interested in what you had to say. He had one glass eye from an accident when he was cutting a new line for the clothesline in the backyard. He missed the rope, and the knife went straight into his eye.

But there was no eulogy; they let the priest do most of the talking.

After my grandfather died, the mandatory Pynchon family holiday visits ceased immediately. His funeral was the last time I saw my two uncles, my aunt, and my cousins all together. No one of this small group, just two generations totaling ten people, wanted to carry on the tradition. The communication dispersed with the get-togethers. I had no reason to call any of them, except occasionally cousin Kara and Uncle Tom. We never saw each other. My mother kept in touch with her brothers on the phone and with rare visits, but mostly this idea of family just went away. We had never felt that connected as a whole together, but I missed them. My Uncle Tom was the closest to me, and we had much in common; I loved our conversations where he treated me like a grown-up and let me ramble on about lesbian s/m, queer erotic magazines, all the bizarre happenings in pop culture. Shocking us all, including the reclusive man himself, he got married, and I really liked his new wife, who was also his literary agent. She was smart, direct, put-together. But she didn't seem so fond of me, my mother, or the rest of the family. Besides, it's easier to blame her than examine what broke the already fragile ties between my uncle and me. We still send each other birthday cards each year. He never was a people person and preferred solitude to most things. Except for my mom, and occasional cards from Kara, my family simply vanished.

Tristan Taormino

FALLOUT

Shortly after the death of my father and my mother's father, I moved out of the Christians' brownstone and six blocks away to a two-bedroom apartment on the south side of Williamsburg. Gabrielle, the first friend I saw after my dad's death, moved in with me. She was going to Hunter College and needed a place to live, but some part of me wondered if she wanted to keep an eye on me.

Gabrielle picked up my mail from Grand Central Station, where I had a mailbox that I opened when my job was around the corner. One day she brought home a thick, stiff white envelope with the name Winston Wilde embossed in navy blue at the top. He was the dapper man I'd met at my graduation, with whom I'd corresponded a few times. I felt an almost inexplicable connection with him. Five months earlier, he had lost his partner, the beloved writer Paul Monette, to AIDS. I sent him a condolence card, but I didn't know what to say. To me, he wrote:

I would never presume to at all be able to come close to replacing your father. But may I propose to sometimes be your Daddy. When you need a Daddy or want a Daddy, I would be honored to be that for you, Tristan. . . . I am holding you in my arms while you cry at my breast, and I'm rocking you. You are a beautiful woman and a fine daughter.

The tears welled up, and I inhaled a short breath. No one in my own family had written such moving, special words in the wake of my father's death. I called him, and we talked about love, grief, this awful plague. He again offered to be what would see us through: Winston wanted to be my queer family, my chosen family, and that was exactly what I needed.

The following October, right around my dad's birthday, we held a memorial service in his honor in Portland. Seth, Ted, and I curated a selection of speakers, readings of his work, and clips from some of the short films he made. We called the service Fallout, the title of one of the films he made with Seth. I was the final reader, and as I stood in front of people who knew him and loved him in the community room of the YMCA, I struggled to keep it together. I read his essay about fighting the United Way for same-sex partner benefits, a poem he wrote to a lover who left him, and one of the first stories in his memoir. Page 6:

1944 Mirror

Late morning, and I am in my parents' bedroom.

Their bedroom set is heavy mahogany with noisy brass handles. There is no dust on the furniture. It is not allowed. On the shiny reddish surface of the dresser drawers, shadow clouds appear and disappear.

The windows are open, and the Venetian blinds have been pulled up, both of them leveled at the same white slat. There are identical twins everywhere: end tables, lamps, starched doilies, ashtrays, picture frames, perfume atomizers.

There is a naked man on the bed with me. I am naked, too; a crawling, naked Scorpio. I don't know who the man is. It does not matter. There is no danger.

Over the dresser there is a large mirror, and it captures and reflects the two of us.

I have no words. No ideas. I feel safe. I am safe. And it is this memory of safety that I will search for.

Then we played a video clip from his short film *Shelter*. He sits against a red wall, facing the camera and wearing a leather jacket, and talks about always telling the truth.

A few years ago, I went to visit my friends—the ones who got married in New Hampshire, giving me the chance to visit the church I once lived in—at their railroad apartment in Red Hook. This once forgotten part of Brooklyn had gentrified: buildings were rehabbed, cute cafés popped up, the streets were cleaner, and you could buy a microbrew ginger beer for $4.95 at the bodega. I walked around the neighborhood and thought about the story I had read at my dad's memorial. My wandering led me to a set of projects that looked exactly like the ones where my father grew up: tall, solid, and imposing on the outside; all high-gloss beige paint and nondescript on the inside, accessible because the front door was propped open with a brick. I didn't have to imagine what his life was like in those early years: I have his own words. Page 24:

I heard a commotion. At first I thought it was static from the radio, but then I heard a familiar voice say, "Shut that fucking music off!" Someone turned the radio off.

In one hopeless moment, I leapt off the bed and did a scrunched-up somersault, pulling the foxy slip over my head as I landed. I jammed the slip under the dresser, and I stumbled, bare-assed, into the hallway. The sun was not as bright as our hallway that day. I was a leap away from the bathroom when my mother grabbed me by the arm and knocked me against the wall. My Aunt Pat yelled, "Kitty, stop it!" My mother's neck was flushed and taut, and her eyes were primitive.

"Kitty, you've got to calm down!"

"Mind your own business, Pat!"

She smacked my face. Then she held both of her open hands up between us and began to pound her own forehead with them. I slid to the floor.

"Get up! What have you done? Are you crazy? What are you doing? Get up!"

She kicked me, and I jumped up.

"Kitty, please!"

"No!"

I ran into my room. She was right behind me. She pushed me down on the bed.

"What did you do last Monday?"

"What? Why?"

She was on the bed now, and she punched my pillow and hit me again.

"Where were you last Monday? Did you go down to the main office?"

"I don't understand. . . . . I. . . . ."

She shoved me against the creamy vinyl headboard.

"Kitty, you're being ridiculous! You know he was there. Why don't you . . ."

"Shut up, Pat!"

My mother raised her hand and snapped it into a fist, but as she came at me, my Aunt Pat grabbed her arm, and I fell off the bed.

Fallout

"Billy Boy, where were you on Monday? I'll take care of this, Pat! Stay out of it!"

My aunt made a helpless gesture and looked away.

"Where were you on Monday?"

"I don't know!"

"Don't lie to me! Tell me the truth!"

She pulled me up off the floor and pushed me into a chair.

"I was at Aunt Tessie's!"

"You're lying!"

"No. . . . . .I was at Aunt Tessie's. . . . . .oh no. . . . .
. yes. . . . . .and then I went swimming. . . . . .I was at the pool. .
. . . . .I told you. . . . ."

"We have to move! They gave us our eviction notice! We have to move in thirty days, all because of you!"

"Why? What did I do?"

"Did you go to the main office on Monday?"

"Monday. . . . . .I. . . . ."

"Monday!"

"I went swimming. . . . ."

"Last Monday!"

"Yes! Yes, I did go down there! I told you I forgot my key. I had to get my bathing suit. Don't you remember? I told you! They were nice to me. That colored lady with the rhinestone glasses; she was so nice. I wanted to go swimming. I told you."

"That colored lady with the stupid fucking glasses is a fucking bitch!"

"Why? Why?"

"You told her I was at work!"

"Yes, I did!"

She slapped me twice.

"Kitty, he didn't know."

I started screaming, and the phone started ringing, and my Aunt Pat ran to answer it.

"She asked me where you were. I told her you were at work. I told her the truth."

"You little rat! You got us in trouble!"

My Aunt Pat yelled, "It's Nino! He wants to know if you want him to bring home some Chinks!"

"Fuck Chinks and fuck him, too! Hang up the phone!"

My mother sat on my bed and cried.

Getting and keeping an apartment in the Red Hook project was based on income. My mother was working illegally, stashing her salary so we could all make the getaway to suburbia. They were afraid of the coloreds. The Puerto Ricans were dirty and noisy. And there were too many juvenile delinquents being found on the roof, dead from dope. We had to escape.

I learned one thing that day. Telling the truth could be hazardous to your health.

It's difficult to read and imagine the terror he felt. Shortly after he came out, he stopped speaking to his entire family and never looked back. In his memoir he wrote about the last time he saw his parents; there was a big blowup, and he vowed to never return as he drove home with my mom. Page 128:

We both knew it was inevitable. There was no other way. Not with my parents. We both knew that if I wanted to grow up, if I wanted to get well, if I wanted to survive, if I wanted to be myself (a frightening possibility), I had to stop having contact with them. I was tired and depressed, and I kept telling myself that if I was going to be crazy, I wanted to be crazy on my own terms.

I appreciate that he tried to cut out the cancer: it was his rejection of Catholicism, heterosexism, misogyny, racism, and homophobia as much as it was a turning away from Kitty, Nino, Patsy, Jodie, Bubby, and the rest of them. He wanted to wash off all their shit and start anew. He felt confident in the absolute denouncement of his family of origin, but I sensed a deeply buried longing to belong to a family. He had a wandering spirit eager to move on to the next city, *and* he was desperately looking for somewhere to settle and feel at home. He carried intense shame about his sexuality plus unadulterated pride about who he had become.

The trauma, the loss, the struggles are imprinted on my DNA. Perhaps what's most painful when I read my father's writing is to reflect on the ways in which the cycle has repeated itself. He and I were both abandoned by our fathers, he had manic episodes like his mother, and my depression is third generation. Because he was often confused growing up about what was true and what was real, he had a dogged dedication to honesty and rejected those who couldn't meet his unyielding expectations. I am trying to intervene in a cycle that I didn't create but that is ultimately a part of me. Like for him, much of my pain, wounds, and baggage remains unhealed. I work every day to be compassionate with myself and others. Some days I do better than others. *I'm trying my hardest, Dad.*

There is a meme that pops up on my social media feed from time to time. It's self-helpy, but it hits me between the eyes: a quote from therapist Stephi

Wagner: "Pain travels through families until someone is ready to feel it." I am my queer father's daughter. I struggle with my own demons and darkness; they are different from his, formidable nonetheless. There was no gay bashing, no toxic gender policing, no fits or fists from my mother. But I felt disconnected from the people around me because I felt things so deeply. It took a lot of time and years of therapy for me to uncover the roots of my insecurity, perfectionism, fear, and unworthiness. There was (is) empty space where a full-time parent, protector, and caregiver would have been, and I filled it with self-blame. I didn't have a fully formed brain or any language when my family broke apart. No one gave me an explanation that I remember. He left because I wasn't enough for him to stay. This knowing bored into my soul and lived in my unconscious and my body for decades, until I realized, acknowledged, and began to work through it. I am still working through it.

I wish the fallout of his death had ended with that memorial service. I wish this part had a happy ending. A resolved ending. A resolved beginning? But there was one more secret to be revealed after Dad died. I remember it happened in the weeks right after his death, but when I fact-checked the timeline with letters, it turns out it was seven months later. Time is so sped up, slowed down, fractured, and abstract during grief and depression—almost nothing about that time is absolutely certain. Ted sent me a breezy, chatty email with this in the final paragraph: "Without really thinking about it a whole lot, Seth and I have become a couple (of sorts) over the last couple months. We actually find ourselves making future plans together." Those plans included selling the condo and moving to Chicago. The revelation was abrupt and hit me hard; it also left me feeling that I didn't have the complete picture. I was missing something.

I don't remember when or if the next reveal came. Toward the end of his life, I think my father, Ted, and Seth had been in a triad relationship, but no one bothered to tell me that crucial piece of information, which would have been good to know. I flashed back to that early morning when I called Seth in a panic after I found my father on the floor bleeding and he drove us to the ER. Then to his studio apartment the day after my dad died, where Gabrielle made phone calls as I lay in Seth's bed and sobbed. I thought Seth was mourning a close friend, but he was, in fact, grieving the loss of his lover. I felt stupid. I felt betrayed. I felt shut out. *Why didn't they tell me?* The excuse that I was a child, perhaps used to justify no one telling me my father was gay, didn't

Tristan Taormino

work this time. It couldn't have been fear of judgment; I was his daughter who was into radical sex who'd been in openly nonmonogamous relationships. I still don't know why, and no one has offered any explanations. I was so sure of this after he died. Now I think I may have made up the triad part. I can't sort it out in my brain and have no one to confirm or deny it.

After I found out about Ted and Seth's relationship, the plan was that the two remaining lovers would leave Portland behind to begin again. In fact, when I got that news, the condo was already on the market. I was flooded with emotions. Decisions and plans had been made without me. I fixated on my dad's stuff again. *What would happen to all of his things?* They would be packed to go to Chicago. A rush of loss came over me. I wouldn't be able to visit his home. I wouldn't have access to these pieces of him. I couldn't let Ted take all that my dad left behind. I was Bill Taormino's daughter for twenty-four years, and his partner of less than four years was taking him away from me. I told someone about the situation, and they had a recommendation, which I followed: get a lawyer.

I could go on about the minutiae of it all, but it doesn't matter now. What followed was a civil negotiation between our two lawyers over the "estate." What my dad left behind was a collection of memories in the form of what a paralegal denoted as "miscellaneous." Photo albums, journals, letters. His CD and VHS collection. Artwork of sentimental value. Furniture that had traveled from P-town to Seattle to Portland, Oregon, to Maine. Pages and pages of his writing. A small brass Boston terrier figurine, a round box with a horse head carved into the top, an old Kodak Brownie Hawkeye movie camera, a small knit bag with rocks in it, three silver bracelets, an Art Deco tie clip, a heavy white stone head of Buddhist female deity Tara, a small map of Red Hook in a tacky gold frame, a baby-blue rosary from drag performer Jimmy James, a clay head I made in kindergarten with holes poked in it for the eyes and a too-wide smile. In that moment I believed it was all I had left of him. Sometimes I still believe that.

"Good news!" my lawyer said on the phone. "Ted agreed to let you have every single thing that belonged to your dad before their partnership. There is just one..."

Caveat: that I sign a legal agreement stating that I would never have any contact with him again. There was one thing my father had told us he wanted at the end of this life, besides a morphine drip: for us to have a relationship that outlived him, for us to remain a family. *Did I agonize over it?* I signed it. I drove up from New York and met a moving van at the condo. Ted sent his identical twin brother as his representative to supervise the packing. So I saw a man that looked remarkably like him, and that was painful, but I would never see Ted again. My stepfather, surrogate father, other father, was gone too.

When I was thirty, for several months I decided I wanted to have kids. I think it was some sort of dramatic hormonal spike that caused me to want to breed, but it passed, thankfully, because I never felt it again. I even asked Dalton, from our beach-house days, if he'd donate sperm. His answer: no. It's just as well. I don't think parenting is one of my callings. And I don't want the legacy of pain or the mental health issues to be passed on yet again, to damage and wound a new set of people. I am an only child, so this particular line of Pynchon-Taorminos (and Clancys, really, whom I know very little about) stops with me. I am happy to leave behind words, images, and ideas for future generations. The queers will inherit them.

Tristan Taormino

A NIGHT LIKE THIS

When I returned to Brooklyn after my father died, I was lost. I needed to pay the rent, so I started working part-time as a receptionist for an architecture firm near the Javitz Center. I needed to get out of bed, wash my hair, and put on a skirt and blouse to fulfill the majority of the job's requirements. But it started to get harder and harder. After several months I simply didn't show up for work. They left voicemail messages for me. I never called back.

I slept all the time. It took me two hours to psych myself up to get out of bed to take a few sips of ginger ale. It took even longer for me to leave the house, so I put newspapers down in the kitchen for Reggie Love to pee on. No food—not a slice of pizza from Ninth Street, an egg-and-cheese sandwich from Bergen Bagels, or Planet Thailand's peanut curry—was appetizing. Brushing my teeth was out of the question because it required too much energy. Going out felt impossible at first and then terrifying. *No one can see me like this.* I listened to the Cure and the Smiths from my high school days. My skin grew paler, and the circles under my eyes darker, so I stopped looking in the mirror. I played scenes over in my head obsessively: the blowup before my hospitalization, my father dead in his bed in hospice, movers hauling boxes out of the condo as the Ted doppelgänger looked on. *Did he die one month ago or six months ago? I am losing track of time.* My thinking was fuzzy, and I couldn't concentrate on any one thing. I cried spontaneously and often. Friends from college came to visit for the weekend but abruptly left after one day. *I am too much.* My mom checked in, and I told her I was fine, which she accepted at face value.

When I'm depressed, the depression subsumes my personhood. A level of exhaustion consumes every cell, and I only have the energy to keep breathing, which feels hard. My body doesn't want to move. The bed is both soothing and uncomfortable. Noises startle me, and my skin feels hypersensitive. The more I sleep, the more tired I get, the less satisfying the sleep is. I don't need to feed myself if I am not a person. Depression feels inevitable, all-encompassing, and permanent.

In the most common recurring nightmare I have (besides the one where I am in a play but have never read the script), I am leaving someplace and going somewhere else. The problem is I have a lot of stuff, I don't have enough bags or boxes to carry it, and I keep losing track of things that are important to me. I begin to bargain: What can I leave behind, what can I come back to get (knowing I can't come back)? When I think I've packed all I can, something appears that's necessary but impossible to take with me. Where are the moats with sharks, the fire-breathing dragons, and the esoteric symbolism? The baggage in my life is represented by actual baggage. What a failure of imagination for my unconscious.

I canceled plans at the last minute because I couldn't face spending time with anyone. I didn't return phone calls, convinced I was a bummer to talk to. As the city whizzed by like a rollercoaster, I was stuck at the top of the Ferris wheel, dangling in the air, with no way down. No one could reach me. I couldn't reach me. The me I knew had evaporated, and a gray outline of her body was left in my bed. I turned inward, but there was no *there* there. *Is this what Ruth's sister felt like before her suicide? I don't have a strong drive to kill myself, but I definitely do not want to be alive. Anything but alive.*

I received condolence cards from so many wonderful people in my life. Invitations to take a break from grieving. They wrote:

You are surrounded by people who love you.

You'll always be in my heart.

I know you will use your courage to teach and inspire those around you.

You're so strong and resilient.

Tristan Taormino

You can only be what you are.

Soon people communicated other sentiments:

You're fired.

You really need to get your shit together.

You don't look well. When was the last time you ate something?

I can't take care of your feelings and mine.

You might question whether your feelings of abandonment are well founded.

We were all in our twenties. What did anyone know about grief?

You are using your dad's death as an excuse to not be there for me and your other friends.

That, from my friend Greg, hurt the worst. Haunts me. I couldn't focus on the supportive ones. I hear his words so clearly, even twenty-five years later. *I'm making excuses.*

Pain can debilitate me, and it does. It knocks me over; it drowns me; it's all I can think about. But sometimes it can be a comfort. I wanted more pain. Squid had full tattoo sleeves on both her arms, short black spiked hair, and thick eyeliner, and her lips were never without lipstick. She was the bass player of an all-girl punk rock band, the Lunachicks, and a tattoo artist at Venus Modern Body Arts in the East Village. I thought she was badass. She had done a sharp barbwire design on my arm in 1993, and I returned to her for a memorial tattoo for my dad. I wanted to get a scorpion in the geometric tribal design that was popular at the time. He was a Scorpio, and all the clichés of that astrological sign really did fit him: intense, passionate, turbulent, secretive. I didn't specify the size of the tattoo I wanted, but I was picturing something that would fit in the palm of my hand. When Squid showed me her sketch, it was big enough to cover nearly my entire thigh. She placed it so the black claws of the scorpion creep toward the start of pubic hair at my bikini line and the long, segmented tail wraps around my thigh, ending just below my butt cheek. I saw her vision and went with it. This was a major step up from the first tattoo she gave me, and it took multiple sittings. But I had suffered, and physical pain did not scare me. The needle bore into my skin like sex: my brain took a break, my body acquiesced, and the endorphins flowed. I knew I could take it. She finished it on the kitchen table in her apartment in Brooklyn. For something permanently etched into my flesh, it offered only temporary reprieve from the ache of the loss I felt.

Tristan Taormino

PUCKER UP

oral, the girl who came to my grandfather's funeral, called me when she returned to New York after being on tour as a backup dancer for avant-garde performance artist Kembra Pfahler and her band, the Voluptuous Horror of Karen Black. It took everything I had to leave the house and meet her at a café in Brooklyn, but I did because she intrigued me. She sauntered in, her small frame dressed in a tight T-shirt that rode up on her round belly and wearing the requisite dyke accessory: a leather wallet in her back pocket with a chain attached to the loop in her jeans. Her brown eyes and smile were mischievous. Her hair was no longer fire-engine red but a flaming orange. Coral couldn't and didn't want to camouflage herself.

"Hey, I brought you something back from the road," she said, as she presented me with a vinyl pink sparkly collar wrapped in newspaper. I was a little confused. *Is she kinky and this is an overture from a dominant? Or is this just a cool thing to wear?* When we had sex that night, blue body paint and glitter circled her armpits, left over from her final show, where her wardrobe consisted of a G-string and tall boots. She was playful and uninhibited in bed, she loved to strap on a dick, and I could make her come like a wild woman. Her style wasn't explicitly butch, but she had an energy that drew me in. Her tough punk rock look masked a softness, a kindness, that made me think she wouldn't hurt me. She was a writer, a disciple and friend of Kathy Acker, and she told me her favorite things to write about were anal sex and death. It was inevitable.

I was beginning to think of myself as a writer too. I had penned my first piece of erotica in college and continued to write after I graduated. Although I called them fiction, they were basically true stories about my sex life, names and details changed and all that. The genre gave me so much freedom to revisit the power dynamics and scenarios I co-created with my lovers and examine the inner workings of my own desires. Good lesbian sex writing was hard to find, but I did in books published by queer presses like Firebrand, Naiad, and Alyson and short-lived magazines like *Brat Attack* and *Venus Infers*. A Different Light, the queer bookstore, was not only a place to find these gems but a central hub of a young queer literary scene, along with spoken-word events downtown. I read my work at places like Meow Mix, the lesbian bar on the Lower East Side, alongside poets like Gerry Gomez Pearlberg and Emanuel Xavier. Many queer writers were getting their words into the world through homemade chapbooks and zines. Zines were at their height in the 1990s, bold, in-your-face photocopied booklets of rantings, poetry, essays, cut-and-paste art collages. If you happened to be fucking some cute queer at Kinko's, then you could get your zine printed for free.

Zines were usually authored by a single person, but I believed that the many radical voices I heard on mics at crowded bars deserved a bigger platform. More queer writers were being published than ever before, but there was a limit to what mainstream publishers were willing to print. The more sex in your writing, the fewer options you had to publish it. This larger recognition for documenting our lives and our histories was happening alongside a LGBT civil rights movement that was gaining some momentum. *The straight world is beginning to recognize us, to tolerate us. This could be the road to ending discrimination against us. Don't push it.*

But I wanted to push it. I wanted to amplify the voices of perverts. I began crafting the idea for a zine called *Pucker Up*. Tagline: the zine with a mouth that's not afraid to use it. I made a list of all the writers whose work I loved, who really spoke to my soul, and I reached out and asked them to submit. Coral was the designer and became my collaborator on many aspects of it. It grew to sixty-four pages. It was difficult to find a printer who didn't blink an eye at a photo of a woman in a strap-on grinding against a man's chest or the words FAGGOT RANT and DIABOLICAL CLITS in sixty-point font. I paid for it with the credit card I had gotten through a glossy flyer I received in my mailbox at Wesleyan in 1993. One of my dad's poems appeared in the inaugural issue:

Figure 35.1 Photoshoot with famed fetish photographer Richard Kern, New York City, 1996. This image appears in his book *New York Girls*.

It has been two years
since we have been together
really together
In fact
it's more like three years
but who's counting?
I am inside this other man
on my back
having safe?
safer?
sex
I am distracted
numb
when suddenly
the Dave and Bill slide show begins
Hellos
Good byes
Reconciliations
Pumping
spiraling
ending
And as this other man
begins to shoot on my chest
I realize he is not on me
it is you he is riding
You
You are miles away
running
your memories buried
and yet
you give this stranger
such pleasure
Was it good for you?

Tristan Taormino

ANAL SEX MADE ME

What's the one topic in sexuality that you're most passionate about? That question began a call for book proposals from Felice Newman and Frédérique Delacoste, the lesbian cofounders of indie, queer Cleis Press. I first met them when they embraced my pitch to edit a new anthology, *Best Lesbian Erotica*, which they began publishing annually in 1996. They wanted to start a series of sex-education guides, but unlike the popular encyclopedia-like tomes that covered everything from masturbation to positions, they were interested in books that focused on one specific topic. I was ready to explore what it meant to uncloak my experiences and ideas; I wanted to write in my own voice and be a guide for others. Plus, I needed a project. I knew immediately what I would pitch. A book I wished I had on my own bookshelf. A book about a subject that my friends rarely talked about, even though we knew everything else about each other's sex lives. A subject about which only one book existed; otherwise, it was covered in a paragraph or two in the sex manuals and some articles written mostly by men and a handful of leatherdykes. I drafted a proposal for *The Ultimate Guide to Anal Sex for Women* and sent it off.

Then I thought about it in some more depth. Could I write an entire book? Did I even have the time? A higher dose of Zoloft and that inherited work ethic propelled me back into the workforce full-time in a well-paying job at a tech start-up. In my interview I showed my future boss a copy of *Pucker Up* and argued that I had a wide set of marketing skills that could be applied to anything; unbelievably, he agreed. But developing campaigns to get people to buy online advertising was not my passion. Writing and anal sex were my passions. I had a lot to say, and experiences to share. Most of what I had learned came from gay men who were open to talking about anal sex, passing down wisdom, and creating community-based guides as a result of the AIDS crisis. But what did I know about anorectal anatomy and the science of STIs? *I will research.* The publishers were probably expecting to launch the series with something a little more run-of-the-mill, like oral sex, so anal would be too out there. I was basically an unknown writer. Would anyone read it? Was anyone as enthusiastic about it as I was?

I set my expectations to "no way," and then I got the email: not only did Cleis want it, but my book would kick off the whole series. Wow wow wow wow wow wow. *Now I have to write a book.* I genuinely loved the process and being so busy further drew me out of my depression. I got to work with one of my favorite artists to do illustrations, a dyke named Fish who drew comics. Fish drew the sexiest line drawings, my favorite being a woman with a strap-on fucking a man. *Pegging* didn't exist in the vernacular yet, but that didn't stop me from writing about it. No advice on grief I've read suggests it, but writing a book about anal sex gave me purpose. It brought joy to my life. I had also discovered a coping mechanism to avoid grief. Work has served many purposes throughout my life—to express myself, to forge new worlds, to pay the bills. But it was also something I had control over to compensate for my fear of loss, a distraction from the darkness swirling inside me. Capitalism can be a hell of a drug if you know how to use it.

In December 1997 UPS delivered a box of twenty copies to my apartment. I turned the lavender cover of the slim volume and read the introduction:

Yes, I admit it—I love anal sex. The first time someone put a finger in my butt, I almost went crazy from the pleasure. The sensations I experienced were so intense, incredible, and heavenly that it was mind-blowing. I felt high from the experience, and I couldn't wait to do it again. The first time I put my finger in someone else's butt, the results were just as fabulous—I felt entrusted with my partner's deepest vulnerabilities, in awe of the ecstatic pleasure I could give.

I cried with joy. I was giddy. I had written a book, and it was there in my hands. I had done what my uncle had done and what my father would have loved to do.

The *New York Times* reviewed my uncle's books, but mine was not one that lent itself to traditional types of publicity. There would be no big poster in the window of Barnes and Noble—"Meet author Tristan Taormino reading from her debut book *The Ultimate Guide to Anal Sex for Women*"—not even the Astor Place location near NYU. When I met with salespeople from the distributor who pitched titles to bookstore buyers, they were frank:

"I am afraid to even utter the title of the book."

"Yes, the title and cover are so . . . racy." The cover featured only text, with the word *anal* in the lightest color, a pale yellow. Cleis was all in to support it, but there were still gatekeepers and sex phobia to get through.

"I don't believe that anyone will walk up to the counter at their local bookshop with this. They would be too embarrassed," said one rep. "And this whole 'buying books online' thing—we don't even know if that's going to pan out."

It was time to put my self-taught marketing skills to work. First: review copies. *How can I get people who receive dozens of books to notice mine?* My friend Kim Airs, who owned the feminist sex shop Grand Opening in Brookline, Massachusetts, sold me fifteen purple jelly butt plugs at the wholesale price. Each sparkly purple plug was shrink-wrapped to a bright blue cardboard backing, to which I affixed the title of the book, printed on sticker paper. I sent the butt plugs with review copies of the book. Drag king Lizerace performed at the launch party at Acme Underground.

My friend Don at my day job encouraged me to mail a copy to someone notorious for being obsessed with anal: Howard Stern, who recorded his popular radio show at the headquarters of K-Rock on Fifty-Seventh Street, a three-block walk from where we worked. I had nothing to lose. A week later, a producer named Gary called to book me on the show. I told my publishers immediately, and they were over the moon. It was not only my first radio show but my first mainstream media appearance.

"We still have no idea which bookstores are going to carry it. But we have a 1-800 number for mail orders, so you should give that out on-air," said Felice. This was unexplored exposure for them too. "We'll have to get to the office very early to sync up with East Coast time. But we will answer those calls."

Don prepped me (he'd listened to every single episode) and went with me to meet his idol. I knew Howard liked to shock and embarrass his guests by saying outrageous things that tripped up even porn stars. The studio was dark, and Gary pointed to a rolling office chair and adjusted the mic near my mouth. Seated across from me, there he was: the lanky man with long, curly hair wearing tinted glasses. He said hello, but not much else, and then someone said, "Back on in 5, 4, 3 . . ." Howard fired away with the questions, and I held strong, answering each one matter-of-factly. He actually asked me

Figure 36.1 Shot for the "Queer Issue" of *Village Voice*, 1999; photo by Dick Mitchell

about specific things that appeared in the book as if he'd read it (or someone on his team had). He wanted to talk about poop, and a track of fart noises played in the background. I remained unshaken.

At a commercial break, all his sleazy vibrato disappeared, and he addressed me directly and respectfully: "Good for you. I hope you sell a lot of books. We want to get your mom on the phone in the next segment. Can we have her phone number?"

I didn't want to seem rattled, so I recited it. Thankfully, she was game and blasé on the air when she responded to his queries about her own anal sex experience.

"Of course I have," she said confidently. My mom did come through for me when the stakes were high.

In the late 1990s, there were several sex-positive feminist sex toy shops in major cities, and one from Seattle, called Toys in Babeland, had recently opened its second store on the Lower East Side of New York (I would eventually work there). The store occasionally held workshops in its tiny, cramped space, where dildos lined glass shelves, deerskin floggers hung on the wall, and all the butt plugs were displayed on a wooden island stained high-gloss red. I approached the owner, Claire, about teaching a workshop based on my book, and a few weeks later, I stood in front of ten people sitting on metal folding chairs and taught an anal sex class. I knew only one person in the audience, a friend who came to support me. I was organized and relaxed, the audience was attentive, and everything felt exactly right in the universe.

A woman came up to me after it ended and said, "Thanks for all the info. And thanks for making me feel less weird."

That evening I knew in my heart what my life's work would be: to write and teach people about sex, hold space for shame-free talk about taboo topics, and create a more sex positive world. *This is what I was meant to do.*

Some fellow writers cautioned me that if I wrote a book on anal sex, I would forever be pigeonholed as "the anal sex girl." That has worked in my favor—once anal became an ordinary topic covered in *Cosmo* and other mainstream media, they all had to talk to the woman who wrote the book. And, as it turns out, that bookstore buyer's skepticism about web shopping in the late 1990s was wrong: people *did* buy books online. Mine was named the number-one bestseller in women's sex instruction by Amazon in 1998; back then, they sent a beautifully designed award certificate, which hangs framed in my office.

ADVENTURE GIRL

"Our love making sessions are imagined to be long, luxurious tongue baths that produce multiple orgasms and little tinkling bells in the background. You know how I feel about those tinkling bells—I'd rather rattle a few cunts." My college girlfriend Jen read me an article by Susie Bright called "Muff-O-Mania." That was my introduction to *On Our Backs*, the sex-positive lesbian feminist porn magazine that began in the mid-1980s. I took the magazine from her hands, as if to confirm what she said was real.

The first time I saw *cunt* in print, it seared itself into my brain and stayed there. The article was accompanied by a photo of Susie with her face between the legs of a woman, bent over and wearing a thong with ruffled trim. There was a tiny salt-and-pepper shaker balanced on each of the woman's ass cheeks. Everything I saw in *On Our Backs* was a feast, a celebration of what feminists fought over in the Sex Wars of the 1980s: butch/femme, sex toys, fantasies, s/m. The words and pictures were a revelation. Dykes in charge of their own bodies, owning their sexuality, saying *Fuck you!* to polite society. It wasn't just jerk-off material: it was a road map to what my life could be.

The publishers also ran Fatale Media, which made porn movies featuring real-life lesbians having authentic sex (as opposed to gay-for-pay mainstream actresses). Until then, my porn had been *The Joy of Sex* illustrations, *Playboy*, the soundtrack of scrambled adult cable channels, and clips playing in the background at parties. Fatale's movies were hot, genuine, edgy, even educational. It was porn you wanted to watch intently. They instilled an important idea in me: you could capture not just a performance of sex but the pleasure the women in it were having. Sexual media could be smart, boundary-breaking, political. *Do I want to deconstruct it or get off to it? Both.* I watched Fatale's *Doing It for Daddy* a dozen times and included a critical reading of the film in my undergraduate thesis.

In 1994 I had submitted my story about a dyke who go-go dances in a bar to *On Our Backs* because being published there would be everything. It was rejected. But four years later, the editor of *On Our Backs* reached out to me with an idea.

"We all brainstormed and came up with this concept for a column. You go out and have exciting sexual adventures—maybe go to an orgy or try some fetish for the first time. You get the idea," she said on the phone. I started dancing around my apartment.

"Then you share this adventure in vivid detail, like we're on the journey with you. Maybe down the road, readers can write in and suggest escapades for you. We'll call it 'Adventure Girl.' What do you think?"

It felt custom-made for me as I actually had a list of sex and kink things I wanted to try. Plus, I could try a few I might not otherwise have access to—in the name of journalism. Being adventurous was the job, as was spilling all the details. (I was paid $50 per article, so *job* overstates its contribution to my income.) My first column was about disrupting an all-male space with lesbian desire (getting a lap dance at a strip club):

> She starts to grind against me, not keeping the distance between her body and mine like I watched the other dancers do, but brushing right up against me, rubbing her face against my cheek, kissing my neck and nibbling on my ear. I like the idea that we're breaking the rules.
>
> "I thought you weren't supposed to touch me," I say playfully, letting her know I am absolutely enjoying it.

The lap dance was followed by a swinger party, a paid visit to a professional dominant, a sexy hazing by the Dyke Uniform Corps, a play piercing scene, and peeing on an adorable submissive butch in a bathtub.

My one-on-one session with Betty Dodson stood above the rest. The author of the game-changing book *Sex for One*, she was a true feminist trailblazer in women's sexuality known as the Mother of Masturbation. Since the 1970s she'd taught hundreds of women in her Bodysex workshops about body acceptance, self-pleasure, vibrators, and orgasms. When I walked into her Park

Figure 37.1 My first time meeting Betty Dodson, World Pornography Conference, Los Angeles, California, 1998

Avenue apartment, I could feel the history. I knew she had rubbed shoulders (and clits?) with Gloria Steinem, Bella Abzug, Betty Friedan, and other leaders of the women's movement, but I also thought about all the ordinary women sitting in a circle on the floor of her living room learning about their vulvas and clitorises. I was in the presence of a pleasure evangelist who laid the groundwork for *all* sex educators, a role model for what was possible. I was a little scared.

Betty was a compact, strong white woman with a round face, spiky salt-and-pepper hair, glasses, and very straight teeth. At seventy, she didn't look a day over fifty, and her secret was clear: not plastic surgery, sobriety, or veganism, just decades of helping other women discover their bodies. And a lot of jerking off.

"Let's take off our clothes and get comfortable!" She was cheeky and disarming. Clients who came (and paid top dollar) to Betty often had a particular sexual issue to address, had never masturbated, or had never orgasmed. I've been touching myself since I was five years old, but who would pass up the chance to learn from an actual legend? Plus, there was one thing, something I hadn't shared with anyone, that I was ready to say out loud and write about publicly. Zoloft made it possible for me to get out of bed and be pretty functional, but that came with a price: reduced sexual sensation and difficulty coming. There

Tristan Taormino

was a time when I could come at the drop of a hat. My usual tricks weren't working. It was taking a lot longer. There was very little information about the sexual side effects of the class of antidepressants known as SSRIs (selective serotonin reuptake inhibitors), and my doctor never mentioned it. Few people talked openly about depression or being on psych meds. The memes and magnets came much later. I felt free of the shame around sexuality that most people had, but I couldn't escape the stigma of mental illness. I felt broken.

I shared my problem with Betty, who responded with compassion along with her bracing honesty: "So it takes more time. Let her take as long as she wants to. Those drugs! Of course no one cares how they affect women's pleasure. That's the old patriarchy for ya. I say just smoke pot, that's what does it for me! We can work on this, you deserve orgasms."

She gave me a handheld mirror and encouraged me to gaze closely at my vulva, find and identify the important parts, stroke it, rub it, play with it, say out loud what I admired about it. I'd read about feminist consciousness-raising groups; I knew what this was. But it was still really powerful to look at a part of my body that society taught me was gross.

"Okay, now show me how you usually masturbate."

Her directness was a turn-on. She squeezed some lube on my fingers, and I slipped my left hand between my legs, crossed my right hand over it, and casually touched my outer labia. I don't go to my clit right away, I need to coax it first. "Yes, just let her wake up before you start anything," she said, as if reading my mind. "Now, squeeze those PC muscles. Do you know what Kegel exercises are?" I did as I was told.

"Good. How does that feel?" she said. It was part of a routine, so it was like second nature.

When I was ready, I made my way up, pressed down with my fingers, and started moving in counterclockwise circles on top of my hood.

"I am into having a lot of pressure on my clit. I know some people like gentler movements. That's why light flicks of a tongue feel good but don't get me off." *When I say pressure, I mean the weight of ten bricks.*

"Ah . . . you're a clit masher." *Clit masher.* "Relying on the pressure can be limiting, though. If you train yourself to come from other kinds of stimulation, you'll be a more versatile lover. Want some penetration?"

I do like having something inside my pussy to apply pressure from the inside as well. I started with a thin Lucite S-shaped toy and then moved on to Betty's Barbell, a heavy metal dildo she designed herself. *I have a one-of-a-kind piece of Betty Dodson sculpture inside me.*

"Let me know if you want something for your butt." I appreciated how absolutely normalized everything about our interaction was.

"Rock your pelvis. Loosen up," she coached. "And don't forget to breathe! Those shallow breaths you're taking, maybe you sort of get a head rush? But that's just temporary. Taking really deep breaths gets your blood pumping so the whole area becomes engorged."

I took a deep breath, then another. My pussy was juicy, and my muscle memory meant I didn't have to think about the motion very much. But it didn't feel like I was headed anywhere.

"I think I need to concentrate," I said. I suddenly felt pressure to not let Betty down. I don't respond to that kind of pressure.

"How about some power?" Betty handed me her tool of choice, the Hitachi Magic Wand vibrator, and the tangerine-size flexible head was cool against my skin. When she turned it on, I jumped.

"That's a . . . lot . . . of power. Too much for me maybe." She handed me a wash-cloth to put between the head and my vulva, which diffused the sensation, and the buzzing began to feel better. I shifted around to get just the right spot, but my brain turned back to the thought *What if I can't come for Betty Fucking Dodson?*

"Get out of your head and just *feel*," she said. I tried to redirect and pay attention to how my body was responding to the vibration.

"It's easier for me to come when I am on my stomach," I explained. Since that first orgasm, it's the way I've masturbated.

"Go ahead," she said softly. There was no judgment in her voice, just permission.

I turned over and began grinding against the vibe. There is such a distinct internal sensation that resides in the nerves and signals between my clit and my brain when I know I am at the edge. My body tensed, I let go, and I was flying. I was in that space where my clit ruled the Earth. Quickly I was back on the ground with my heart pounding.

"Good girl," she said. I went home and wrote it all down.

In the nineties, sex journalism of any kind was still a novelty. Sex writing was not considered *serious* writing. It would be another decade before there were a bevy of sex experts, bloggers, and journalists published everywhere from college newspapers to mainstream women's magazines. In 1999 there was only one smart and popular show in town: Dan Savage's advice column, which I read in the *Village Voice*.

The *Village Voice* was not simply one of the papers in New York City; it was an institution covering politics, city corruption, LGBTQIA+ communities, plus underground music, experimental theater, avant-garde art, anything and everything *alternative*. It was the *New York Times* of my people. I found myself in the *Village Voice* offices on Cooper Square after Doug Simmons called to set up a meeting. It's not every day the editor-in-chief of your favorite publication wants to meet you. I was thrilled for the opportunity to just be in the building. Maybe I would run into famed gay columnist Michael Musto in the elevator.

"We want to move Dan Savage's column out from among the 1-900 ads and into a different part of the book, and we'd like something to run opposite it," said Doug. He was a tall, effusive guy with full eyebrows and smile lines around his prominent mouth. He was wearing a band T-shirt that I thought was very punk rock. Yeah, it was definitely not the *New York Times*.

"We're thinking of a first-person sex column. There was one in the *Observer* a few years ago by Candace Bushnell, but we'd like something edgier, with a little more meat."

I knew the column, "Sex and the City," which followed the life of a straight, white, upper-middle-class New York girl. They turned it into an HBO show.

"We had a meeting, and your name came up several times from staffers who knew your work from various sources: your books, your workshops, and *On Our Backs*."

The publisher, Don Forst, a charming, well-dressed older white guy with gray hair that had turned white at the temples, asked, "How would you feel about writing a sex column for us?"

Was I actually parlaying my work at a lesbian porn magazine into a byline at the Village Voice?

I let it sink in.

"I would love that! Are you thinking about something along the lines of 'Adventure Girl'? Because I could also do musings on the state of various issues in the world of sex, trend pieces, profiles . . ."

"It would be your column, so we would give you a lot of room to make those decisions as it, and your voice, develops," said Don.

We decided I would get my feet wet by writing an article about the International Ms. Leather Contest, which I was attending in a few weeks. Before I left the meeting, Don had one final question: "Do you think you might run out of things to write about at some point?"

I smiled. "You have nothing to worry about."

MY GAY BOYFRIEND

My relationship with Coral became domesticated and devoid of desire; I told her I thought we should live separately, but that was a cover story for me wanting to break up with her. I found an apartment across from Prospect Park on the southwestern edge of Park Slope. I was depressed but no more so than usual. I wanted to be on my own. But I didn't want to be alone. I professed to everyone that my new sexual orientation was not queer or bi but simply first come, first served: whoever had the guts to approach me had the best chance of getting me. I was single and flexible.

At a queer writers' event, my friend Alexander introduced me to his ex-boyfriend Michael, an outgoing guy with a stocky build, wavy brown hair, and hip glasses. He was a handsome, smart, charming Jewish architect, like the gay cousin to my Cornell boyfriend Ethan. We clicked immediately and became fast friends; we watched movies and had marathon meals where we'd tell each other about our sex lives in exquisite detail. I loved having blow-by-blow gay sex recounted to me, and he was clueless but curious about what dykes did in bed; some sexual tension rose up in these moments, and it was playful and queer. Although I am confident that I can persuade people to play for any team, Michael definitely loved men.

We were waiting in line for tickets at the Angelika Film Center one night, and I spun around to tell him something. Our bodies collided, but it didn't feel awkward. Then he kissed me. It was a deep, passionate kiss. His full lips pressed against mine, and the scrape of his five-o'clock shadow surprised me. I leaned into him, going with it without considering what was happening. We stepped back from each other.

"Um, what are you doing?"

"Really?" he smiled broadly.

"But you're gay!" I retorted.

"So are you, Miss Don't Fence Me In," he returned, unflinching. "I seem to recall someone claiming that she was first come, first served." I scowled; he had me. He touched my hand and said, "Do we really need to talk about this? I think you're sexy, and I want to kiss you, okay?"

"When was the last time you were with a woman?" I asked (already knowing the answer from a previous conversation but somehow needing to hear it again).

"Um, like eight or nine years or something. It'll come back to me. Like riding a bike."

"That's not what I—" He cut me off with another delicious kiss.

The first time we had sex, it was like being dropped into one of my favorite gay porn movies, starring him as the hunky leading man. His hairy chest, his buff arms, and his long-distance cyclist's thighs. He undressed me, and I marveled at the sure way he moved into my body. The way he held his cock in his hand. And what a cock! When I saw it, I blurted, "Wow, the boys must love you!" No wonder he had no trouble picking up guys, all the inches they wrote about in their personal ads were there.

Many of my boy crushes in high school and college eventually came out, and stories from other people echo my experience. Still closeted queer folks of different genders can be drawn to one another by a kind of desire that is enrobed in queerness, yet still unknown to us. But Michael and I were both way out of the closet, so this wasn't that. *I have a gay dad. Fuck the unconscious, let's wake her up and really do this!*

His gayness didn't resemble Dad's in specific ways. I was drawn to his energy, to a different kind of masculinity. I realized I had flawed expectations. He will be my personal stylist. We will bond over musical theater. *Nope.* I will get all the anal sex I could ever want—and not nice, well-paced anal sex, but throw-me-down-on-the-bed-and-fuck-me-like-you-mean-it anal sex. (Clearly, I had watched way too much gay porn.) *Nope.* I would get genuine curiosity about my body and my pleasure. I would get genuine love and connection. I would get a taste of my own medicine.

One of my gay boyfriend's favorite things to do was fuck people he didn't know. He cruised men in the locker room at his gym and bathhouses. He played safely, so I didn't worry about him. He'd come home late at night, smelling clean from a recent shower; crawl into bed; and describe the details of his hookups. *He was the one who made a move on me. He was tall and lean like a dancer. His cock was short and thick enough to stretch my mouth open. He told me he wanted to eat my ass.* He indulged my voyeuristic thrill, then fucked me like he meant it.

No one knew exactly what to make of us. It was 1998! People assumed he was gay and I was his fag hag friend, or some read us as straight, which freaked us out.

"Oh, so you're both bisexual," people concluded.

"No, he's gay, and I'm a dyke." That was another element of the dynamic between Michael and me: my femme identity didn't feel in danger; it wasn't changed because of who I was with. I would usually introduce him as my gay boyfriend, and I could see people trying desperately to process the phrase. In fact, I referred to him as Gay Michael because right before him, I had had a mad, passionate affair with a straight guy named Michael, another Jewish architect. He lived in San Francisco, he proposed, I said yes, and we fucked in Grand Central Station to celebrate. The engagement was brief. He became Straight Michael, and Michael became Gay Michael, so it was easy to tell them apart in a story.

Gay Michael and I went to LA together so I could introduce him to Winston, who lived in a gorgeous house in the Hollywood Hills with a dungeon that had padded walls. It was important for the two central gay men in my life to meet. Winston had become Daddy Winston to me since my father's death. He was pursuing his doctorate in sexology, which brought us even closer because I was excited to learn about the field from him. Our relationship is imbued with queerness, leather, power, and sex, but it's not sexual. Daddy encompasses many things: a teacher, an adviser, a role model, sometimes a judge. He tells me he is proud of me when I accomplish something. He let me shoot a porn movie at his spectacular, secluded house in Idyllwild, where performers had a four-way on his California king. He holds me when I cry and gets mad because I don't call him often enough.

Michael scored us an invite to the wrap party of a long-running TV thriller in which his ex-boyfriend played a serial killer. We met another cast member at the party, I'll call him the Actor, and after we explained our situation to him, he was mesmerized.

"Wow, that is so cool," said the Actor. "You're the future!"

Tristan Taormino

Figure 38.1 Michael with Winston Wilde and his dog Buddy, Hollywood, California, 1998

Apparently we were the very near future, because we took him home that night.

He confessed he was bi-curious and ready to take the plunge because the two of us were so charming and nonjudgmental. Michael and I hadn't seen each other for a week, so we were looking forward to a reunion fuck, and we were happy to bring a third along. On the way back to his place, the Actor was flirty with us both but seemed nervous. He offered us something to drink as we sat down in his living room.

"So, before we, um, start . . ." he began.

"Listen, this doesn't have to be some big . . . we can go at your pace," I reassured him.

"Thanks," he said. "Obviously I haven't been with a guy before. But I want to tell both of you, before we get into . . . anything . . . so no one is surprised. My dick . . ." he trailed off.

We sat across from him, waiting for what was coming next.

"Well, past partners have said it's big. Sometimes *too big*. It can be hard to...." He was searching for the word. He settled on: "Accommodate. So I guess I wanted you to know?"

My instinct was to roll my eyes so hard, but I'm not mean, so I just listened, silently judging him. *God, men and their dicks. Can't wait to see what this one's definition of big is...*

We moved to his bed, where we sat on our knees and took turns making out. Clothes came off. When I was ready for the reveal, I slipped his boxer briefs down his legs, and there it was: the biggest dick I'd ever laid eyes on. I'm sure the look on my face said everything. I am cock hungry but also incredibly pragmatic. I know my body's limits, and this was definitely beyond what I could take. I turned to Michael.

"Holy shit," he said. "That thing should have its own zip code."

Michael's primarily a top, but he's not one to pass up dessert when it's right in front of him. We both smiled and laughed softly. I kissed the Actor. Michael dipped his head down and took the enormous cock in his mouth like a champ. I watched. I could do this all day. The Actor got shy about reciprocating with Michael and eventually lay back and watched as the two of us fucked.

A few weeks later, Michael and I went to P-town together. A decade had passed since I'd been there. Commercial Street seemed the same, just with new faces. Northern Lights Leather, the store where both my father and I worked, was still doing a brisk business. I felt sadness for the many men I was surrounded by in my teen years who died of AIDS. It felt weird to be there without Dad. Michael wasn't excited to go to drag shows, which is where I wanted to be, to relive those formative moments of my youth. After that trip I saw a future with us as partners. It was clear I was ready to go all in—all in to what, I didn't know, but all in. He wasn't. He really did envision himself in the long term with a man. It was my turn to be heartbroken.

Tristan Taormino

HEART/THROB

After the breakup, I got back out there. I ran with a pack of leather femmes who went out cruising for butches. I attended Lesbian Sex Mafia workshops. I went to parties like the Clit Club and Squeezebox. I bought my first latex dress, which clearly outlined my nipple piercing. I performed with my friend Sherry at a club called Aspara, where we were often naked as I spanked her ass and licked her bald head. I hung out at Don Hill's with drag queens and club kids. That was when the meatpacking district was home to s/m and sex clubs, before gentrification pushed them all out. In 1999 some parts of New York City were still affordable and powered by zines, outlaw art forms, and freaks.

In 1998, brilliant performer-activist Annie Sprinkle invited me to be a part of an event called Liberty Love Boat to celebrate freedom of creative sexual expression. She was in New York with her show *Herstory of Porn*, and she knew from her decades of work that she was in danger of being censored. Everyone took the ferry to the Statue of Liberty dressed as mermaids, sailors, and whores; one woman held a sign that read "GET SEX BACK ON 42ND STREET WHERE IT BELONGS." The performance-cum-rally was a response to Rudy Giuliani's campaign he called "Clean Up New York" because it was catchier than "Desexualize the City." It had been going on for a decade and included the Disney-fication of Times Square to make it tourist friendly. Laws were passed to rezone adult businesses and used to shut down sex shops, massage

Figure 39.1 With Annie Sprinkle at the Castro Theater, San Francisco, California, 1999

parlors, and peep shows; increased policing pushed out the sex workers, drug users, and homeless people.

I was on the ferry with my femmes, and we all noticed a hot butch/butch couple dressed in navy whites. Yum. We introduced ourselves.

Val, the shorter, dark-haired one in full leather, put her arm around a thin, muscular, masculine woman with hair the color of a nectarine that was shaved on the sides.

"This is my boy Red."

The girls and I flirted and landed an invitation to serve them while they watched the game at a house in a quaint Queens neighborhood. We mostly got them beers and crawled around on the floor naked hooked to a TENS unit that delivered little shocks to our bodies whenever they wanted.

Val and Red were both skilled, experienced kinksters, and I felt like I hit the jackpot when they took me on as their girl. They tried to turn me into a more proper *submissive* submissive, which I admit I wasn't very good at, but I followed orders most of the time. I was really into the well-crafted scenes they concocted—like when Val pierced my chest with about fifty needles and then tied the ends together with ribbon to look like a corset. Until that point, I'd only had maybe five needles at once. When other people talked about flying high on endorphins from a really good flogging, I didn't get it, until play piercing. The first prick and burn, feeling the needle slide through your flesh until it pushes its way out of you. It transports me to a place that transcends my body.

Our triad was nonmonogamous: we played with other people, Red had a leatherdaddy in San Francisco, and Val was dating a woman named Blaze.

One night, Val sat us both down and said, "Sadly, I think this thing with the three of us has to end. I'm really in love with Blaze, and we want to be monogamous."

It was unexpected and left Red and me, both submissive to Val, wondering if we would continue our relationship. Red was seven years older than me, a real grown-up with her shit together: she'd had the same job with the phone company for years and organized her life around friends, kink, and pleasure. The leather chaps and paddles got me in the door, but a steady, grounded partner is what really appealed to me. We went on an ice-skating date with some friends, entirely ordinary compared to what we usually did together, and decided to give it a go.

Living up to her fiery name, Red had one of the most voracious sexual appetites I've ever encountered (still). On many occasions, I fisted her in

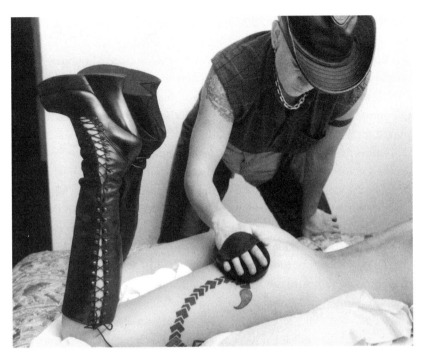

Figure 39.2 s/m scene with my partner Red, 1999; photo by Janet Ryan

both holes at the same time. She was never not erotically ambitious, and she eventually got her whole hand in my ass in a hotel room at a kink event. She was a squirter, and the first person who made me squirt (it was in front of a room full of people during a workshop). When she dressed me up as a pony, I happily wore a rope harness, a butt plug tail, and my lace-up Fluevog boots with hoofs as I trotted down Fifth Avenue for the Gay Pride Parade. She was like my ex Jen in that way: all kinks were on the menu, treated equally with respect and reverence.

Red took me to the Michigan Womyn's Music Festival, which was my first and last visit to the famed event on 640 acres known as The Land. In the 1990s, women's space, as it was defined by feminists in the 1970s, was becoming a more contested idea. Some feminists, like those who ran Michigan, were hanging on to the notion that only "womyn-born womyn" should be allowed in such spaces. It was fucked up. For us queers, gender had always been ours to play with, craft, and name for ourselves. By the time I visited, Camp Trans was going strong across the street in response to the festival's

Tristan Taormino

Figure 39.3 Dressed as a pony with Red, Gay Pride Parade, New York City, 1999

blatant exclusion of trans women. At the same time, more people who were assigned female at birth were coming out as genderqueer, boydykes, and trans. I saw some of them as they moved proudly on The Land, casually grabbing their packages; as long as they didn't identify openly as trans men, they were welcome. That was confusing.

Some people came to Michigan to see dozens of musicians, like Le Tigre and Bitch and Animal, but plenty came for the uninhibited outdoor sex. On a schedule of offerings that included "Healing through the Voice of the Mother," Red and I taught workshops where I fisted her and she put a clear Lucite butt plug in my ass, inviting people to see inside my rectum. After our squirting class in the woods, we spontaneously decided to host the First Annual Ejaculation Contest on a big blue tarp. The category is . . . Quantity. Speed. Distance. Style. A leggy redhead gushed so much fluid, she left a sizable puddle on the plastic covering.

A shy, silver-haired fifty-something butch said, "I only began ejaculating after I turned forty. I don't know what's going to happen, but I'm gonna give it a try." Paired with a complete stranger (one of our generous volunteer ejaculation helpers), she squirted her way to the speed championship in what seemed like fifteen seconds. These kinds of intergenerational moments

Figure 39.4 (left to right) Sini, Carey, me, and another friend, Michigan Womyn's Music Festival, 2000

made me see why people revered the event—if only the organizers' gender politics would evolve with the times. Michigan was representative of many women's organizations and events at that time, including leather ones, that were grappling with these issues.

Red and I both loved public sex, but in New York City, space is a commodity, sexual spaces hard to find, and sexual spaces for people who are not cis gay men practically unheard of. Val ran a women's S/M play party at a commercial dungeon in an office building in Midtown, but it petered out. Mayor Giuliani's reach extended far beyond Forty-Second Street. So many gay men's bath-houses had been closed by the city at the start of the AIDS crisis in the mid-1980s to "protect the public's health" (which was homophobic bullshit), and Giuliani was intent on eradicating the ones left standing. Gay bathhouses are such a vital part of queer men's history and culture, but an equivalent didn't/ doesn't really exist for women. The trick back then was to get a men's club to agree to close for a night so we could get a taste of the debauchery. Red made her case to the managers of Le Mirage, a men's sex club on Houston, down the block from dyke bar Meow Mix, where my ex Coral used to host a queer punk night called Xanadu. We started producing a sex and S/M party once a month called Throb. We welcomed all women and trans folks.

Tristan Taormino

Figure 39.5 with Red (middle) and a friend at Leather Pride Night, New York City, 1999

On a typical night, after checking in with the door person, I'd swing through the social area to make sure there were enough snacks out, including mini cheesecakes my mom made for each party.

Queers chatted before heading further inside or came there to unwind after an intense scene. The big open play space had a St. Andrew's cross, spanking benches, several slings, and a few mattresses. Downstairs was a much smaller area with a gang shower perfect for water sports but, sadly, rarely used for that purpose. At first, our partygoers didn't get right down to it like in gay men's communities, where cruising is a national pastime. Many were still figuring out what it meant to be in a queer public sex space. We were the offspring of the women of *On Our Backs*, *Samois*, Lesbian Sex Mafia, Betty Dodson, Gayle Rubin, Patrick Califia, Susie Bright, Annie Sprinkle, and others who created and documented radical sexual communities. I thought we'd created a new space to fulfill our own desires, but it was actually cocreated by all the different people who came there to feel seen, to feel free. It felt like home.

TURN ME ON

"Turn your face toward me so we can see it better," I said gently.

I was in an apartment in Fort Greene where a statuesque woman with black pinup-style hair wearing vintage lingerie was on her knees unbuttoning her partner's pants.

"That's it. You guys look amazing. Keep going."

It had been less than a decade since I'd seen my first issue of *On Our Backs*, the one with the butch wearing army fatigues in the desert on the cover. Eight years later, I graced the cover myself with a pictorial inside of a hot butch and me getting it on at a gym. Then it happened: my gig as Adventure Girl turned into a dream offer from the publisher, and I took the reins as editor.

When Debi Sundahl, Nan Kinney, Myrna Elana, and Susie Bright put out the first issue of *On Our Backs*, they created a new ethos of dyke eroticism. The aesthetics and stories morphed with the times, but the basic foundation remained: to make a hot porn magazine by and for real dykes with no holes or kinks barred. To represent racial, ethnic, age, gender identity, sexual expression, and body diversity. In their motorcycle boots and stilettos, these outlaws kicked down the door, facing rejection, censorship, and obscenity seizures at the Canadian border. I wanted to both honor them and leave my own mark on the magazine that was built by my role models. It was a serious legacy to live up to.

My experience with my zine prepared me for most of my tasks except one: to cast, style, and direct photo shoots. The casting part was fairly easy since I had a deep pool of perverts to tap; I recruited friends, lovers, strangers

Figure 40.1 From my *On Our Backs* pictorial, New York City, 1998; photo by Michele Serchuk

who caught my eye at Throb parties, plus lots of the models came to us. We shot mostly real-life partners, everyday people. I'd done some sex and fetish modeling when I first got to New York, which helped me relate to their experience. When Richard Kern gives you ten enemas in one day, you remember what it's like to be vulnerable in front of a camera. The creation of an *On Our Backs* pictorial was feminist and collaborative, something that contradicted typical ideas about porn making. The models were in charge of the scenario, hair, makeup, wardrobe, and toys, and they did what they wanted. It was in the small moments of laughter, spilled lube, a pause to negotiate, or a harness adjustment where I saw people unguarded and open. It felt really intimate. Precious even. The pictures were naturalistic and brimming with chemistry. This queer sensibility, passed down through each iteration of the magazine, deeply informed my work in mainstream porn for years to come.

Following the models where they wanted to go meant confronting an interesting dilemma: some didn't want to be completely naked. It wasn't like a celebrity wanting to be coy (and respectable) with a well-placed sheer scarf for *Playboy*. Some were brave enough to pose because they knew they'd be seen mostly by other queers (an upside of our limited distribution and not yet having a significant web presence), but they still didn't want their cunts in the centerfold. Plus, I didn't want to exclude anyone in the community, including folks who identified as genderqueer and trans. It was about prioritizing respect for the models' boundaries and their genuine self-expression. I am someone who likes to dress up for sex, so there is lots of appeal in jock straps, garter belts, chaps, and latex dresses. But I still had to make the case to the staff that the magazine needed to reflect how the culture was evolving.

When I got to *On Our Backs*, your fingers still got a little inky from the cheap printing when combing through an entire issue in one sitting. Readers desperately wanted to see these images in glossy full color. I did too, but there simply was not enough ad support, since most came from queer-owned independent businesses. I felt inspired by small-budget magazines from the 1990s like *Bad Attitude*, *Quim*, and *Venus Infers* and wanted the mag to retain its community cred and DIY vibe, but I was also ready to set a new bar. Dykes deserve gorgeous porn too. I was interested in exploring more fantasy, camp, glamour, and playfulness on the covers. With some strategically placed hay bales, we transformed a leatherdyke couple's suburban backyard into a ranch where a sexy transmasculine white couple posed as cowboys. A Black butch/femme couple did a pussy-shaving scene in a barber chair, paying homage to that Cindy Crawford/k.d. lang *Vanity Fair* cover.

An astrologer once read my birth chart and said I was *living my dharma*. Making pornography is part of my life's work. It's one iteration of my mission: to create and hold judgment-free, affirming space for pleasure. I imagine other worlds by cocreating temporary vessels where sexual expression is not just respected but valued, sealed off from the negativity and shame society heaps on sex. In those vessels, authentic desire and passion can thrive. Antiporn feminists get one thing right: making it is a radical, political act.

Working keeps my depression at bay, and working on so many things I loved was rewarding. But my depression had its own timeline and logic, and it worsened, even during a time of great abundance in my life. Therapy seemed to only get me so far. My doctor increased my Zoloft dose (again), a strategy that worsened the already sick irony: it kept me alive but killed my libido. I felt insecure that Red and I were not having as much sex as she wanted. Besides the meds, I experienced a new sensation: being disconnected from my body or from her or both. It was disorienting; my connection to my body was something I had always been able to count on. I sometimes felt like Red's expansive, enormous sexuality might swallow me whole. Other times, she wasn't completely attuned to my desires, like when you plug something into an outlet but you realize you've got it upside down. It's so close to being right.

People were beginning to recognize my name, which felt thrilling, especially in a city populated with such brilliant media makers. But there were times that I didn't live up to my own hype. It appeared that Tristan Taormino was having nonstop, sexy fun, which didn't leave any room for me when I struggled to get out of bed in the morning. It was lonely. I began to cultivate a skill I learned from my mom. *Smile though your heart is aching.* I tried out ways to turn on the sexpert when I was in public, something I can still do. I can feed off the energy of an audience to fuel and propel me, but it's temporary and becomes more difficult the older I get.

Grief comes and goes but never recedes completely. As my father would say, it lives in every cell of my body. At Hampshire College, as I was getting ready to tell a story about him onstage, a banner behind me came flying off the wall, and the audience gasped. But I don't get these signs often, like people do on TV. There is no romanticized guardian angel floating above me. I miss our phone calls filled with figure-skating competition reviews or drafts of letters to the editor (rants, really) read aloud. I want to hear him tell me he's proud of me. There isn't even family to call and reminisce, *Could you imagine how Bill would go to town on the Republicans?* Instead, there is just absence, sadness. I read one of his poems, wanting to hear his voice:

> Lie
> Down
> Let me hold you in place
> by the back of the neck
> Let me move myself
> so that your mouth will understand
> how we are connected
> how I am trying to give
> Lie
> Down
>
> Watch
> *Me*

So that your mouth will understand how we are connected. I wanted to be connected to myself and to something bigger.

BUTTMAN IS
ON THE PHONE

"When are you going to make a movie about this?"

I continued teaching more anal sex workshops to promote my book, and this question came up repeatedly. I liked the idea of creating a how-to video, but when I thought about sex-education films, I flashed back to health class: a doctor in a lab coat pointing at a diagram of the reproductive organs, a sperm fertilizing an egg, and terrifying pictures of STI-ridden genitals. These images felt so disconnected from actual bodies and pleasure. I'd also seen a film with more white coats talking, cut with couples having sex in blurred focus in the background. Legendary porn star and registered nurse Nina Hartley had her own line of educational videos that featured her and other performers demonstrating tips and techniques. I'd seen *Nina Hartley's Guide to Better Fellatio* from 1994, and I thought she was charming, and her message was clear: sex is fun! I remembered the lesbian-produced video *How to Female Ejaculate*, where a group of women sat in a circle talking about squirting, then masturbated to demonstrate it. Sex ed could be educational and entertaining.

I wanted to make an anal sex video that not only taught viewers *how* to do it but was so sexy and hot, it inspired them to run out *and do it*. I dreamed of combining the excitement of a porn movie with the information of an instructional book. There would be no soft focus; the butt was already shrouded in mystery, which contributed to all the cultural baggage and myths around it. The ass would be center stage, well lit, and celebrated. I had a vision, but what about the cash? Like many aspiring filmmakers, I had two options: go independent or mainstream.

I could probably run up my credit cards (again), ask my friends and their friends to work for little or nothing, and put it together with duct tape and hope. But then how would I get it out there? On my own, I could sell it to my readers, workshop participants, and sex-positive stores like Toys in Babeland and Good Vibrations, but that was preaching to the converted. I wanted to reach as many people as possible, so I decided to try for a mainstream adult film company.

I wrote a proposal, and the keywords were *anal, educational, hot,* and *for women.* Daddy Winston and I went to the World Pornography Conference in LA, where I met Nina Hartley herself, plus academics, historians, performers, and insiders. I was introduced to a guy named Brendan who worked for the industry trade publication *Adult Video News,* and we hit it off; I told him about my idea, and he coached me on the main players. When I got back, I sent a copy of the book and my proposal to the top companies. When I got one rep on the phone, he seemed stuck on sexy *and* instructional ("those two don't go together") as well as for women ("that stuff doesn't sell very well"). I was an outsider to their world, pitching an idea that defied well-established, marketable categories like "big-budget feature" or "barely legal." I envisioned my film to be a hybrid of several genres: female driven, instructional, and gonzo. Gonzo porn is a documentary style where there are no scripts or plots; it is traced back to 1989, the year I graduated high school. Performers talk to the camera, and spontaneity and chemistry are prized over fancy production values. Gonzo appealed to me as a viewer and a potential producer. Don't give performers elaborate dialogue, props, and costumes because it only distracts from their talent: delivering a scorching sexual performance.

One of the pioneers of gonzo is the legendary John Stagliano. John created the wildly successful *Buttman* series, of which I was a fan. John was the titular Buttman, the guy behind the camera indulging his obsession with women's asses. He liked the way they moved, the way they looked in G-strings, the way they could take a dick. It has been drilled into our collective mind that porn is made by and for straight men and can't possibly appeal to women, but that directly contradicted my experience. I identified with Buttman. I wanted women to show me all the things their asses were capable of.

In 1999, I was sitting on my father's couch with my laptop glowing in front of me when the phone rang. I had gotten my dad's furniture and artwork out of storage when I moved to my new apartment in Brooklyn. Looking at his stuff every day, I bounced between feelings: it was strange, it was normal, it was comforting, it was painful.

A voice said, "Hi. This is John Stagliano."

It had been several months since I mailed out the proposals, but I hadn't gotten any responses. I held my hand over the receiver and squealed, "You guys!!!! Buttman is on the phone!!!" My heart was racing.

Reggie Love and my Boston terrier Jordan were curled up side by side, nestled at my feet. Before I broke up with Coral, we had adopted Jordan, and I got custody in the split. She was AKC registered, with a champion father, but after a streak of second-place finishes that signaled she was not bound for stardom, she was retired to live the rest of her life as a pet. Both dogs lifted their heads at my yelling, then went right back to dozing off.

"I read your proposal and your book, and this idea of yours is very interesting."

He read my proposal and my book.

"Are you going to Vegas?"

I remembered from the conference that there was some big event for porn in Las Vegas. *I'll figure out the details later.*

"Yes, I am," I replied, trying to sound convincing.

"Perfect. Why don't you come by the booth, and we'll sit down and talk about it."

"Okay. A particular time or day?"

"Show up early, before things get crazy, and we'll make a plan."

"That sounds great," I said. "I'm really looking forward to it."

"Me too. So I'll see you then."

I logged into my AOL account, found the search feature, and typed "porn Las Vegas." The first result: the Sixteenth Annual AVN Awards at Bally's. I remembered the guy I met in LA, Brendan, who worked for AVN. I found his business card and dialed his number.

"I just got off the phone with John Stagliano."

"You did?" He sounded as surprised as I was.

"He wants to meet with me in Vegas. I assume you go since AVN puts on these awards. Could . . . Can I possibly crash on your hotel-room floor?"

"I have a double. You can sleep in the extra bed."

The awards were just one part of a four-day trade show, and Brendan got me a media pass. When I entered the convention floor, it was sensory overload. Movie box covers blown up so that the starlets were life size. Hanging from the beams of the convention center, twenty-foot-tall banners of women in lace panties or nothing but high heels. Boobs the size of the moon in the sky. I took in their airbrushed skin, their obviously enhanced cleavage, their pouty looks. The male gaze served them up on a platter. I didn't have any sense of the scope of this world. Each company had a booth, some tastefully decorated, others less slick. In one with sleek chairs and leather couches, several men sat at a table with spreadsheets and calculators; they looked like they sold microwaves. At the front of the booth was a flawlessly made-up blond whose picture hung above her. She was trying to get back into a tall chair, teetering on seven-inch Lucite heels, wearing a crop top with a company logo on it and a tiny white skirt. A short man helped her up, and when he stepped away, I could see a line snaking around the corner of other men waiting for a glossy 8 × 10, an autograph, maybe a photo if they were lucky.

I made my way past other lines like it, a sea of men with the occasional woman, until I got to John's company, Evil Angel. It wasn't decorated like a sultry wine bar, more like a clubhouse at a sports stadium. Painted signs listed the directors' names—Rocco Siffredi, John Leslie, Joey Silvera, Gregory Dark—and their nominations and previous wins. I was intimidated on several levels: there was an obvious legacy to live up to here, and there were no women's names. *Was I way out of my league?* I was intrigued to meet the man behind one of the most decorated, profitable companies. My research had led me to a revelation that made him stand out for another reason: John was open about being HIV positive. A not-so-quiet rumor circulated that John got HIV by bottoming to a trans woman in Brazil, and he didn't exert a lot of energy denying it. It was a big deal at the time, especially for someone on the "straight" side of the industry. Gay and bi men and trans women were walled off on their own side with different companies, STI testing protocols, and films. It's a binary that persists in the mainstream industry today, as do heterosexism, homophobia, ableism, and racism. Although he stopped performing, John dared to push back on several taboos and did it without shame. I respected him for it. He and I had more in common than most people knew.

Teaming up with him offered me a special opportunity: his well-established fan base would watch my movie based on his reputation. *Just another smokin' hot anal sex movie.* In the process they might also learn a few things. It was my Trojan horse.

He had Italian good looks, with sun-weathered skin and blue eyes. He used to be a Chippendales dancer back in the day, and his body was older but still toned. I had a pang of jealousy when I saw him because he looked . . . healthy. He was diagnosed two years after my father died, when the Cocktail,

Figure 41.1 With Nina Hartley (left) and John Stagliano (middle), AVN Awards, Las Vegas, Nevada, 1999

a combination of two types of antiretroviral treatments, was available. It changed the landscape for people living with HIV, decreasing viral loads, boosting the immune system, and transforming the disease into a manageable chronic condition.

"I'll fund it, and I wanna shoot it," he said in our meeting. "Since you've never made a movie before, I'd like you to have a codirector, someone to help you."

A year earlier, at the World Pornography Conference, Brendan had hosted a small sex party in his hotel room. The majority of the people there were in the industry, and I fangirled over Sharon Mitchell, who put five fingers in my ass wearing a condom, since no one had a glove. I lay down on one of the beds and started making out with a performer named Julian who had sweet eyes and light brown skin. He stopped kissing me, and I turned to my right, where a thick, pale white guy with a buzz cut had several fingers inside a performer I recognized. "Hey," I said. It seemed polite given that we were right next to each other.

"Hi," said both of them in unison.

"I'm Tristan."

Tristan Taormino

"I'm Ernest," said the man, and he worked his hand inside her. "We should talk after."

"I'm Chloe," said the redhead with big round eyes and her legs splayed open. Minutes later, her eyes started to roll back in her head, which I also recognized—she was known for her explosive orgasms.

He was Ernest Greene, a director best known for his BDSM videos and strong credentials in his personal life: a highly sought-after pro domme told me he was one of the kinkiest kinky people in LA. He edited *Hustler's Taboo*, Larry Flynt's hardcore fetish magazine. When we were both upright and clothed, he said he'd read my book and we should keep in touch.

"How about Ernest Greene?" I asked John.

"Oh, the fetish guy? I like his stuff. Yeah, I think that will work."

The pieces were coming together, but there were a million things I didn't know. John was taking a chance on me, someone with no filmmaking experience. How was I going to make it all happen?

THE LEARNING CURVE

My Boston terrier Jordan's bug eyes followed me as I packed a suitcase. What does one even bring? She was exceptionally fast and agile for what breeders classify as a nonworking dog, and she reminded me of Chipper, tenacious and underestimated. We had quickly become bonded in a way I'd never experienced with another dog. In the moment before a mood engulfed me, before the tears actually came, she was by my side as if we shared the same nervous system. She helped regulate my emotions, and I needed her to ground me during this new adventure.

Ernest Greene, John Stagliano, and I had had a series of phone calls where we talked budget, casting, logistics. They approved my final script, a loose outline of what I wanted to accomplish in each scene. Finally, Jordan and I boarded a plane to LAX (Reggie Love stayed home with a friend), then took a Super Shuttle to Ernest's apartment. He had graciously offered to put me up during production but squinted at the arrival of my companion; he had allergies and asthma and wasn't fond of dogs. He begrudgingly agreed to let her stay. He lived in a big building on Highland Avenue, just past the Hollywood Bowl.

"I hope your trip here wasn't too bad. I'm excited we're making this picture. I think it's going to be really good," he said as he ushered me out of the elevator. He was dressed in black jeans and a black long-sleeve button-down shirt that was neatly ironed. He opened the door to a living room with a dark green leather couch trimmed with round metal studs and a small spiral staircase leading to a loftlike area. The walls were covered with erotic artwork, including an original Olivia drawing.

"Let's get you situated in the guest quarters." He led me past a bedroom, through an open door, to a dungeon. I saw a gynecological exam table with stirrups in one corner, an imposing metal cage a few feet from it, a St. Andrew's cross to the right, and, in the center, a black padded faux leather table with bolted silver rings every few inches all the way around it.

"The bondage bed is quite comfortable. So I'm told," he said without a hint of irony.

"This is amazing," I said, my eyes taking it all in.

"We all need a place to indulge ourselves," he said with a grin. He had the refined manner of Red Reddington, the character in *The Blacklist* played by James Spader, with an unapologetic taste for luxury and sadism. I pictured him surveying his work on a submissive woman bent over the bed with thin red cane stripes marking her ass cheeks. I imagined they would be spaced in a neat, orderly fashion given the precision of the decor. The walls were filled with hooks for floggers, spreader bars, bondage cuffs, coils of rope, canes, paddles, and other things I couldn't name. On one hook, a ball gag hung on top of a leather hood with a zipper at the mouth. The closet in the corner was open and lined with leather and latex dresses, skirts, and tops. Each item was in its place and meticulously arranged. It looked like a movie set, but his reputation preceded him: none of it was for show.

"Let's get some dinner. There is a sushi place I like around the corner. We still have a lot to go over," he said. I wheeled my suitcase past the bed.

"Thank you, Ernest, this is really generous of you. Let me take Jordan for a walk first."

Three days later, we pulled into a small, nondescript industrial park in Van Nuys in the San Fernando Valley to film the first scene at the Evil Angel office. The setup for the opening scene: I pitch my idea to John, but he is reluctant. He says he will only greenlight it if I can work my magic on a performer he hasn't been able to cast in his movies because she doesn't do anal.

"If you can teach someone like Ruby to love anal sex, then I'll make your movie," he said in our improvised back-and-forth. My theater experience came in handy. In walked Ruby, a tall woman wearing a body-hugging blue dress with short curls of strawberry blond hair tamed by a headband. She didn't look like what I thought of as that typical California Barbie doll and wasn't wearing full-glam makeup. She had never done anal before on camera—that part was 100 percent real.

"Hey," I said. "Thanks so much for being in my movie."

"Sure. I eventually was going to do it and thought this would be a good way. John says you wrote the book!" She seemed nervous, which intensified my nerves. *No pressure.*

This would be a hands-on lesson.

"The idea is that we're going to mess around until you're really warmed up first, then eventually get something in your butt."

"Tristan brought a briefcase full of sex toys, and you can pick whatever you want!" interjected John, who was fiddling with something on the camera.

"We will go at your pace," I reassured her. "Just talk to me." *Action.*

I went down on her, smearing all the gooey red lipstick the makeup artist had applied (a carnal sin in porn, I should have had blowjob lipstick—the kind that stays put no matter what). When I finally got one finger inside her ass, it was tight, like clamped-down tight. I've had my fingers up so many asses that I can tell what kind of day you've had and what the future holds (for your ass). It's a gift. Her hole said to me, *I'm not sure about this,* when I wished it exclaimed, *I'm so excited to meet you!* The reality part of gonzo kicked in. She was not going to fake it, nor did I want her to.

We took a break, and she asked John, "Could I have a little wine or something to calm my nerves?"

He produced a short clear plastic cup with what was probably Chardonnay from a box. I was not in favor of this tactic, but I didn't want her to feel judged or more anxious. *This is not how I thought my first porn scene would go.* We got back into it, but it wasn't sexy-hot; it was start-and-stop, slow at times, potentially not going anywhere. I lost confidence; Ruby lost confidence. Judy Garland would say, *They want a show!* Ruby knew this too, so we collaborated to make it work.

"The editing will make it look better than you're feeling right now," said Ernest to comfort me. I hoped the other scenes would be smoother than the one with Ruby.

During the casting discussions, Ernest had said, "We've got to go with players who can give *a strong anal performance,*" and I agreed and wanted even more: open, honest people who truly loved anal sex, could communicate and demonstrate why, and were into this unique project. I compiled a list of favorites I'd seen in action, Ernest made suggestions and knew what men would pair well with what women, and John threw in a newcomer couple who were in town from Europe. Plus, Ernest got Chloe, the anal queen and my number-one pick because her performances were brimming with intensity and authenticity; she'd just won Female Performer of the Year at the AVN Awards.

I had visited the porn set of *Nikki Nikki Bang Bang* and found that besides the sex, the elements of a shoot mirrored those of any film: you had to deal with location issues, various personalities, sound snafus. There was a lot of waiting around. But there are specific things pornographers know about the art of the tease, body angles and positions, capturing connection, sex as a vehicle for storytelling, and how to make a tight shot of genitals look gorgeous. I didn't know how to do any of that. But I had Buttman and Ernest, and I was prepared for a steep learning curve.

I was determined to challenge not only sex-education conventions but those of traditional porn films; I wanted more authentic portrayals of fucking, women's pleasure, and real communication. Every performer I know uses lube for anal, but the final cut doesn't show moments that are messy, awkward, or noneventful (even though sex can be all those things). I wanted to *see* them using this very necessary ingredient, modeling it for viewers. When I asked the female performers what could make their scenes more pleasurable, there was one common answer: a vibrator. My heart skipped a beat. *That seems easy, and Betty Dodson would be so proud.* The reason you don't see more vibrators in porn is that they obscure what the camera doesn't want to take its eyes off: pussy. Plus, vibrators sound like there's a blender in the background, and if you cut that noise out in post, out go the moans, ohhs, and dirty talk with it. Vibrators and other toys would be abundant on my set. Also, no skimping on warm-up (usually called *foreplay*, a word I hate because it implies there is a main dish and it's always intercourse). I wanted to show it all: different kinds of stimulation, working up to penetration, those moments where they talked to each other.

I've eavesdropped on performers talking on set about their scenes over Gatorade and bags of Famous Amos cookies. Conversations between sex workers are layered and fascinating, and they demonstrate to other people how to talk about sex in a straightforward way:

Don't pull my hair or get rough.

Go as slow as you can in the bj, that's what really gets me rock hard.

You can call me a slut, but don't call me a cow.

Pretend you never learned the word fingerbang: *don't finger me hard, I hate it.*

I like my balls played with.

Can we start in cowgirl? That helps me get into it.

I like to start rubbing my clit from the very beginning.

Just look me in the eyes and I will let you know if you need to slow down.

If I get quiet, it doesn't mean I'm not into it. It means I'm concentrating.

The problem is, you never see these conversations *on camera*, but I wanted to.

Then Ernest, John, and I had to talk about a porn staple: facials. Most scenes culminate in an external cum shot; more often than not, a semen splat on her face. Feminism taught me that the facial was a visual representation of male-centered pleasure. Certainly the look on the woman's face doesn't always scream "I am loving this!" The fact that every scene ends in the man's ejaculation (wherever it lands) reproduces heteropatriarchy at its basest level. But I feared this might be a fight I couldn't win. John and I compromised: cum shots in, facials out. It felt like a victory, although I have a much more nuanced view on facials these days.

It was standard that directors and performers tested for HIV and STIs each month, and you couldn't work without a current negative test. In porn the only safer-sex barriers that existed were condoms (they knew nothing of gloves or dental dams), and their use was rare. John toed the party line: "Movies with condoms don't sell." This brought up so many complicated feelings for me. How was this okay with the performers? Did they really feel protected? The irony that John was HIV positive but didn't promote safer sex in his films confused me. I ran it over and over in my brain. Naturally, I thought about my dad and the thousands who had died of AIDS. I remembered how passionate I was about Queer Nation's safer-sex messaging, the posters we plastered around campus. And I knew from my personal life that latex could be sexy. I was a sex educator first, and condoms needed to be in this movie. *But this might be a deal breaker for him.* We decided on another compromise: everyone would use condoms except for the real-life couple, whose relationship would be established on camera. My movie was the first released by his company with condoms (I even managed to get some latex gloves in there).

Figure 42.1 Shooting the cover with the cast of *The Ultimate Guide to Anal Sex for Women*, Malibu, California, 1999

Before we began each scene, I talked to the performers about what I envisioned:

"I'm interested in seeing more realistic sex, like you'd have at home. I want to see stuff you usually don't do in other movies—use lube, stop and start again, have real talk with your partners, and give them direction about what you want." I gave them the beats I wanted to hit.

"But make it hot," John chimed in.

"Do what you do best and be yourselves," added Ernest. Ernest emphasized to me that performers are good at their job and a smart director sets up the right conditions so they can do it. He was steady, even, stepping in only when he had an idea that ultimately made it a better film.

In many ways, the performers didn't need much more direction after John called, "I'm rolling." *They are professionals.* If anyone tells you that watching attractive people fuck isn't a sweet part of directing, they're lying or really jaded. It's a privilege to see them, to be let in on how other people express their sexuality. Several times in my career, I've gotten caught up in what's happening and forgotten to check the lighting, the frame. Plus, I didn't want to be off camera barking orders (I've seen directors do that, and it's unpleasant).

We shot the rest of the film at John's house in Malibu. I brought Jordan, and she stayed in the garage among mountains of boxes; her short black-and-white body was hard to spot under stacks of *Rocco's True Anal Stories.* We shot one scene a day. John was excited to try out a new performer named Nacho Vidal, a tall, well-built Spanish guy with bad tattoos and a steely look in his eye who had been discovered doing live sex shows in Barcelona. His real-life girlfriend, Jazmine, had flawless brown skin, a black bob, and an outstanding ass. The heat between them was raw and palpable. Nacho cast a kind of spell on her as he spoke to her in Spanish and pounded her aggressively.

Next up was Chandler, who had a girl-next-door look and low-key way about her; she was the youngest in the cast and still getting her feet underneath her. Her boyfriend drove her to the set and stayed to watch her scene with Sydnee Steele, a tall brunette with big fake boobs and an exceptionally large clit. Sydnee articulated exactly what she wanted and wielded a hot pink double dildo with such finesse. Another scene featured Inari Vachs, who was intelligent and gave a confident, sloppy blow job. I could tell her star would rise soon, and she had already developed some emotional armor that was difficult to break through. Jewel Valmont (later known as Ava Vincent) had a thicker body with pale white skin and an infectious laugh. During Jewel and Inari's three-way with Tony Tedeschi, he fucked Jewel in piledriver position, and they both made it look effortless, which it is not. Tony had long hair and a strong body; he clearly respected his partners, checked in with them.

Chloe had a slight dancer's body with no curves and tiny tits. As the result of a childhood accident, she'd lost all feeling in her clitoris. She was unafraid to speak openly about this deeply painful experience and how she found acceptance and pleasure without what is considered essential to women's sexuality. She was a boss with a sexy, husky voice who approached her work with an impressive combination of gusto and nonchalance. She prioritized giving a performance *and getting off.* She was paired with Kyle Stone, the most ordinary-looking, unassuming guy whose desire was driven by a hunger to please Chloe by fucking the living daylights out of her until her eyes rolled back in her head. Off camera, he was a witty conversationalist who took pride in his work without the need to gloat about it.

I was in awe of how different they all were and the meaningful moments we had while working together. I was grateful that they had a part in making my book come alive in this way. I was wide-eyed as I unlocked the next level in my own sex education on the road to knowing, seeing, creating. And it wasn't over yet.

FEMINIST GANG BANG

The alarm beeped at 7 a.m., and I sat up in Ernest's bondage bed with Jordan curled up behind my knees snoring.

"This is the big one," I said to her. She crawled into my lap and leaned against my chest. It was time to start our routine. After I walked her and showered, I put on what had become my uniform: a black stretch-cotton miniskirt, lace-top thigh-high stockings, black velvety high heels with a bit of a platform, and a push-up Victoria's Secret bra under a tight lacy V-neck top. I'd worn it six days in a row because the film takes place in one day, and sometimes the camera caught me coaching or pumping lube into someone's hand. I duplicated my hair and makeup as best as I could. I grabbed the last blueberry muffin from a six-pack that Ernest got at Von's. Then we made the long drive from Hollywood to the hills of Malibu and strategized about the day.

We began by shooting a big group scene where I teach my anal sex workshop to the performers, and they each go off to try out what they learned. Nina Hartley arrived on set to be my demo model. A classic beauty with thick blond hair and an hourglass figure, Nina starred in the first porn movie I ever watched all the way through, *Suburban Dykes*. As I shot my film, I was aware that I was standing on the shoulders of many feminists who had paved the way for my work, but Nina was right there in the room, bent over, giving witty narration as I put a lavender-and-white-swirled butt plug in her ass.

At the end of the workshop, John began shooting stills. We got in various poses, and suddenly the cast members began to undress me. They were ready to practice what they had learned on me in an anal gang bang. I acted shocked, but, in reality, I had orchestrated this finale.

Moments before the undressing began, I stood holding a clipboard and reviewed a long list of detailed instructions for each performer:

Nina, I love your dirty talk. Let's kick it off with dirty talk and spanking.

Chloe, start with fingers in my pussy, and I will suck Tony's cock.

Chandler, you're next, my pussy, then Inari with that curved blue dildo and the silver vibe on my clit.

Chloe, fuck my pussy with a strap-on—the black dick right there. Later on, that can end up in my mouth.

Kyle, you be the first cock in my pussy, then Tony, then Nacho.

Jazmine, warm my ass up with the green butt plug, then Jewel take over with the copper-colored one.

Fuck my ass in this cock order: Kyle's, Sydnee's strap-on with the red dick, Tony, Nacho.

I told them what to do to me, so I could feel safe and surrender to the experience.

John asked me, "Did you go to Vassar or something?"

He knew I went to Wesleyan, but I got his point: he was acknowledging me as an East Coast, college-educated woman, a feminist with a to-do list. I was supposed to be an anomaly in porn (in actuality, I wasn't). He said I looked like I was organizing a pep rally. In many ways, he was right: I wanted every performer to be as excited as possible and for viewers to feel our collective enthusiasm.

The cast exchanged knowing looks with each other as I went through my list, and Chloe jokingly said, "Okay, Tristan, we'll do exactly what you want." And then they did. They went in the right order and used the toy assigned to them, which I coordinated to gradually step up to the serious penetration that was to come. They were peeling away my leaves, headed toward the soft center, and I was having the time of my life. Tony's sex style represented his personality: charming with the right amount of swagger, and we had such intense eye contact and later on some kissing. He made me come when he was in my pussy. Sydnee strapped on a sizable silicone red dick (named Champ by its lesbian manufacturer) and fucked me in an intuitive and mind-bending way that I didn't want to end. It was like she'd known my ass for a lifetime.

Figure 43.1 Jazmine (at my butt), Nina Hartley (at my head), and the rest of the cast of my gang bang for *The Ultimate Guide to Anal Sex for Women*, Malibu, California, 1999

Only later in editing would I learn that John's camera only caught a snippet of it because he was filming Kyle making Jewel squirt, so my favorite part was never captured on videotape—a pleasure mandala whisked away by the ocean. Because there were so many people in the room and only so many of them could be on me at once, inevitably, it became an orgy. As I got fucked, six inches from my face, Inari was going down on Jazmine. I could hear the sounds of others in ecstasy. Kyle's was the first dick in my ass, and he worked his magic. I came hard, the kind of cum where this high-pitched primal voice emerges from me that I don't even recognize. I think I actually kicked him when I came. Then Tony took his turn and suddenly, *I* was in piledriver position, like Jewel had been, folded in half on my back with my ass straight up in the air. Getting fucked by people who fuck for a living can be a gift.

Since we were going in dick-size order, Nacho was up last. He fucked my pussy earlier but it was pretty short lived. I'd already seen him fuck; I was intimidated by his big cock and his dominance, which wasn't anything like I was used to. His energy was slightly off, like a bit of empathy was missing.

Tristan Taormino

I felt it in my gut, like he'd rather annihilate me than rock my world. The rest of the cast had taken such care of me, been so present and thoughtful, I didn't want to shift out of that space. I asked to take a break and pulled Nina to one side. My butt cheeks were sticky from all the lube. She handed me a baby wipe and paper towel without me asking. She was the respected veteran and the Mommy of the group I'd assembled.

"I might be losing my nerve about Nacho," I said. There was no time to mince words.

"Okay," she said, without judgment. "What's up?"

"Well, his dick is huge, so it's going to be a physical challenge, but there is something else: I feel like if I ask him to stop, he might not. He has one speed, which I think is not my speed. He's aggressive in a way that scares me a little."

Nina motioned Inari over and paraphrased me.

"Listen, you do not have to do anything you don't want to. Full stop," said Inari firmly.

"Agreed," said Nina. "Is there a way we can help you or make it feel safer?"

"Well," I said, "this conversation is already making me feel better."

"What if me or Inari . . . like got back there and held onto his dick, using it like a dildo," said Nina. "We will have the control. Then he can't just go wild or too deep."

"And I will have my eye on him the whole time. If he starts to be a jerk, I will step in," Nina said. They were both crystal clear. So many thoughts raced through my head.

Don't embarrass yourself by backing out now.
You're being a wimp, suck it up and do it.
Nothing bad will happen to you, except maybe a sore ass.

I summoned that fearlessness I had internalized from my riding days. I channeled my resilience. I looked at the women around me.

They will make sure.
I can stop whenever I want.
He won't be a jerk in front of all these people.
This is my fantasy, and if it doesn't include him, it doesn't include him.
I do like a challenge.
I am in charge.

I listened to my body, breathed into my gut.
"Okay! Let's do this!"

"But, Nacho, you've got to be gentle," I said playfully. "I can't take it like Jazmine can!" He nodded half-heartedly. I got back on all fours on the circular platform we were fucking on. Nina and Inari took their places behind me.

Inari cooed to Nacho, "I can't wait to see your dick in her ass, and I want to put it there." That actually turned me on, and I felt my clit jump.

"You look so sexy," said Sydnee, unaware and unprompted.

Inari, wearing a blue latex glove, wrapped her hand around his cock and guided it slowly inside my opening. Her hand stayed there for the rest of the scene. My ass was plenty warmed up and open; it had been fucked for more than an hour by then. Sydnee pressed the pink pocket-rocket vibrator against my clit, and I positioned it exactly where I wanted it. I started to melt from the sensations in my ass, the vibe buzzed against my clit, and I was back in it. I sunk into the feeling, I thought about how big his dick was, but this time I framed it differently: the thrill and the fantasy. *He can tear you apart.* Nina's voice in my head: *But he won't.*

"Okay, Nacho and you guys, let's get the pop," said John. "Where do you want them to come?"

I flipped over and said, "My chest."

Tony, Kyle, and Nacho stood over me holding their erections and jerking off. They came one at a time, shooting their cum and landing close to my breasts. I was blissed out. The whole thing felt epic. But not done.

"Buttman, there's one person who hasn't been in my ass. Someone get John a glove," I said spontaneously, calmly. Ernest made eye contact as if to say, "I don't know what's happening next, do I?" John held the camera in one hand, and Nina worked an aqua latex glove over the other one. Someone squeezed lube on it. He slid three, then four fingers inside me.

"Oh my goodness" is all he said.

When people think of a gang bang, a common image comes to mind: a straight cis woman surrounded by straight cis men ready to ravage, use, and demean her. But it's past time to reclaim this trope, on camera and off. It's a scene where one gets done by many, and the rest is up to you. The doers can be any body type, gender expression, sexual orientation, and ability. The types of sex they have can be diverse. Penises are optional. The vibe can be reverent, focused, silly, or dominant, if that's what the person in the center wants. There are few spaces in the world for women to take charge of and claim our right to be the center of sexual attention on our terms. Whether we want to call the shots or surrender or both or neither, that space is ours for the reimagining.

Tristan Taormino

Figure 43.2 Signing autographs for fans at the AVN show, Las Vegas, Nevada, 2000

Figure 43.3 Celebrating my two AVN Awards with Red, Las Vegas, Nevada, 2000

I thought a lot about it before I decided to have sex in my movie. It was a decision that would affect the rest of my career. I've talked to women who are intimidated by porn performances, so even if they believe the pleasure is real, they can't relate because *those women are professionals.* I needed to prove that any woman can enjoy anal sex, and I represented everywoman. Plus, I was a slutty exhibitionist, so my gang bang was a fantasy; the entire movie fulfilled that early goal: I was a teacher *and* a *Solid Gold* dancer. And the emerging marketing genius in me knew I had a unique hook. Traditionally, a female performer paces her career in the industry in a certain way: first solo sex, then girl/girl, then boy/girl, then anal, then groups or gang bangs, and so on. I don't know anyone else who made their debut in a ten-person anal orgy. *Well, this should cut through the noise and get the movie some attention.*

It did. In 2000 the movie won numerous awards, including Anal Video of the Year at the AVN Awards. I happily walked onstage to accept the trophy, a delightfully tacky plastic gold-tone female form with wings glued to a faux wood pedestal. Later they sent me the real one, which has the name of the award and the movie title on an engraved brass plate. My name, etched in a utilitarian font, looks nearly identical to my name on the brass plate on the back of my saddle. I thought to myself: *Mine.*

EPILOGUE
MY FATHER'S EYES

He says that families are people we choose to have in our lives,

so it's by elegant chance

that he is my daddy and I am his daughter and on top of it all we're family.

FROM MY POEM "REBIRTH" (1995)

Shame and silence run in families, like eye color or skin that easily burns in the sun, but I am determined not to inherit them. Scientists who study epigenetics believe that trauma in our past or in our ancestors' pasts can leave markers on our DNA—a kind of molecular scar, like raised skin you might rub your finger over again and again to help you access a memory. If that's the case, adultery, forbidden love, heartbreak, secrecy, and pain were already part of me when I got here. My faraway ancestor, the lay theological scholar, wrote in his banned book that he didn't believe in predestined fate: we can earn our salvation, we just have to work for it. I may be failing.

In *The Queer Art of Failure*, gender theorist Jack Halberstam writes about failure as "a practice that builds upon queerness in the sense that queerness is always a failure to conform, to belong, to cohere. Rather than reorienting queerness, we should embrace failure." We think of failing as a bad thing, but maybe it's what we were meant to do all along in order to shift the culture and write our own histories. Confusion is also something no one is supposed to strive for, yet it was a part of my father, his partnership with my mother, and our relationship. Confusion does not have to be the opposite of clarity; it can be a space of knowing multiple things at once, even those that appear contradictory. Like being in love and terrified of love, feeling unsure yet committed, wanting to hold on and ready to let go. When something is confusing, it often requires imagination to help us through it.

My lover has their dick in my ass. I'm facedown on scarlet sheets with a purple vibrator buzzing against my clit. They push their arm across both my shoulder blades. They call me *good girl*. They are pumping and groaning like an orgasm is coming. Theirs or mine, I don't know. I'm just pulsing flesh and nerve endings. I'm in my body, in the moment, but then I'm not. I picture a man on top of my father, grunting and coming inside his ass. The moment when the HIV virus permeated a mucous membrane, found its way to his bloodstream, and he became infected. I don't even know if that's the way it happened. I read this line in an article: "The mucous membranes are vulnerable but not defenseless." I try to dismiss the thought, snap out of it, return to the pleasure. These days, I usually can. I am vulnerable but not defenseless.

"You have his eyes," someone once said. His eyes were what drew you in; they showed you everything about him: love, desire, curiosity, confusion, mischief, sorrow, anger, and hope. They told lies, and they told the truth. But I don't actually have his eyes. I think people want to pick one thing—to say, *We see the family resemblance.* He had bright blue eyes that sparkled at you. Deep blue reflective glass that showed you who you are. I can see how my mother fell in love with him and, later, how many men did too.

Mom has blue eyes also, but they are subtle, grayer, muted, not like his. As the child of two blue-eyed people, I don't have blue eyes. Something about chromosomes and dominant genes. They probably expected me to have blue eyes, but when I pushed my way out of my mom, I was already defiant. My eyes are a pale mossy color that turns into wet, bright grass when I cry. Sometimes they are a dull grayish green. Gray like steel beams or a smoke-colored cat. Gray like those days when you can't move, where you lie still under a blanket, unable to face anything.

Tristan Taormino

Still it's hard to look in a mirror without seeing my father. Not just the sensitive Irish skin and dark hair that peppered early with salt. The pain behind the eyes. The stories we can choose to reveal or not. We both have the porcupine-like armor of an artichoke: sharp and formidable on the outside but, as you move in closer, something softer and more sensitive. Just when you think you're all the way in though, another layer of the artichoke appears—barbed quills that you have to reckon with in order to get to the tender, nourishing heart. Something to savor is so close to something you could choke on. Even though it's the best bit, a part of the heart can't be eaten.

I didn't get my father's eyes, but I did inherit his life stories and his way of seeing the world. I carry his shame, secrecy, and silence with me, and it's heavy. He saw the tall brick projects in Red Hook, the stern Catholic school nuns in black and white. Army barracks in olive drab and mud brown. The red lips of Judy Garland in the restored version of *A Star Is Born*. The pink sequins of a drag queen's dress. The creamy color of cum on a stranger's skin. Which is like the color of his skin. And mine.

Like an old film projector, the kind where you can step in front of it and block the image, his eyes shined pictures of Brooklyn summers, classroom punishments, basic training, and Hollywood movies. Reading his memoir, recalling his stories, is like looking through a child's Fisher Price View-Master, each image slightly blurry no matter how much light there is, each one framed with an old-fashioned white border. Sometimes the stories he left for me are like looking through a kaleidoscope, repeated shapes and colors but mixing together in new patterns each time I look.

Eleven years after his death, I contacted my second cousin Dolores, whom he had reconnected with when he got sick. She put me in touch with his half sister, my aunt Joanne. We emailed, and then we talked for the first time on the phone. Joanne was a spitfire, sharp tongued and funny; she had a husky voice like his, although it was from years of smoking. She sounded familiar. Like the rest of his family, she hadn't seen me since I was a baby, and we both wanted to plan an in-person visit. Months before that visit, her father, my step-grandfather, the man whose name I have, died. On the steps of Our Lady Star of the Sea in Carroll Gardens at his funeral, I finally met the Taorminos and Barbas—my aunt, my first, second, and third cousins. It was surreal. They brought me back to a reception at a brick row house in Brooklyn, where they fed me three different kinds of rice balls from the buffet table. This family, brand new to me, embraced me with such love.

The stories my father wrote about his mother are hard to read—her fits of uncontrollable rage, her sadistic methods of discipline, recurring scenes of crazy and crying (hers and his). My grandmother was domineering, moody, and often ill but was never treated for any psychological disorder. The signs were there, but there was much less awareness about mental health issues, and there was a tolerance in the family to resign themselves to accepting people's eccentricities. My aunt Joanne, a psychiatric nurse, told me their mom was diagnosed with bipolar disorder when she was in her sixties.

"Mom was nuts. But once they started her on Depakote, everything really did even out."

He didn't know her then. He believed he had run far enough away from her, from them, to release the tethers of history and DNA. I'm not sure if that's even possible. He didn't want to be anything like his mom, but he could be. He could scare me.

The queer descendant of a queer person is not an exact copy. My dad's story is his, but it is also a snapshot of a queer history that we share. His favorite things became my favorite things. It was only later that I understood that his pleasures were tropes of gayness (a particular kind of white, male, middle-class, urban gayness). We both loved to escape through movies. He had an enduring crush on Montgomery Clift and identified with him in his closeted torment, his tragic star quality. I inherited his photograph of Montgomery and Elizabeth Taylor on the set of *A Place in the Sun*. It reminds me of us, the way Liz Taylor looks, young and happy, the way Montgomery holds her arm so gently but deliberately. The way his eyes stare off in the distance, imagining another life. My father wrote a one-line review in his journal: "A great film about wanting more."

Like many gay men of his generation, he grew up acutely aware of homophobia in his family and in the world at large. "Fags are sinners, fags are perverts, fags are bad" was drummed into my father's head like an unyielding techno song in a gay bar with a neon sign in the window. When he was young, he took pleasure in his adventures with other boys in the neighborhood but felt forced to hide his desire, deny it, and hate it. When he finally came out, he faced a world that wasn't yet ready to embrace him with open arms.

I am a Gen X post-Stonewall baby. I knew actual queer people and saw role models in the *Advocate*, *Out Magazine*, *On Our Backs*. The high school gay-straight alliances, queer proms, a bevy of out public figures, *Will and Grace*, and *RuPaul's Drag Race* would come later. But there was enough. Enough

Tristan Taormino

for me to be embraced and supported. Enough for me to learn about and meet the ones who came before me. Enough to feel like I belonged. When I came out, a chosen family was waiting for me. My dad was deeply invested in LGBTQIA+ rights, and he sometimes marveled at just how far we had come. But I wonder if it ever seemed bittersweet to him that I came of age in a time of more visibility and acceptance than he could've imagined when he was my age. Perhaps I am living the life my father always wanted. Or a version of it. Perhaps.

He gave up so much to be gay: his family of origin, his friends, his religion, his safety and security on the street. And me. For years, he didn't believe he could have his desire and his daughter. I bear the wound of being twice abandoned by him, first to a life of being his true self, second to the disease that decimated queer communities. My dad was/is part of my queer history and *our* queer histories. My father exists in who I am today: a girl who likes anonymous sex, figure skating, dandies, and leatherdaddies.

It still feels like my father knew and understood me in a way no one else can. A particular kind of loneliness wells up in me knowing someone I feel so in sync with isn't here. He was my best friend, my mentor, my teacher. I was the object of his adoration and affection, and he was mine. I am his spitting image, the charming queer girl to his queer boy. He instilled in me a belief that drives me: I can do anything I set my heart to, and I can make this world better for people like us.

When I used to pack for each visit, I always brought my coolest outfits to show off to him. Each morning, I strutted into the kitchen like I was on a catwalk, posed for a proper look, poised for his approval. We never tired of the ritual. His eyes followed me, lit up with glee.

"You. Look. Fabulous!" It was my moment to shine, to be adored. I relive those times now with lovers, dressing up, anticipating the moment when she or he or they will survey every inch of me, drink me in with their eyes, compliment me. Sometimes they say, "You're beautiful, little girl. Come here and sit on Daddy's lap."

I have searched for my father's eyes everywhere. At makeshift theater stages, down Castro Street, around a circle of activists in metal folding chairs, on the L train to Bedford Avenue. At women's sex parties held in gay bathhouses, in dungeons secretly hiding in Midtown Manhattan office buildings, on porn sets among silky slips and panties, at a public health conference presentation on the evolution of HIV treatments. I want someone to see me, really see me. Sometimes all the eyes can see are fuchsia lips and fishnet legs. Or I gaze into a pair of eyes that shows me a smart ass. Or someone squints, trying to make out a soul struggling between devastation and ecstasy. I am all these things, and I want the eyes to see *that* complicated person. Eyes that look and love and understand.